Precautionary Polit

Urban and Industrial Environments
Series editor: Robert Gottlieb, Henry R. Luce Professor of Urban and Environmental Policy, Occidental College

For a complete list of books published in this series, please see the back of the book.

Precautionary Politics

Principle and Practice in Confronting Environmental Risk

Kerry H. Whiteside

The MIT Press
Cambridge, Massachusetts
London, England

MIT Press books may be purchased at special quantity discounts for business or sales promotional use. For information, please e-mail <special_sales@mitpress.mit.edu> or write to Special Sales Department, The MIT Press, 55 Hayward Street, Cambridge, MA 02142.

This book was set in Sabon by Graphic Composition, Inc. Printed on recycled paper and bound in the United States of America.

Library of Congress Cataloging-in-Publication Data

Whiteside, Kerry H., 1953–
Precautionary politics : principle and practice in confronting environmental risk / Kerry H. Whiteside
p. cm. — (Urban and industrial environments)
Includes bibliographical references and index.
ISBN-13: 978-0-262-23255-5 (alk. paper)—978-0-262-73179-9 (pbk. : alk. paper)
ISBN-10: 0-262-23255-3 (alk. paper)—0-262-73179-7 (pbk. : alk. paper)
1. Environmental risk assessment. 2. Precautionary principle. 3. Political participation. I. Title. II. Series.
GE145.W47 2006
363.7—dc22

2006044939

10 9 8 7 6 5 4 3 2 1

Contents

Introduction

In 1996, a new trade dispute began to roil relations between the United States and Europe. Civil disobedience and popular demonstrations erupted across Europe to a degree unseen since the United States proposed to modernize the North Atlantic Treaty Organization's (NATO) nuclear weapons systems in the early 1980s. This new controversy provoked concerned statements by presidents and prime ministers. There were urgent meetings between the top trade representatives of both continents and intervention by some of the highest courts in Europe. Frustrated with the lack of progress in resolving the dispute, the Bush administration decided in 2003 to challenge the European position before a supranational body, the World Trade Organization.

Oddly, the controversy involved something that could hardly seem more trifling. At issue was the fate of a soybean.

How could a humble legume—a crop mainly used to feed cows and pigs—fuel widespread public demonstrations and tense political confrontations? The answer is: this was no ordinary soybean. It was a *transgenic* soybean, a product of genetic engineering. And it ran into the precautionary principle.

One measure of the significance of that principle is this: precaution has held in check the commercial interests of the largest economic power in the world. Europe blocked the importation of transgenic crops, at least until it could develop new regulations consistent with the precautionary principle. Moreover, for the first time in an era of rapid technological innovation, not just a single product, but an entire, newly developed mode of production has had to endure delays in its global commercialization. Those delays were justified not because the technology had been *proven* harmful but because *uncertainties* about its potential for harm had not yet been adequately investigated. Those are unprecedented effects in the history of environmental regulation.

The precautionary principle is most widely known through its formulation in the Rio Declaration on Environment and Development of 1992. The declaration holds that "where there are threats of serious or irreversible damage, the lack of full scientific certainty shall not be used as a reason for postponing cost-effective measures to prevent environmental degradation."[1] The principle in this form—the form I shall be referencing throughout this book—stands in opposition to a regulatory posture that justifies action only in cases where the scientific proof of harm is well developed and the benefits of regulation demonstrably outweigh the costs.[2] "At its core lies the intuitively simple idea that decisionmakers should act in advance of scientific certainty to protect the environment (and with it, the well-being of future generations) from incurring harm" (O'Riordan and Jordan 1999, 23). The precautionary principle applies especially in situations of environmental risk where by the time unambiguous scientific evidence of a serious problem becomes available, the danger may already have materialized and perhaps become irreversible. A strategy of anticipatory preventive action is necessary to avoid a disastrous outcome.

The precautionary principle was enshrined as a key feature of environmental law throughout the European Union (EU) in the same year as the Rio Declaration. Other treaties making reference to it now include the United Nations Framework Convention on Climate Change of 1992, the 1996 Protocol to the Convention on the Prevention of Marine Pollution by Dumping of Wastes and Other Matter, and the 2000 Cartagena Protocol on Biosafety (Sadeleer 1999; LaFranchi 2005, 683–687). By some estimates, "precaution is emerging as a guiding norm in international environmental law on a global level" (Centre for International Sustainable Development Law 2002). Another threshold of significance was crossed in February 2005. France inscribed the precautionary principle in its constitution, alongside the 1789 Declaration of the Rights of Man and of the Citizen. The steady advance of the precautionary principle stems from a growing awareness of the seriousness of humanity's environmental predicament and the limits of our understanding of how to manage the risks flowing from it. Decisions relating to such matters as the dissemination of new biotechnologies, nuclear waste disposal, and greenhouse effect mitigation, to name only a few, fall within its scope.

This book is a study of the precautionary principle—its meaning, rationale, and policy implications along with the controversies it has provoked.[3] It is also an argument in favor of it, particularly in its "deliberative" form.

The ideas here are addressed in the first instance to readers in the United States. Here, the precautionary principle is not widely appreciated. While in Europe the precautionary principle has become a household word, on U.S. soil the occasional academic article defending it seldom finds an echo among the general public. The rare book-length essays about it in English have been mainly negative (Sunstein 2005; Goklany 2001). Too often, however, U.S. critics pay insufficient attention to how the principle has been debated, refined, and elaborated, particularly in Europe. In part that is because the very concepts of risk assessment are handled differently on the two sides of the Atlantic (Jasanoff 2000). The U.S. idiom of "science-based" risk regulation and cost-benefit analysis tends to be quantitative, driven by marginalist economic reasoning, and can be unabashedly technocratic in its political implications. Europeans find more place for history, sociology, and philosophy in their analyses. More so than Americans, European policymakers approach environmental affairs speaking a language of "duty," "care," and "democratic participation." Finding a common language with which to discuss environmental protection is urgent, precisely because of what is at stake in precautionary action. As defended here, the precautionary principle targets environmental problems with potential global consequences. Only concerted international action stands a chance of avoiding them. Therefore, finding the principled grounds of consensus is vital, especially among the most powerful economic blocs in the world.

The precautionary principle is a particularly intriguing case of international consensus building because the reasoning supporting it proceeds not just from knowledge but equally from *doubt*. More commonly, consensus building is a matter of bringing people together by getting them to recognize some relatively well-established truth about a state of affairs. "High deficits weaken currencies," so members of the EU agree on the need to control deficits before adopting the euro. "Genocide is occurring in Bosnia," so NATO members could (belatedly) be brought to see the need to intervene. In contrast, a precautionary attitude arises when we are forced to acknowledge that we are making decisions with potentially serious consequences, but at the time our knowledge about whether those consequences will actually occur is quite limited. The precautionary principle concentrates attention on the uncertainties and ambiguities that emerge at the interface between humanity and nature. It fashions policy out of skepticism.

To a greater degree than Europeans, Americans have trouble entertaining such skepticism. In my previous work (Whiteside 2002), *Divided Natures,* I argued that English-speaking environmental thought tends to assume that a well-defined "nature" is the proper object of environmental concern. While there are major controversies within English-speaking environmental thought over whether our reasons for valuing "natural" entities are essentially human-centered or not, all sides tend to agree that there is a nature *there* to value. This shared assumption, I maintained, diverts attention from one of the most vexing features environmental debate: often there is substantial uncertainty over the very *identity* of nature. Scientists disagree over whether certain types of environmental deterioration are really occurring. Even if the occurrence of a certain troubling phenomenon is not in question, its extent is. Or there is uncertainty about whether the phenomenon is part of a "natural cycle" or is humanly caused. Controversies surrounding global warming, the dangers of growing genetically modified crops (often called genetically modified organisms, or GMOs), and the possible associations between cancer and exposure to industrial chemicals all have this structure. Not just valuing nature but even knowing what it *is,* is in question.

One of the best reasons for Americans to pay closer attention to European ecological thought is that it better captures this dimension of our environmental predicament. Where nature's identity becomes uncertain, environmental concern takes the form of exposing the origins of those uncertainties, laying bare their questionable implications for the distribution of power in society and cultivating a multivalent, skeptical attitude in the face of overconfident assertions of the human "mastery" of nature.

What fascinates me about the precautionary principle (and the reason that this work follows—dare I say it?—"naturally" on my earlier study) is that I see it as the clearest concrete manifestation of that alternative way of framing environmental concern. The precautionary principle problematizes both humanity and nature. It is a public recognition of the fact that what we call nature is not *simply* "there." Rather, its identity emerges gradually and often confusedly. Diverse research programs, innovative forms of environmental monitoring, social protests, demographic tracking, and political regulation all play roles in solidifying the sense that an environmental problem even exists. The precautionary principle represents a reasoned effort to take account of the complexity of the processes—social as well as scientific—through which environmental problems become known and hence become subject to regulation. In the five chapters that follow, I present the precautionary principle from a series of vantage points, each of which draws out the practical and philosophical dimensions of this way of viewing environmental risk.

I begin by recounting the controversy over GMOs. I chose this issue as my main case study not because GMOs are *known* to be dangerous but precisely because they are *not*. One way to justify precaution would be to start from examples where significant harms have already occurred and then show how precautionary action might have prevented them (European Environment Agency 2001). This book takes a somewhat different path. Since the hallmark of the precautionary principle is that it calls for action under conditions of uncertainty, it makes sense to confront the reader with a case that is still open. The question regarding GMOs is, Faced with dispute and doubt about their potential harmfulness, what do we do? The United States and Europe have offered very different responses to that question. Where U.S. regulators quickly convinced themselves of the safety of transgenic crops and consequently allowed them to be grown on a massive scale, Europeans saw many areas of insufficient testing and potential danger. Greater precaution meant reinforcing multidisciplinary research, implementing traceability and monitoring requirements, and organizing new modes of democratic consultation.

Europeans have been particularly troubled by the possibility of slowly developing, large-scale damage to human health and/or the self-replenishing properties of ecosystems. These very properties make for risks that are difficult to perceive and calculate, particularly in their early stages. Europe's precautionary politics is grounded in a conviction that humanity faces new types of risk, requiring specially adapted modes of regulation. Chapter 2 explores this conviction by contrasting it with the assumptions underlying science-based risk assessment of the sort favored in the United States. Presenting this contrast in the form of arguments, pro and con, between proponents and opponents of the precautionary principle allows me to probe the strengths and weaknesses on both sides. As a proponent myself, I maintain that precaution should be understood as a demand for *better science* and more self-conscious *political judgments* about how to select appropriate policies from a graduated scale of potential precautionary measures.

Such nuance too easily gets lost in the climate of increasing polarization between the United States and Europe of recent years. Since the 1980s, U.S. presidents have routinely championed deregulation and so-called free trade—or what Europeans sometimes pejoratively label liberalism. The Bush administration's systematic opposition to any talk of precaution—discussed in chapter 3—makes the prospects of an international consensus on environmental protection seem remote. Yet I show that historically, U.S. regulators have been more precautionary than recent politics suggests. At the same time, Europeans are responding to some U.S. concerns by becoming more careful about how they operationalize precaution. Convergence is possible. The larger question that remains is whether the precautionary principle *necessarily* modifies the liberal philosophy embodied in existing international trade regimes.

If precaution challenges something so fundamental as contemporary understandings of liberal social relations, a closer examination of its philosophical premises is warranted. Chapter 4 evaluates two competing theories of precaution. Hans Jonas's "principle of responsibility" (1984) foreshadows the precautionary principle in arguing that humanity faces new ethical responsibilities toward future generations because modern technologies have the unprecedented potential to destroy life. This philosophy emphasizes the special competence of scientists to manage this situation. Coming from the opposite pole, Bruno Latour sees precaution as part of a larger project of "bringing the sciences into democracy." (1999b) His version highlights social contingencies and factual uncertainties in the development of scientific research. I conclude that Jonas's thinking better expresses the ethical attractiveness of the precautionary principle. But Latour makes a useful contribution by emphasizing why there are so many uncertainties in scientific understandings of environmental phenomena and suggesting that wider deliberative practices are necessary to help societies respond to them.

A deliberative interpretation of the precautionary principle is the topic of chapter 5. I explore the relationship between precaution and expanded citizen participation in regulatory processes. My contention is that precaution should be regarded less as a matter of a priori democratic ethics than of achieving environmentally positive results. I look at three ways that participatory innovations can contribute to such consequences. Then, in conclusion, I argue that the precautionary principle is best conceived as an instance of social learning on a world scale. In the last couple of centuries, there has been increasing international recognition of the value of democracy and human rights—probably because they help humanity better adapt to social complexity and the intensified need for social cooperation. Likewise, the precautionary principle expresses an increasingly broad acknowledgment that our advancing—but incomplete—understanding of humanity's impact on the environment requires new rules of behavior that will be respected by all. For the first time, progress consists in recognizing our *inability* to master the world. The precautionary principle is a key ethical expression of that recognition.

Precautionary Politics

1

Precaution at Work: The Case of Agricultural Biotechnology

In October and November 1996, freighters delivering the first shipments of transgenic soybeans from the United States docked in European ports. Greenpeace mobilized quickly. Activists chained themselves to lock gates and cranes in Liverpool. They beamed spotlights on cargo ships entering Hamburg. They prevented dockworkers from unloading cargo in Antwerp. Their goal was to draw attention to the fact that unlabeled GMOs were about to enter the European food distribution system. The media picked up the story. There were articles about Frankenfoods: the monstrous, uncontrollable products of science run amok. Some reporters drew parallels between GMOs and the failure of regulatory authorities to protect the public against mad cow disease—a terrible brain-destroying disorder caused in humans by eating beef from cattle fed on reprocessed sheep tissue (Joly et al. 2000, 30–31). "Warning: Mad Soybeans" ran a headline in a French newpaper (Alerte 1996).

In spite of the protests, the EU calmly followed its established procedures and took the next step in the ongoing process of authorizing transgenic crops. In December 1996, its scientific committees gave the green light to member states wishing to make genetically modified (GM) corn available for consumption and cultivation in Europe. The crisis deepened. On January 27, 1997, Greenpeace-led activists protested in front of multinational food company offices across Europe. Some EU member states, notably Austria and Italy, refused to allow any GMO imports. France suspended imports of GMO products until it could review and revise its regulatory legislation.

Still the controversy refused to die down. In November 1997, the French government announced a new, more cautious policy—but one that still allowed the importation and cultivation of GMOs. Greenpeace and other environmental organizations then brought suit before one of France's highest courts, the Council of State. They charged that the government's policy violated the precautionary principle, which France had adopted in 1995 to conform to EU mandates. In September 1998, the council agreed. As a "precautionary action," it quashed the government's authorization to grow GM corn and remitted the controversy to EU authorities. For the next three years, the EU instituted a virtual moratorium on GMOs as it struggled to define more precautionary regulations for marketing them. Requirements for GMO labeling and monitoring for environmental effects were finally incorporated in an EU directive in March 2001.

This chapter is a case study of the application of the precautionary principle. The advantage of starting from a case study is that it exposes some of the real-world complexity involved in judgments about environmental protection. Later chapters will take up more abstract arguments about such matters as the difference between precautionary politics and science-based risk regulation or the relative merits of competing ethical justifications for precaution. But before deciding which of those positions is more convincing, it is important to observe how regulatory politics works in practice. Shifting definitions, political maneuvering, and suppressed questions are all part of the messy reality of a regulatory system. Those practical shortcomings can, at times, justify new approaches.

By contrasting how the United States and Europe have chosen to regulate transgenic crops, I show how the precautionary principle can reshape public policy. The example of GMO regulation illustrates what conditions trigger the use of the principle, how it is put into operation, and why it has such powerful political effects. It also provides a first indication of the principle's chances of continuing its development as an international norm of environmental risk regulation—one capable of eliciting cooperation between countries in the face of new types of global environmental risk.

GMOs: Their Nature and Potential

Genes carry the information that organisms use to grow, survive, and reproduce. If a tulip is yellow or red, it is because of information encoded by genes on its chromosomes. If a plant produces a poison to discourage a potential predator, it is because one or several genes contain "instructions" for the manufacture of the toxin in question.

Since genetically based traits can make organisms more or less useful to human beings, people have been engaged in a sort of biotechnology ever since the first plants and animals were domesticated some ten thousand years ago. Selecting and crossbreeding particularly robust plants or healthy animals alters the genetic composition of the chosen species. Genetic manipulation by these methods, however, is slow, imprecise, and limited to traits available within the species. It is slow because people must raise generation after generation of the target species in order to select for the desired trait. It is imprecise because in the process of crossbreeding, thousands of genes are transferred, not just the particular gene desired. Undesirable traits originating from the nontargeted transfer may then make the crossbred organism much less useful for human purposes. As Harvard biologist Richard Lewontin (2001, 81) explains, "If one attempts to introduce disease-resistance into an especially high-yielding variety of wheat by crossing that variety with one that has the disease resistance but not the high yield, the result will be a variety with improved resistance but lower yield." Finally, crossbreeding techniques are limited because they depend on the mode of reproduction of the species in question, whether asexual (as in bacteria) or sexual (as in most plants and animals). This means that the only genes (and hence the only traits) that could be selected for were ones already present in other individuals of the same species (or in a few cases, very close relatives). Gene transfers were not possible between individuals or species that did not interbreed (Reiss and Straughan 1996, 4–5).

What is revolutionary about genetic engineering is that it radically overcomes these limitations. Suppose a plant breeder wants to develop a yellow tomato. With recombinant DNA technology, as Jane Rissler and Margaret Mellon (1996, 9–10) note, "any organism—even a butterfly or a daffodil—[can be] a source of the yellow trait . . . [as long as] the gene that determines yellow color has been identified and isolated."[1] The possible combinations are startling. In order to promote the ability of potatoes to resist certain bacteria, genetic engineers have managed to insert chicken genes into them; scientists have created bacteria that manufacture human insulin; and researchers have added flounder genes to tomatoes to increase the fruit's ability to resist cold.

Genetic engineering refers to processes by which scientists extract DNA corresponding to a particular gene from one organism—bacteria, plant or animal—and transplant it into the cells of a target organism (usually of a different species). Genetic engineering seeks to make traits from the donor species appear in the recipient species. Because donor genes get incorporated in the genome of the recipient, the new trait is then passed along to subsequent generations.

The potential uses of genetic engineering are so diverse that it is difficult to characterize this technology in general terms. It seems that almost any desirable trait that one can imagine might be added to some organism. A few examples, grouped in broad categories, may suffice to give an idea of the scope of the possible benefits.

- Added convenience: Fruits and vegetables can be made so that they have a longer shelf life, and are less susceptible to damage from handling and shipment.

- Enhanced nutrition: Plants can be engineered to increase their protein or vitamin content. The most famous example is so-called yellow rice—transgenic rice designed to remedy vitamin A deficiency in populations that consume little meat.

- Pharmaceutical uses: GM corn has been made to synthesize the blood anticoagulant produced naturally by leeches. Human growth hormone is now manufactured by transgenic bacteria. U.S. researchers have investigated GM bananas that could carry a deactivated form of cholera protein in order to convey resistance to cholera.

- Adaptation to challenging environmental conditions: Crop plants can be modified so that yields are higher and so that they are more resistant to adverse environmental conditions. Scientists in North Africa are working on drought-resistant date palms. Cereals that can tolerate salinity stress and soil acidity are in the works.

- Reduced environmental impact: To protect the environment from polluting practices associated with modern intensive agriculture, crops can be modified to contain their own pesticides or to need less fertilizer. Trees grown for paper pulp can be remade so that less chlorine is needed in the paper-production process. GM plants can manufacture raw materials for biodegradable plastics.

- Environmental cleanup: Transgenic organisms are even envisioned that will help remedy existing environmental problems. It may be possible to take heavy metals out of industrially contaminated soils by planting potatoes that have been genetically modified to absorb specific poisons.

Any regulatory proposal—like the precautionary principle—that might slow down or stop the development of GMOs must take these potential benefits into account. GMO proponents argue that it is absurd to oppose GMOs on environmental safety grounds without considering that transgenic crops might offer humankind's best hope of combining high agricultural production (to feed this planet's burgeoning population) with the reduced use of polluting pesticides and fertilizers (Goklany 2001, 51–52; Miller and Conko 2000, 100–101).

On the other hand, those who are more GMO skeptical point out not only that there are potential dangers but also that most of the much-vaunted benefits are still largely hypothetical. It turns out that many desired genetic modifications are, in practice, more difficult to realize than thought at first (Rissler and Mellon 1996, 14). At any rate, by 2004, hardly any of the more exotic applications have been commercialized. Just two engineered traits account for over 90 percent of the worldwide biotech crop acreage (International Service 2004). The most common form of genetic modification makes crops resistant to a broad-spectrum herbicide like Monsanto's Roundup. Farmers can then control weeds in their fields by spreading the herbicide over their entire crop. The other agriculturally favored use of gene splicing involves creating plants that manufacture their own pesticide. A gene from the soil bacterium Bacillus thuringiensis (Bt) can make crops manufacture in their tissues a substance that while harmless to humans, kills certain insect predators.

Is Anything Wrong with GMOs? Reasons for Precaution

Many people have immediate ethical reactions against "tampering with nature" in the brazen way practiced by genetic engineers.[2] That is why headlines about Frankenfoods caused so much stir in Europe. Still, no one should underestimate the complexity of morally evaluating GMOs. Our moral intuitions about why it matters that something is natural may not be very coherent. Arguments that GMOs are unnatural quickly run up against the reply that all crops subject to widespread cultivation have been selectively bred for many generations, if not millennia. Traditional breeding techniques have thus profoundly altered their genome relative to that of their "wild" ancestors. Yet no one objects to such techniques on principle. Nor can natural be equated with healthful, since many wild plants contain toxins that are dangerous to human beings. Surely the case for or against GMOs turns significantly on questions regarding their safety and utility—empirical matters about which our ethical intuitions give little reliable guidance.

But as regards empirical studies of transgenic crops, there is a complication that has to be recognized from the start: even prominent scientists disagree about the risks involved. Award-winning geneticist Louis-Marie Houdebine (2000, 154) insists, for example, that "the GMOs that have been proposed [for commercialization] have easily undergone tests for toxicity and allergenicity, without raising the slightest concern." In the United States, a prestigious panel of the National Academy of Sciences (1987, n.p.) did not hesitate to declare that "no evidence based on laboratory observations indicates that unique hazards attend the transfer of genes between unrelated organisms." On the other hand, well-known French plant biologist and ecological activist Jean-Marie Pelt (2000, 78) raises question after question about the long-term effects of GMOs in order finally to ask whether anyone has really evaluated the global consequences: whether GMOs may modify the course of natural evolution; whether they will cause the emergence of new pathogenic agents for plants and animals. Barry Commoner (2002), one of the leading scientific ecologists in the United States, challenges the "central dogma" on which molecular biologists ground the practice of genetic engineering: the premise that "an organism's genome—its full complement of DNA genes—should fully account for its characteristic assemblage of inherited traits." If, as he believes, gene expression depends on additional factors in the chromosome's cellular environment, then "alternative splicing of the bacterial [Bt] gene might give rise to multiple variants of the intended protein . . . with unpredictable effects on ecosystems and human health." Uncertainty and scientific controversy loom large in any discussion of GMO safety.

So what are, or might be, the dangers? Even before considering any specific risks, one should note three factors that when combined, make genetically engineered crops into likely candidates for precautionary treatment.

The first factor is their sheer novelty. The first successful instance of genetic engineering took place in 1971, when biochemist Paul Berg combined genetic material from a bacteria plasmid and a monkey virus. It is not an exaggeration to say that until then, in the entire three-billion-year history of the evolution of life on this planet, genes were recombined almost exclusively by the slow, species-bound processes of asexual and sexual reproduction, with the survivability of the resulting traits determined by trial and error in the harsh conditions of natural selection.[3] In 1971, however, Berg broke the species barrier. He opened the door to creating new organisms out of widely separated species, and doing so in the space not of years or generations, as in traditional plant breeding, but a few weeks. Molecular biologists marched through this door in 1973 by introducing DNA from a toad into an E. coli bacterium. By 1978, the transgenic manufacture of human insulin was accomplished. The first GM plants for agricultural use were developed in 1983. In 1994, the first such plant—the Flav'r Sav'r tomato—went on sale in California. Later that year, a virus-resistant squash was also approved, followed soon thereafter by insecticide potatoes (Rissler and Mellon 1996, 11). In the case of this agricultural biotechnology, it took just twenty-two years to move from the creation of life-forms without biological precedent to a set of banal commercial products that with little fanfare, settled into supermarket bins in the United States.

The contrast with the regulatory approach to pharmaceuticals could hardly be more striking. Even where decades of research and experience make the biological mechanisms affected by new drugs reasonably well understood, each and every new drug molecule is subjected to so much testing on animals and humans that it takes, on average, fifteen years to move from its discovery to its commercialization. For GMOs, the time frame between the invention of a new life-form and experiments with it is a matter of months, and few animal tests are carried out (Lepage and Guery 2001, 33–34). The precautionary question that arises from the newness of GMOs is, Can the broad range of potential health and environmental effects of such unprecedented creations be well understood in so short a time?

Second, the fabrication of GMOs is an imprecise art. Bits of DNA clipped from one organism are transferred into another, often by a bacterium or virus, sometimes simply by being shot into cells with a special air-gun. Even if the transgene is integrated into the cell (which frequently it is not), exactly where it ends up on the recipient's genome is anybody's guess. Sometimes the process produces the desired traits in the recipient species; often it fails. Even when experiments succeed in transferring a particular trait, the resulting organism sometimes behaves surprisingly. Transgenic plants have been known to express the desired trait, only to revert to their original form in a growing season or two. This phenomenon, known as gene silencing, is still poorly understood. Gilles Seralini (2000, 18, 20), a professor of molecular biology at the University of Caen, explains the source of much uncertainty:

> We understand neither the detailed structure of the DNA of highly evolved organisms that will be genetically modified, nor a fortiori their complicated functioning. Among plants and higher organisms, only a relatively small number of individuals, within a small number of species, have had their hereditary legacy deciphered. . . . We are intervening in the genome of living beings without having a global, and precise, vision of their structures and functioning.

Seralini (80) worries that genetic engineers too often embrace a simplistic view of cellular operations: one function and one protein correspond to one gene. That is why it is possible to hope that by moving a gene from one organism to another, the desirable trait taken from the donor organism will appear in the recipient. In reality, it is usually not so simple. Many traits apparently require the interaction of multiple genes as well as other factors in their cellular environment. Even the National Academy of Sciences (2000, 61), when reviewing the U.S. regulations concerning biotech plant foods, recognized that the "introduction of transgenes into plants typically involves random integration of DNA into the nuclear genome," with the potential for "unintended consequences." Because "unintended" can also imply "unwanted" and perhaps dangerous, special care seems warranted.

The third factor inducing precaution is that by introducing GM crops, we are changing the nature of the human food-supply in potentially massive ways. Again, even without evaluating whether those changes pose specifiable dangers, it is important to emphasize their seriousness. We are changing the *nature* of the food supply. Recombinant DNA technology alters the *genetic identity* of the crops that farmers grow and the foods we put on our plates every day (Teitel and Wilson 1999, 1–5). If transgenic crops hold all the potential that their promoters claim—ease of cultivation, improved transportability, enhanced nutrition, and so forth—it is likely that in the space of a decade or two, they will largely displace nontransgenic species in world markets. This process is well underway with some crops. In 2004, biotech soybeans represented 56 percent of the worldwide soybean acreage—as opposed to none ten years earlier. Twenty-eight percent of the world's cotton crop was transgenic—up 21 percent from the preceding year. Moreover, transgenes spread unintentionally as well. It has proven impossible to keep transgenes from flowing into the environment beyond the fields where the biotech plants are being grown (Barred from

Testing 2004; Genes 2004; Les pouvoirs 2001). Pollen carried by insects and the wind ends up fertilizing other related species. Seeds are moved and hoarded by animals. Soil bacteria incorporate, replicate, and transfer genetic material. GMOs will not stay put. So it is not only the crops in this or that field that are being transformed. This technology is destined to alter the course of the evolutionary processes that generated the plant traits on which human nutrition depends. Because living organisms replicate the DNA they contain, this diffusion, once begun, continues automatically. It is likely in many cases to be irreversible.

Are these factors alarming? It has to be said that after ten years of commercial cultivation, no significant damage has been seen. Even GMO-detractors admit that there are no bodies to point to, that there has been no biotech Chernobyl. Still, there is something about the newness and power of this technology that gives one pause. Before we irreversibly alter the world's food supply—and the path of evolution in many ecosystems—isn't there cause for being *especially* careful?

Specific Risks of Growing and Consuming Transgenic Crops

Yet it is not just vague unease that triggers precaution. Biologists, food nutritionists, ecologists, and social scientists have raised numerous, more specific questions about the long-term safety of GMOs in regard to human health and the environment. There are two broad categories of questions.

First, do transgenic plants cause any adverse health effects in the animals—especially human animals—who consume them? Although there is no evidence to date that any commercialized GMO product has hurt anyone, there is reason for continued vigilance. For the peculiar characteristics of transgenic products create new potential sources of danger. For one thing, the randomness inherent in the process of gene insertion could cause unexpected problems. As Lewontin (2001, 82) remarks,

> Tomatoes are delicious, but you would be ill-advised to eat the leaves and stems because they contain toxins. It is not impossible that a genetically engineered tomato might, by bad luck, start to produce toxins in the fruit. Thus the process of genetic engineering itself has a unique ability to produce deleterious effects and . . . this justifies the view that all varieties produced by recombinant DNA technology need to be specially scrutinized and tested for such effects.

In the same category of unwanted dietary effects are GMOs that provoke severe allergic reactions in some people. An experimental soybean that was genetically engineered to contain a Brazil nut protein (to make it more nutritious) caused a reaction in people who were allergic to Brazil nuts (Nordlee et al. 1996). This might be no greater cause for alarm than learning that peanuts cause a severe allergic reaction in some people. These individuals learn to take special care to avoid foods containing peanuts and their derivative products. The difference is that with genetic engineering, the allergy-provoking gene might end up—unknown to consumers—being spliced into just about anything: soybeans, corn, squash, or wheat. Peanuts were never so promiscuous.

Related worries about the ingestion of GM crops come from the use of antibiotic marker genes in GMOs. In the 1990s, scientists routinely added a gene for antibiotic resistance to plants with which they were experimenting. This facilitated the task of identifying individuals that had integrated the desired transgene. This practice has since been abandoned, out of fear that the antibiotic resistance gene might be incorporated by other bacteria, in the intestines of consuming animals or the soil. GMOs might thus contribute to the growing problem of antibiotic-resistant infections. In addition, there is some evidence, albeit controversial (but almost all evidence regarding GMOs is controversial to some extent), that certain transgenic soybeans are less rich in nutrients associated with protection against heart disease and breast cancer (Teitel and Wilson 1999, 47–50). Meanwhile, there are concerns that the active molecules in pest-protected GMOs may mimic certain hormones in humans, with the possibility of effects on the reproductive system or the growth of cancer cells (Seralini 2000, 85).

The second broad category of safety concerns relates to the environmental effects of GMOs. What are the chances that biotech crops might adversely affect the ecosystems in which they are located? Again, much depends on the specific genetically engineered traits in question. It is best at this point to focus on the most widely imparted traits: herbicide resistance and biopesticide production. Growing herbicide-resistant crops carries with it the danger of developing "superweeds." Transgenic crops spread their pollen to surrounding areas. If they have native relatives among the wild floras, they can form hybrids—hybrids that become herbicide resistant too (Lewontin 2001, 83). These hybrids then show up in farmers' fields and cannot be controlled by the preferred broad-spectrum herbicide. Moreover, certain transgenic crops like sunflowers and rapeseed themselves are capable of becoming weeds in their own right, much as exotic plants like kudzu have sometimes invaded ecosystems where they were transplanted. Some of today's most pernicious weeds were intentionally introduced as crops or ornamental plants (Rissler and Mellon 1996, 36–40). At any rate, predicting the potential weediness of a plant is an imperfect science. There can be a long delay between the first cultivation of a plant and its becoming a weed—two hundred years in the case of proso millet (Reiss and Straughan 1996, 147–150). So it is quite possible that some GMOs will end up being invasive and persistent to an unanticipated degree. In addition, as herbicides are more widely applied, herbicide-resistant specimens are likely to emerge by the process of natural selection. In all these cases, farmers could then no longer count on using a broad-range herbicide to protect their crops.

In a similar fashion, the widespread use of Bt biopesticide crops may accelerate the evolution of insects resistant to this relatively benign pest-control agent (Zhao et al. 2005). Meanwhile, beneficial species, such as "soil-inhabiting insects that degrade plant debris containing the insecticidal toxins" from Bt crops may be hurt (Rissler and Mellon 1996, 42). One famous article reported in the journal *Nature* (Losey, Rayor, and Carter 1999) demonstrated that Bt pollen can, under certain conditions, kill monarch butterfly caterpillars. While subsequent studies have minimized the significance of this finding, they have not necessarily laid to rest its troubling implication: biopesticides can harm the development of nontarget species. As these crops are cultivated in ever more diverse ecological contexts around the world, the possibility of a more serious, unanticipated harm increases.

Finally, the spread of transgenic agriculture may have adverse effects on biodiversity. This is because unlike traditional crossbreeding, genetic engineers are seeking to give plants traits that increase their survival rate. Their competitive superiority in resistance to pests and diseases may enable them to "replace native species—with the result that the makeup of the community is altered or local species or subpopulations are driven to extinction" (Rissler and Mellon 1996, 41). This possibility is especially disquieting in relation to effects on centers of crop diversity. These centers are regions in the world where the ancestor species of today's crops still exist. Mexico, for example, harbors relatives of the varieties of corn that are cultivated at present. When crops are threatened by new environmental stresses (diseases, pests, and drought tolerance), plant breeders and genetic engineers turn to these ancestor species as the source of traits that will enable crops to fight the threat. The inability to keep biotech crops from spreading means that natural reserves of biodiversity will gradually be invaded by transgenes. In 2001, scientists discovered that GM corn had already spread into native corn varieties in fifteen localities Mexico, in spite of that country's ban on growing biotech crops (Genetic Modification 2001). Centers of crop diversity are already under great pressure from the expansion of modern agriculture. GMOs may worsen this trend, as biotech crops replace wild species or as transgenes flow into their populations (Rissler and Mellon 1996, 113–115).

Regulating Transgenic Crops: The American Way

Given so much uncertainty and this array of potential problems, it seems wise to take precautions. One thus asks, Are there sufficient safeguards in place so that problems can be detected and eliminated before they enter the marketplace? Are GMO producers systematically testing for such potential problems? Is there a legal structure in place to enforce compliance? If there were an unexpected problem, could its source be located? Would it be possible to clear the distribution system of the problematic goods? Are citizens being given information that would allow them to decide if the risks involved are ones they want to take? Precaution is a matter of pursuing these questions with a care and thoroughness that is proportional to the seriousness of the potential dangers. In the United States, GMO regulatory policy moved from precautionary to permissive in the space of less than ten years.

When Berg completed the first successful experiment in gene splicing in 1971, the United States was in a phase of environmental regulatory activism. In the same year as the first Earth Day (1970), Congress passed the National Environmental Policy Act to mandate environmental-impact assessments of major government projects. The Environmental Protection Agency (EPA) was created in 1971. The Federal Water Pollution Control Act of 1972 sought to prevent toxic discharges into U.S. waterways. And there was growing public attention to a widening circle of issues such as nuclear power safety, resource exhaustion, and species protection. In this context of environmental concern, Berg took the lead in urging scientists to explore the possible dangers of genetic engineering. In 1974, under the aegis of the National Academy of Sciences, he published a letter calling for a moratorium on certain types of gene-splicing experiments until the possible dangers could be better assessed. His efforts culminated in a 1975 meeting at the Asilomar Conference Center in California. The Asilomar conference issued a preliminary regulatory framework for GM research, which was then elaborated on in official detail by the National Institutes of Health (NIH) in 1976. The United States was thus the first state in the world to regulate recombinant DNA technology. Essentially, the NIH framework prohibited experiments on especially dangerous (for example, cancer-producing) organisms, forbade the deliberate release of GMOs into the environment, and called for devising various types of containment measures for experiments with less dangerous organisms (Gottweis 1998, 83–99). Grounded in uncertainties rather than known dangers, these regulations had a distinctly precautionary flavor.

From this relatively stringent start, however, U.S. policy rapidly evolved in a more permissive direction. There were no GM accidents in the first years of research, so guidelines were revised in 1978 and 1980. The requirement of registration with the NIH was dropped. In 1982, it became possible to get authorization for the deliberate release of GMOs into the environment following a multitiered review process (Gottweis 1998, 101–102). But these requirements applied only to federally funded research. By the early 1980s, industry had become seriously interested in the commercial potential of recombinant DNA technology and so had begun doing much research on its own.

The Reagan administration sought to accelerate this trend by lessening the regulatory burdens on biotechnology companies. The EPA was, at first, not entirely in step with this philosophy. In 1984, it announced plans to regulate biotechnology under existing laws applying to insecticides and "toxic substances." The White House intervened to chart a different course. It convened a special, interagency working group to establish federal policy. This move allowed the White House to keep the EPA from assuming predominant regulatory responsibilities in the field of biotech regulation. It also allowed a framework for biotech regulation to be hammered out in meetings that were not open to the public (Lynch and Vogel 2000).

Key features of U.S. policy in regard to GMOs were established in the working group report, *The Coordinated Framework for the Regulation of Biotechnology*. First, biotechnology regulation is not under the auspices of a single department. Three agencies divide oversight. The U.S. Department of Agriculture (USDA) is supposed to ensure that GM crops do not harm traditional agriculture. The USDA's Animal and Plant Health Inspection Service regulates transgenic plants only if they are seen as having the potential to do damage. The Food and Drug Administration (FDA) concerns itself with any possible human health effects of GM food. It examines the safety of foods, feed additives, and drugs. The EPA evaluates the potential effects of plants engineered to contain pesticide genes. Implicit in this decision to split regulatory responsibilities is the key assumption of U.S. regulatory policy regarding transgenic crops: genetic modifications per se entail no special dangers that would justify treating them as a unique category (Joly 2000, 53). As the National Research Council (1989; cited in Jasanoff 1995) subsequently formulated this doctrine, "The *product* of genetic modification and selection constitutes the primary basis for decisions . . . and not the *process* by which the product was obtained." There is no cause to regulate a product merely because it was created by the process of gene splicing. Special care need be taken only in regard to products that have potentially troublesome characteristics (for instance, they contained genes from a known allergen, or they had been engineered to produce a hormone).

At this point, one of the most ironic developments occurred in recent regulatory history in the United States. At the very time when the Reagan administration was implementing its deregulatory agenda, the infant biotech industry lobbied the government to get itself regulated. In 1986, executives from the leading biotech company, Monsanto, approached Vice President George Bush. The *New York Times* (Redesigning Nature 2001, p. A1) reported what happened next, and why:

> The company wanted its new technology, genetically modified food, to be governed by rules issued in Washington—and wanted the White House to champion the idea. "There were no products at the time," [recalled] Leonard Guarraia, a former Monsanto executive who attended the Bush meeting. . . . "But we bugged him for regulation. We told him that we have to be regulated." Government guidelines, the executives reasoned, would reassure a public that was growing skittish about the safety of this radical new science. In the weeks and months that followed, the White House complied, working behind the scenes to help Monsanto . . . get the regulations it wanted. It was an outcome that would be repeated, again and again, through three administrations. . . . If the company's strategy demanded regulations, rules favored by the industry were adopted. And when the company abruptly decided that it needed to throw off the regulations and speed its foods to

market, the White House quickly pushed through an unusually generous policy of self-policing.

At the very end of the (first) Bush administration, when the first biotech foods were ready to be marketed, Vice President Dan Quayle announced reforms that declared, in essence, that biotech foods were no different from other foodstuffs. There was no need for the FDA to review each and every one of them. Nor were companies required to perform premarket safety tests on them. Companies were simply invited to seek a voluntary—and confidential—consultation with the FDA when they were about to launch a new GM food (Hart 2002, 80). GM food need be labeled as such only if it "differs significantly from its conventional counterpart" (FDA 1992). Except in such cases, there was no reason to keep GM products separate from conventionally derived ones along the whole chain of food distribution. Meanwhile, the USDA established criteria for exempting many GM plants from needing special authorization.[4] In 1995, the EPA consulted with its Scientific Advisory Panel and approved in quick succession Monsanto's applications for a Bt potato, corn and cotton (Hart 2002, 115). It was essentially this regulatory regime that prevailed right up until the time when the first GM crops were brought to market in the United States—and exported to Europe.[5]

In light of the uncertainties and potential hazards mentioned earlier, many features of this regulatory regime seem unduly incautious. What deficiencies stand out?

- The United States sought relatively little testing of GMOs, either for the long-term health effects on the animals that consume them or the adverse environmental consequences. Biotech companies are not required to run controlled tests to see if animals eating GM foods suffer any damage to their health (Hart 2002, 100). Monsanto concluded that their Roundup Ready soybeans were safe for consumption after studies, none lasting longer than ten weeks, on a few species of animals (Seralini 2000, 82). There were no controlled experiments on primates or humans. The field tests of GMOs have been similarly limited. The sponsors of field tests are not required to monitor the ecological effects of their crops—and few of them do (Rissler and Mellon 1996, 123).

- Scientific uncertainties were minimized in the rush to bring GMOs to market. Many scientists had, and continue to have, doubts about the adequacy of GMO testing. Of particular significance in sustaining uncertainty are the differences in understandings of nature between different scientific disciplines. Molecular biologists, who do their work in controlled laboratory environments, often see more predictability in the objects of their analysis than do ecologists, who study the interaction of bacteria, plants, animals, climate, and soil under complex "natural" conditions (Levidow et al. 1997, 477). One way to contain the uncertainties about GMO safety is simply to limit the range of scientists invited to evaluate them. So while field trials of bacteria designed to prevent frost damage to crops were approved by an NIH committee in 1983, that committee's confidence was underwritten by the complete absence of ecologists and botanists from its membership (Reiss and Straughan 1996, 116). It was conditions such as these that by 1986—just thirteen years after the first transgenic organism had been created—allowed Monsanto executives to decide that their products were completely safe and ready to be brought to market.

• The government offers little in the way of independent evaluation of industry's claims about safety. Having found GM food to be "substantially equivalent" to conventionally grown food, the FDA argues that there is no need for it carry out an assessment of every GM food product. Under any circumstances, it lacks the resources to do so. The federal agencies charged with overseeing agricultural biotechnology generally rely on safety assessment data provided by the parties seeking approval for their product. (Lewontin 2001, 82). To reach its regulatory decisions, the USDA does not generate its own experimental data; it has to base its judgment on extrapolations from the scientific literature (Rissler and Mellon 1996, 123).

• The whole process of designing regulatory structures was closed to the public and largely shaped by the very industry that was to be regulated. The chief accomplishment of this lack of transparency was to get the government to favor the doctrine of "substantial equivalency." The substantial equivalency doctrine means that consumers never even get to choose whether to consume GM products or not. GM and non-GM goods will be mixed because no substantial difference separates them. Yet a poll in 1999 found that 81 percent of the U.S. public would prefer to see GM products labeled as such (Brave New Farm 1999). This discrepancy between policy and public judgment is a concern not only from the perspective of consumer rights but from that of appropriate precaution as well. For policies allowing the undeclared mixing of GM and non-GM products are precisely the ones that make it impossible for anyone with suspicions about GMOs to track their effects. They obliterate the possibility of detecting early warning signs of health or environmental danger.

• The methods of cultivating GM crops and disseminating products derived from them does not allow for monitoring or recall. This is not how the U.S. government has proceeded in the case of drugs or food additives. These products are meticulously labeled, and their distribution is tracked. Then, when an unanticipated problem arises, it is at least possible to trace the problem back to its source and remove the dangerous product from sale. Biotech products in the United States are generally unlabeled and untracked. So, if after a number of years, any of the potential risks to human health do happen to materialize, it will be extremely difficult to discover the role of the transgenic product in the risk and then remove the product from distribution.

• U.S. regulations lack a global dimension. Such as they are, U.S. regulations are designed to protect U.S. consumers and their environment. Thus, when studies are done of a crop's potential weediness, for example, it is tested relative to environmental conditions in the United States. Yet GM seeds and crops are destined for global distribution. Companies like Cargill and Monsanto are multinational, and fully intend to ply their wares in countries around the world—including regions that are the ancestral centers of crop diversity. There is no guarantee that plants that can be safely grown in the United States can with similar safety be grown elsewhere. Much depends on whether there are sexually compatible plants in the region. Examples of nonnative species unexpectedly proliferating in a new environment and outcompeting many native species are in the background of worries about GMOs as well (Reiss and Straughan 1996, 147–148). One response might be that it is up to the importing countries to evaluate any dangers that GMOs might pose to local floras. A persistent problem, however, is that recipient countries often lack the resources to undertake their own risk assessments. So the global market in biotech crops has been launched, with few safeguards against unwanted, irreversible, and perhaps global effects on biodiversity (Rissler and Mellon 1996, 111–119).

Regulating Transgenic Crops: European Experiences

In the 1970s, Europeans roughly followed the lead of the United States in the regulation of biotechnology. The European Molecular Biology Organization had been established in 1963. Its representatives attended the Asilomar conference and subsequently sought to promote the NIH guidelines throughout Europe. The rapid relaxation of those guidelines in the United States removed most of the pressure to adopt a uniform law for the European Community as a whole (Gottweis 1998, 107–109.) Thus, in the 1980s, different European states were free to adopt procedures that conformed to their own institutional traditions and political priorities. Two countries, Germany and France, played especially powerful roles in moving Europe toward increasingly precautionary forms of biotechnology regulation.

Before the GMO crisis broke out in 1996, the French state was closely involved in promoting agricultural biotechnology. From the 1970s on, it worked closely with the agrofood industry to accelerate research on recombinant DNA technology. Unusually, it gave industry substantial space for self-regulation. By the mid-1990s, France led Europe in deliberate-release field trials of GMOs and accounted for the majority of requests for commercial applications of GMOs in the EU (Cheveigné, Boy, and Galloux 2000, 31–32). In this period, the media rarely took notice of GMO experimentation in France. Indeed, in 1994, the Swiss biotechnology firm Novartis deliberately chose France as the market in which it would introduce GMOs into Europe, precisely because it was pleased to find a government supportive of biotechnology and a public seemingly prepared to accept the new products without qualms (Marris and Joly 1999, 102). This is important to remember in light of later events. When France took the lead in resisting GMO imports into Europe in 1998 and 1999, disgruntled U.S. politicians accused it of using "protectionist" policies to shield its agricultural sector against more technologically advanced forms of farming. But in fact, the French government had long hoped not to protect traditional agriculture but to modernize it, and hence to keep France competitive in this lucrative field of international commerce. Indeed, what sparked the 1996 crisis was not France's rejection of GMOs but rather its having pushed the European Commission to give final authorization for marketing a form of Bt corn that also contained an antibiotic marker.[6]

Still, unlike the United States, at no point did the French assume that GMOs should be handled in the same regulatory framework as traditional crops and foods. The French government's whole structure of regulation rested on the supposition that the process of genetic modification, not just its products, deserved scrutiny. Its regulatory front line for GMOs was established in 1986 when the Commission for Biomolecular Engineering (CGB) was constituted. Until 1992, consulting this commission before deliberately releasing any GMO was optional; nevertheless, GMO developers always sought its advice (Commissariat Général du Plan 2001, 48). The CGB examines the health risks that a plant might cause (for example, toxicity for people or animals); it compares the nutritional value of a GMO to traditional varieties of a plant; it assesses the probability of cross-species breeding. Then it delivers a consensual finding to the National Assembly (Dossier de l'Environnement 1996). A second expert body, the Commission for Genetic Engineering (CGG), examines the scientific procedures used in producing a transgenic organism and then classifies the organism according to the degree of risk that it might pose to human health or the environment. This classification determines whether experiments with GMOs must be done in more or less confined spaces (Ministère de l'Économie 2000). With the French public demonstrating no particular concerns about plant biotechnology in the 1980s, these regulatory bodies were able to make decisions in the absence of almost any citizen input (Cheveigné, Boy, and Galloux 2000, 173).

In Germany, genetic engineering has long been more controversial. As a result, German laws moved in a more precautionary direction many years before the controversy of 1996. Germany is usually acknowledged as the birthplace of the European version of the precautionary principle. Its origins in the *Vorsorgeprinzip* in the 1970s will be discussed further in chapter 3. What is important in the present context is that in the 1980s, the newly influential Green Party was able to seize on established standards favoring preventive action in environmental protection and use them to create pressure for the careful regulation of all GMOs.

These efforts (and those of many other organizations) bore fruit in the 1990 Act for the Regulation of Questions of Genetic Engineering. This law covered all phases of work with GMOs, from the laboratory to production, transportation, and disposal. It defined safety levels for different types of transgenic organisms. Different safety levels then required different levels of confinement and, in most cases, public hearings before commercialization could begin. Risk assessment responsibilities were assigned to the Central Commission for Biological Security (ZKBS). The ZKBS included not only experts—among them, two ecologists—but also "social" representatives from organized labor, business, and environmental protection organizations. It had to evaluate every deliberate release of GMOs, including the experimenters' methods for monitoring the effects of the GMOs and their emergency plans (Gottweis 1998, 266–293).

The German law served as a model for subsequent European Community legislation on plant biotechnology (Cheveigné, Boy, and Galloux 2000, 31, 52). In view of the imminent commercialization of GMOs, the European Community had to find a consensual position among a group of nations, some of which were far more sensitive to agricultural biotechnology than others. Denmark and Holland, like Germany, were already cautious; the United Kingdom was somewhat supportive, as long as procedures were "transparent" (Hermitte and Noiville 1993, 401). The compromise position was established in Deliberate Release Directive 90/220, issued in April 1990. It combined a uniform requirement that GMOs, as such, undergo risk assessment before release into the environment, with an allowance for national variation in the mode of assessment. As David Vogel (2001, 7) explains:

> Applicants who wanted to conduct field tests of GMOs were required to apply and submit an environmental risk assessment to the "competent authority" of the country where testing will occur. [The directive] further required another application to each Member State to market genetically modified products and granted each Member State the right to object to such marketing within their borders. Under Article 16, any EU member state may "provisionally restrict or prohibit" the use or sale of a product if it has justifiable reason to suspect that an approved product poses a "risk to human health or the environment."

In order to harmonize the assessments of the (then) fifteen members of the European Community, a procedure was accepted whereby a country desiring European Community authorization would have to submit its assessments for comments, requests for additional information, and possible objections (Commissariat Général du Plan 2001, 52).

As the German case shows, European nations made decisions about how to structure biotechnology regulation in the context of an overarching commitment to precaution (Vogel 2001, 7; Commissariat Général du Plan 2001, 51). Indeed, in 1992, the European Community incorporated the precautionary principle into its most general statement of the means by which it intended to achieve a "high level of environmental protection."[7] This statement governed the efforts of member states to adjust their national-level biotechnology regulations in light of European Community–level directives. European states recognized an *obligation* to evaluate this powerful new technology with an eye to *anticipating and avoiding* possible adverse consequences.

How could this obligation be fulfilled in relation to such a new technology? From the start, European states applied general lessons learned from twentieth-century experiences with roughly analogous issues. Experience taught that biodiversity can be harmed when nonnative species spread invasively in new environments. As novel organisms, GMOs might have similar, unpredicted tendencies. Experience with persistent organic chemicals suggested that any lasting substance introduced into ecosystems might end up affecting even distantly removed organisms. That lesson counsels precaution with transgenic crops because they are persistent in a more active sense: they are self-reproducing. Experience with pesticides, asbestos, and nuclear radiation showed that there may be long latency periods before the damage to human health and the environment become apparent. Transgenic crops, too, might have unforeseen long-term consequences on living things that consumed them every day. Certainly this could not be ruled out, given the poor understanding of the conditions of gene implantation, gene expression, and plans to create organisms with pharmaceutical properties.

Europe's precautionary view of transgenic crops is epitomized in its commitment to regulate not individual *products,* but everything that comes from a *process* of genetic engineering. This commitment signals an awareness that regulators are dealing with an incompletely understood technology that is destined to become part of large-scale ecological processes. The novelty of these creations and the complexity of the environmental circumstances in which they will be used mean that questions about their safety are surrounded with significant uncertainties. That is why European states created systems for categorizing GMOs according to their degree of possible environmental danger and included diverse forms of expertise in arriving at those evaluations. All GMOs had to be assessed before they could be brought to market.

Even though this regulatory apparatus had a precautionary orientation, it still did not satisfy many European citizens. Italy, Luxembourg, and

Austria refused to allow trade in the genetically engineered corn that the EU had officially authorized. In France, civil disobedients repeatedly uprooted transgenic plants from experimental plots. Then at a European Council meeting in June 1999, France, along with Denmark, Greece, Italy, and Luxemburg, got the European Union to adopt a virtual moratorium on all new authorizations of GMOs for deliberate release (Europe Information Service 2000). Subsequent events and debates suggested that several important features of precautionary policy were still missing.

First, precautionary concerns prompted greater attention to the composition and rules of functioning for regulatory bodies. Although Europeans—unlike Americans—had set up specialized regulatory panels to examine the safety of all GMOs, they did not necessarily take measures to ensure that these bodies operated independently of the preestablished interests of the state or industry. France's CGB, for example, originally had a much more elitist composition than Germany's ZKBS. The French committee was heavily weighted toward scientists. Observers noted that the few nonscientists rarely commented on the committee's decisions (Dossier de l'environnement 1996). An internal ethic led committee members to seek a consensus around the assumption that its purpose was to encourage the development of biotechnology in France (Joly et al. 2000, 29). So one reform was to enlarge and recompose the CGB so that the consensual assumption would not always prevail.[8]

Links to private interests were recognized as a potential problem as well. As Marie-Jose Nicoli, president of a French consumer protection organization, once noted, "In certain areas, the most well-informed scientists belong to the private sector. It is hard to find a specialist on GMOs who has no links with an agrochemical firm" (quoted in Experts 2001). There can be no question of excluding people with such affiliations, for they are often precisely the ones with the scientific competence necessary to understand the complicated dossiers involved in GMO evaluation. One thing that can be done, however, is to require all members to reveal their ties to the relevant industries in a formal declaration. Another thing is to allow dissenting members of such bodies to append separate opinions to their panel's reports. There is also greater likelihood of there being fruitful dissent if committee membership is widened to include a range of specialists—particularly plant biologists and environmental scientists (Roy 2001, 48–49). All of these changes (implemented by the French government in 1998) have a precautionary bearing insofar as they stimulate further inquiry and enable external observers to track potential controversies, even if these have not yet been consecrated by a consensus of experts.

Second, European experience led to enhanced precaution in the form of seeking greater citizen participation in the regulatory process. In this area, Denmark has led the way (Joss 1998, 3). Since 1987, the Danes have held "consensus conferences" around such issues as information technology, transportation policy, and biotechnology. Consensus conferences are carefully organized public events in which citizens question scientists about the stakes in some matter of scientific/technological controversy and then issue a policy-oriented report on their conclusions. Some fifteen other countries with different political traditions have decided to borrow the Danish model of consensus conferences. Conferences on biotechnology were held in 1993 in Holland and in 1994 in the United Kingdom; in 1996, German citizens panels debated policy responses to climate change (Davidson, Barns, and Scibeci 1997, 339; Mironesco 1998, 338; Hörning 1999). In November 1997, as public skepticism about GMOs continued to grow in France, the French prime minister called for a consensus conference on the subject. That event, which took place in June 1998, ended up being only the first in a series of experimental forms of public consultation about regulatory matters that were usually left to legislators and their scientific advisory panels (Whiteside 2003a).

How new forms of citizen participation can have precautionary effects is illustrated by the French example. In a public forum, the citizens' questions got scientists to admit to uncertainties, or at least disagreements, about the environmental effects of GMOs (Marris and Joly 1999). Among the panel's policy recommendations was a complete ban on the use of antibiotic marker genes.[9] Initially, the French government did not follow the citizens panel's recommendation (Husset 1999, 114). But by 2000, when the prime minister was anxious to give his government credit for its popular consultations, he changed his policy. Today, the addition of antibiotic marker genes to GMOs is generally agreed to have been a bad idea. These genes were originally added not to produce any commercially desirable trait in the crops but just to facilitate scientific experiments with them as mentioned earlier. The molecular biologists who made this decision—and the closed risk-assessment bodies that approved it—did so with little appreciation for how genes might move in the environment (Hart 2002,

95–96). It is thus significant that a nonexpert citizens panel played a role in a precautionary turnabout on this part of GMO regulatory policy.

Third, precaution mandated the labeling and traceability of the novel products. Before 1997, EU regulations—like those in the United States—pertained only to the premarket testing of GMOs. It was assumed that once GMO producers and various regulatory authorities concluded products were safe, then they were safe, period. The moratorium that began in 1999 stemmed from several countries' insistence that the EU adopt a mandatory labeling policy. Labeling requirements are precautionary in the sense that they take more seriously the possibility of regulatory lapses and unexpected developments. As noted earlier, labeling seeds and consumer products as GM is an essential condition for tracing problems, should they occur, back to their source. It allows people with allergy concerns, for example, to choose non-GM products. If some completely unexpected syndrome were to develop, it would be possible, as with tainted drugs, to circle in on the source and withdraw the product.

In January 2000, the EU announced a labeling requirement applying to foods containing 1 percent or more GM ingredients. The EU's reforms were capped off in March 2001 with a new directive to replace the GMO regulatory policies it had adopted in 1990. Directive 2001/18 included such measures as follow-up procedures for marketed products along with a provisional, ten-year authorization for sale, the prohibition of genes for resistance to antibiotics, and taking account of indirect effects on agricultural practices. For countries like Austria, France, and Italy, writes French sociologist Alexis Roy (2001, 35), "the process of revising the European directive constituted . . . an opportunity to orient that reform toward greater consideration for the precautionary principle . . . and inserting more of the public's concerns into the scientific evaluation of risks."

The Nature of Precaution

There are no simple answers in the field of agricultural biotechnology regulation. The potential benefits that innovation might bring are so significant that banning GMOs permanently is out of the question. At any rate, the transgenie is out of the bottle, so to speak. Even if some nations wanted to ban GMOs, the economic advantages that they bring are such that some other nations would surely continue to grow them. Not only the United

States but also China is vigorously pursuing biotech agriculture on a massive scale (Chine 2002). Through environmental processes of dispersion as well as international commerce, transgenes will spread on an ever-wider scale. One way or another, we will have to live with them. On the other hand, recombinant DNA technology has more than enough potential for harm to human health and the environment that even its staunchest defenders dare not argue for dismantling every regulatory safeguard. If Bt soybeans turn out to be entirely safe, no one can be certain about the effects of the *next* generation of GMOs. Scientists are working on creating "immunofoods" that manufacture pharmaceuticals—cancer drugs and growth hormones—for human consumption. Who knows what will happen when these plants are eaten by soil bacteria, earthworms, insects, field mice, and so on (Rissler and Mellon 1996, 42–43).

One thing that makes GMO regulation such a useful starting point for a discussion of the precautionary principle is that it helps us avoid certain simplistic dichotomies that too often cloud environmental thinking. Much environmental thought vacillates between anthropocentrism and ecocentrism—that is, between grounding environmental concern either in human interests or in terms of the interests, rights, or well-being of nonhuman entities (Whiteside 2002, 58–65). Both perspectives fall short in helping us think about how to react to agricultural biotechnology.

Ecocentrists argue in favor of the "moral standing of the nonhuman world," claiming that we humans have an obligation "to ensure that it, too, may unfold in diverse ways" (Eckersley 1992, 26). Often ecocentrists say that natural things, from individual organisms up through ecosystems, strive to preserve themselves and flourish *on their own terms;* they must express their own *nature.* Nature consists of self-generating, self-perpetuating, and self-realizing systems of complexly interacting life-forms (and the nonbiotic environment on which they depend). On occasion, this style of argument is put forth in defense of the precautionary principle itself (O'Riordan and Jordan 1995, 196; Attfield 2003, 145; Eckersley 1999). A prevention-oriented conception of environmental protection is necessary, in this view, precisely because it lets natural entities continue to exist, rather than making them adapt to human-imposed changes.

Ecocentrism has difficulty capturing the nuances of debate surrounding genetically engineered organisms. GMOs seem to be the antithesis of nature as ecocentrists understand it. For GMOs have no *natural* self-identity.

Human purposes fashion them, right down to their genes. And their unnatural identity is, allegedly, what makes them dangerous to natural ecosystems. If pesticide beets might become a noxious weed, for instance, it is because genetic engineers have given them an advantage unlike any that has evolved naturally in related plants in the environment surrounding farmers' fields. It is hard to see what an ecocentric precautionary principle could do in relation to transgenic organisms except ban them completely.

Such reasoning runs up against a host of difficulties. An absolute, principled objection to GMOs would seem to rule out even highly beneficial ones that are kept in confinement. Today, most supplies of human insulin and human growth hormone are synthesized industrially in vats by GM bacteria (Reiss and Straughan 1996, 99–103). If unnatural is bad, how can we avoid condemning such products? Furthermore, if we reject GM crops in the name of protecting the identity of natural things, we are led back, not to nature, but to some other highly developed form of biotechnology. Even the most environmentally benign forms of sustainable agriculture are highly unnatural, in the sense that they require focused human intervention to select plant varieties, keep out pests, and maintain nutrients in the soil. Whether an agricultural practice is, on balance, desirable or undesirable depends on answers to a complex set of questions. These are partly empirical (Is there really less impact on surrounding ecosystems? Does organic produce really carry fewer health dangers for consumers?) and partly ethical (What are our obligations to future generations? Does sustainable agriculture create a more harmonious way of life in the community?). In neither case are the questions plausibly settled by referring to a priori intuitions about what is natural.

It might seem that having criticized a self-balancing nature as a standard of environmental value, we are free to evaluate GMOs strictly in terms of their benefits and costs for us. Yet this anthropocentric alternative is problematic too. The difficulty is not that anthropocentrism is inherently antienvironmental. Any possible harm that might eventually have a negative impact on human life can count in an anthropocentric evaluation (Hayward 1998; Barry 1999). Damages to ecosystems on which human well-being relies, harms to people's leisure or aesthetic interests, imposed losses on future generations: all of these belong on the balance sheet. The problem is that anthropocentrism, just as much as ecocentrism, presupposes that we know what nature is and how it behaves. Characteristically, an ecologically enlightened anthropocentrist would call for sustainable agricultural practices by avoiding soil erosion, diminishing the use of pesticides, and so forth. Such practices are grounded in the notion that natural processes of assimilation and recycling can absorb human impact and rebound from it, but only to a limited extent. The goal of anthropocentric environmentalism is to fit a rightly understood nature into the broader scheme of human interests so that we do not inadvertently diminish nature's ability to satisfy our preferences.

GMOs challenge this nature as well. Debates about the conditions of gene expression at the cellular level, gene flow in the environment, allergenicity, weediness, and so forth are debates about *what nature is*. That is, they raise questions about whether various changes let loose in the world *really will* behave in expected ways. Depending on how some GMO *actually* behaves in a number of contexts, the bottom line of its balance sheet may be hugely positive—or hugely negative. Focusing on whether human interests are the ultimate standard of environmental value obscures even more fundamental questions: How do we come to know what nature is? And what are our obligations as we work through the process of trying to understand it?

Precaution is this uncertainty made self-conscious. As a result, precaution cannot prejudge environmental risks on the grounds that certain changes are unnatural. Nor can it make decisions about technologies as a function of their so-called sustainability. Rather, precaution obliges us to examine and discuss the innumerable linkages through which we come to know nature. It diversifies the contacts at the interface of nature and humanity. It problematizes and opens to discussion the values that are implicit in the scientific framing of environmental issues.

Europe's handling of GMOs suggests what this alternative way of thinking looks like. Precaution mandates transdisciplinary research. It avoids assuming that just one or a few sciences can pose all the right questions in relation to something that becomes part of the environment at large. When authorizing new technologies, precaution means first devising strategies that allow time for experience to accumulate in small-scale settings before releasing them into the larger world. It then monitors them carefully and plans for potential emergency situations. Precaution also means rethinking the very notion of the public interest. It causes us to examine the social values implicit in political systems where elected representatives often defer to the advice of experts. Precaution calls for reinforcing the independence of regulatory bodies and opening risk assessment to new types of democratic scrutiny. Through precaution, we become more skeptical of knowledge claims about the environment, more reflective about our relationship with nature, more attentive to the long-term consequences of our way of life, and perhaps, more receptive to new modes of political participation.

Not unexpectedly, those wide-ranging implications are troubling to many in government and business, particularly in the United States. Instead of the precautionary principle, they advocate science-based risk regulation in a "cost-benefit state." Their arguments deserve a hearing—and a response.

2

Debating Precaution

In the course of the U.S.-European negotiations over GM crops, Christine Todd Whitman (then head of the EPA) found the precautionary principle "concerning" because its premise is that "whatever it is you're doing, you've got to stop." Producers might be ordered to halt an allegedly dangerous activity, not because there was scientific evidence of harm, but simply because someone feared that there might be. That is not how science should be used in risk assessment and management. Whitman insisted that "science should be at the heart and soul of every decision that you make relative to protecting human health and the environment" (quoted in Federal News Service 2001).

It was odd to hear cool, dispassionate science associated with the "heart and soul" of decision making. It was revealing too. The precautionary principle at least makes its opponents own up to the fact that in contemporary policymaking, "science" is integrated in decision-making processes in ways that make it much more than a neutral counselor to power. It offers a soul—an arrangement of virtues, and perhaps even a set of ends. That might be fine, if we know we are choosing these ends and they are the ones we want. Before deciding, however, we need to acquaint ourselves with the virtues of science-based risk management. We must ask, When we put science at the heart of decision making, are we effectively accepting not just a method of risk evaluation but a particular *ethic* of risk taking? If so, is that ethic antiprecautionary? Did Whitman mean to endorse a principle like this: whatever you are doing, you must be allowed to continue, no matter how serious the potential consequences, as long as scientific evidence confirming the danger remains unavailable, uncertain, or controversial?

Both sides, for and against the precautionary principle, need to confront the implications of their position. The time has come for genuine debate.

Therefore, be it resolved that the international community should adopt the precautionary principle as a guiding norm for global environmental protection.

Ideally, a systematic debate is a clarifying moment. Debate helps separate critique from caricature. It can also help reveal the most broadly persuasive reasons for one position or another. Several conclusions, I will argue, emerge from the confrontation of views over the precautionary principle. First, the principle has a core meaning. It applies most clearly to a particular category of new risks—ones that are large scale and develop slowly, often with irreversible consequences. Second, the precautionary principle is not to be equated with prohibiting the source of the risk. The precautionary principle calls for a wide range of potential regulatory actions—actions that can be proportioned to the degree of uncertainty and gravity associated with the risk. Third, contrasting the precautionary principle with science-based regulation is seriously misleading. The history of GMO regulation suggests a far more complicated situation than a rational, scientific United States facing off against a fear-driven Europe. Precaution mandates *more* science, more investigation. It is also a call for doing science *differently*, with more dialogue between practitioners in disparate disciplines and more transparency in relation to the nonscientific community. Does that open the door to irrational or politicized risk-management, as charged by the opponents of the precautionary principle?

Let the debate begin.

The Case for the Precautionary Principle: Taking Account of New Risks

Why do we need a supplementary dose of precaution in our methods of assessing and managing risk? The short answer is, because existing methods are inadequate in the face of new environmental risks. The long-term, delayed, global dangers created by powerful new technologies can exceed the ability of current strategies to contain them (Bourg and Schlegel 2001, 48–51). We need the precautionary principle for special situations in which ordinary assumptions about risk management do not hold.

Perhaps the most significant lesson to emerge from the study of ecology in the twentieth century is that humanity now acts on a scale that affects the well-being of every life-form on this planet. We have become a "planetary geological force," in the words of one of the pioneers of scientific ecology,

Vladimir Vernadsky (quoted in Deléage 1991, 270). Human activity is changing the course of many of the complex cycles and processes that sustain life—at least life as we know and desire it. The uncontrolled emissions of gases like carbon dioxide and methane are modifying the heat-trapping capacities of the earth's atmosphere. The potential consequences include massive alterations in the distribution of plants and animals across the face of the planet; under some scenarios, vast territories could become uninhabitable. The leaking of extremely stable chlorine and fluorine compounds ("CFCs"—used as refrigerants, among other things) into the air appears to degrade the ability of the upper atmosphere to absorb ultraviolet rays. The higher levels of solar radiation that reach the earth's surface are fatal to some organisms and cause skin cancer in humans. Industrial chemicals are accumulating in the environment across the entire globe. It seems likely that humans and many others species will suffer disease, early death, and reproductive dysfunctions as a result. The genetic diversity that has sustained evolutionary adaptation over the past three billion years is in serious danger of depletion. By some accounts, pollution and habitat destruction are causing species to disappear at a rate comparable only to the prehistoric mass extinctions brought about by volcanic eruptions and asteroid impact. These sadly familiar trends are evidence that we face "new risks" whose features do not conform to our usual expectations about risk management. Their newness makes itself felt in four respects.

First, the magnitude of potential damages is unprecedentedly large. Indeed, the very term magnitude is potentially misleading in describing the seriousness of these consequences. Magnitude suggests that a figure can be put on the value of these consequences, and that if we can just reconcile ourselves to paying a figure of this size, then we have rationally taken account of their relative importance in the whole scheme of choices we make in our lives. But human activity is now so powerful that it can damage vastly beneficial ecological services that nature has furnished freely to every previous generation. Such services include the purification of air and water, the recycling of organic waste products, climate regulation, the regeneration of soil fertility, and the evolutionary creation of new species and all the potentially useful bioactive substances that they produce (Ministère de l'Écologie et du Développement Durable 2003). Attempts to put a price on the value of these services require the papering over of many uncertainties and using so many patently inadequate methods of cost calculation that the results are, at best, extremely controversial.[1] At worst, they are simply absurd, because many of these ecological services are irreplaceable. While some effects can be mitigated or substitutes can be found in local situations, the idea that we can compensate for all of these effects (if only we pay enough) is a fantasy (Ewald 1997, 111).

Effects on the scale of climate change or the depletion of the ozone layer confound existing approaches to risk management. In the past, when people have faced dangers like fire or flooding, they have pooled their risk by buying insurance. Based on experience with the risk, insurers are able to calculate premiums and, from their total revenues, make payouts to the relatively few policyholders who are struck by misfortune. New risks, however, can be too large or uncertain for insurers to handle (Les risques orphelins 2001, p. 58). It is notable that while many governments delay acting to reduce greenhouse gas emissions, the insurance industry is getting increasingly worried about unmanageable liabilities arising from climate change (Canada Stunned 2003, p. 19).[2] Where insurers dare not go, governments step in. In effect, government regulations—or their absence—determine the degree of risk that citizens will have to live with. But individual nation-states cannot control risks on the scale of the new ones either. Problems like climate change and ozone depletion are global, and they are the result of collective action. Protective action by one or a few states will not suffice to correct them. Precaution stems from a recognition that there is a general obligation to avoid this sort of problem occurring in the first place.

Second, damages from new risks can take many years to become evident and then their effects can last for generations. In dealing with "old" risks, we have commonly assumed that damages were punctual and that nature as a whole was essentially unalterable. While persons, property, or even a small territory might be damaged by risky human activities, nature could always recover in fairly short order. Injured bodies heal, burned forests regrow, animal populations rebound after the hunt, and pollutants are neutralized as they disperse in the air or water. Those expectations have been modified by the discovery of pathologies that manifest themselves slowly, occurring through long processes of accumulation and environmental diffusion. Biological and ecological processes like the development of tumors or desertification can take place on a timescale that spans decades, centuries, or even millennia. A recognition of "new" risks stems from realizing that reversing these processes—if they can be reversed at all—takes similarly long periods. It is now thought that the Montreal Protocol to phase out the use of chlorofluorocarbons has stopped the further degradation of the ozone layer. But its restoration will take another fifty or sixty years. Species loss is an even more dire case. "People may have increased the rate of global extinctions by as much as one thousand times the 'natural' rate typical of Earth's long-term history" (United Nations Millennium Ecosystem Assessment 2005, 12). An exterminated species is gone forever. The loss is irreversible. If we do not take precautions, we may leave our successors with no choice but to manage a world made dangerous and more frail by our actions.

Third, for many reasons, new environmental risks can be vexingly uncertain. Sometimes a technology is so novel that there simply has not been enough time to test its effects in the wide range of circumstances in which it will be used. GMOs are a prime example. As we have seen, there can be substantial scientific disagreement about potential risks. In other cases, the very scale of potential problems and their slowness to materialize greatly complicates efforts to understand them. Long-term data are lacking or are of poor quality. In the case of climate change, it is the complexity of interactions between the atmosphere, oceans, and land that make it impossible to make precise predictions about the rate or extent of climate change that may occur in the next century (Bourg and Whiteside 2003, 156–157). Natural systems often have "tipping points" in their capacity to maintain their equilibrium in the face of environmental change. They appear able to withstand changes—until a threshold is crossed that sends them into sudden decline. It is suspected, for instance, that the climate system behaves in a nonlinear fashion. Global warming could precipitate abrupt changes in ocean circulation patterns or the breakup of the Artic ice cap (Brown 2003, 146). Such tipping points often "cannot be forecast by existing science" (United Nations Millennium Ecosystem Assessment 2005, 15).

Scientific uncertainty is also likely to be a problem when disease results from repeated, low-level exposure to a pathogen. Where environmental conditions are suspected of contributing to diseases like cancer and asthma, so many factors intervene between exposure and pathology that causal paths are extremely difficult to trace. Uncertainty stems, too, from controversies over the extent to which observed trends can be extrapolated. At what level of exposure does a poison cease being toxic to human beings?

In many cases, uncertainties remain in experimental results because toxicity studies use animals such as rats, rabbits, and monkeys whose physiology is not identical to that of humans (Bro-Rasmussen 2003, 94). In addition, while ecological studies require comparing information gathered in disciplines ranging from biology to geology to atmospheric chemistry, the use of different measures and different experimental protocols in each discipline makes combining data from all of them difficult. While the scientific community can foresee several possible lines of evolution of the phenomenon, consensus can be elusive (Ewald, Gollier, and Sadeleer 2001, 43). Finally, there can be *irreducible* indeterminacy in the behavior of complex systems (O'Riordan and Jordan 1995, 199). That is, indeterminacy results not from inadequacies in our observational methods but from the chaotic nature of the phenomenon itself.

Recognizing all of these sources of uncertainty changes the status of science in the process of risk management. The typical posture in risk management is to demand scientifically verified evidence of a problem before regulating it (Hermitte and Noiville 1993, 393). In the types of cases just mentioned, however, scientific consensus is likely to be slow in coming, partial, contested, and fallible. Requiring the usual standards of scientific proof before acting may well let the problem develop to a serious, perhaps irreversible stage. Moreover, making government inaction the default whenever there is scientific uncertainty gives the advantage to those who wish to impose environmental risks on others while avoiding regulatory oversight. The chemical industry, for example, has a record of generating consistently low-end estimates of the toxicity of chemical emissions (Gottlieb et al. 1995, 179). In cases where uncertainty is exploited in that way, quantitative risk assessment is not simply grounded in "sound science." It becomes a political tool used to promote deregulation. The precautionary principle, on the other hand, changes the default position: uncertainty becomes the ground for additional caution, not for business as usual.

A fourth consideration should be added to this list: some of the most serious potential environmental risks have characteristics that dull our faculties of moral evaluation. This greatly weakens our political will to address them effectively. Perhaps the most enduring justification for popular government stems from Aristotle's (*Politics* 3:11) observation that the people can judge policy because they feel its effects most immediately. Such reasoning has considerable merit in many cases where social interaction causes immediate and perceptible dangers. People become indignant when they see others' rights violated, or when they witness irresponsible or unjust behavior. From these moral reactions spring demands for protective action. Political movements urge legal reform. Manufacturers of defective products are taken to court. Businesses like the insurance industry arise to provide compensation for residual risk. But it is often the case that the new risks systematically fail to trigger moral responses in proportion to their gravity. Many of these risks are invisible or their effects become manifest so slowly that our senses barely register them. Unlike a choking air pollutant such as sulphur dioxide, the "greenhouse gas" carbon dioxide is odorless and tasteless. At low levels it is not toxic to human beings. So it is not easy to feel the urgency of reducing emissions of it. Our moral senses are further dulled when the environmental complexity blurs the lines of responsibility. Who is to blame when the self-replenishing capacity of an ecological system is surpassed by overuse? No particular commercial fisher is at fault for the precipitous decline of a fishery. Fishing becomes a problem only in relation to the aggregate activities of fishing operations and the ecosystem's own capacity for self-renewal. So one and the same action—catching a certain number of fish—may or may not be a problem, depending on factors outside any individual's intentions or actions. In the absence of clearly malicious or negligent activity, the moral inclination of modern, liberal societies is to let individuals do as they please.

Furthermore, the incentive structures surrounding new risks favor displacing responsibility. Where there are dangers of long-term environmental damage, today's decision makers get the benefits, while future generations pay the costs. It is notoriously difficult to get people to take moral responsibility for situations that are geographically and temporally distant (Dana 2003). Of course, awareness of this human foible is hardly a recent discovery. Long before anyone talked of a precautionary principle, we knew that all too often, people carelessly create risks for their neighbors, as when a landlord fails to repair an unsafe electrical system in rented apartments. We have long known that people underinsure themselves or indulge in short-term pleasures, such as smoking cigarettes, while underestimating the long-term risks. Indeed, entire polities behave in similarly negligent ways. Many Western democracies are having trouble adjusting their social security systems because today's voters would rather have money to use for their own consumption than tax themselves for the benefit of the coming generation.

Although the moral obtuseness engendered by opportunities for responsibility shifting is troubling enough in such examples, its seriousness is multiplied many times over by precautionary situations. The future-generations problem of global warming applies most seriously not to our children or perhaps even our grandchildren but to our grandchildrens' children and all their successors. Yet as John Passmore (1974, 91) has shown, the reasoning supporting modern theories of moral obligation, from utilitarianism to rights-based philosophies, seems to lead to the conclusion that our duties pertain only to our "*immediate* posterity." Our sense of responsibility for much ecological damage is further weakened by the inefficacy of ordinary perception in tracking down causation. While it was hard enough to prove the dangers of inhaling secondhand smoke, at least the pollutants were visible, irritating, and traceable to a particular source. It is much harder to notice the presence of trace toxics in our food and water when they remain invisible, cause no apparent damage in the short term, and reach us through the most circuitous of environmental routes. And one can easily understand how difficult it is to get citizens of one country to accept responsibility when their activities damage the environment of other countries. We don't even do all that well in relation to our fellow citizens. Inhabitants of the eastern United States have complained for decades about pollution originating from coal-fired power plants in the Midwest, without being able to get the midwestern states to solve the problem (Environmental Defense Fund 2004). Policies regulating global risks face even greater obstacles. These policies cannot even count on feelings of a shared national destiny and kinship that make citizens care (imperfectly) for members of their own community.

To these morally disarming effects, we must add that new technological risks are often associated with benefits that are prodigious and tangible. Fossil fuels power most of the material conveniences of industrial civilization. Every consideration for the welfare of today's population seems to argue for maintaining that stream of advantages. Likewise, whatever the risks of transgenic agriculture, its promoters promise unparalleled good consequences: new medicines, less use of pesticides on crops, or the end of famine in Africa. It is hard—*morally* hard—to urge caution in the face of such claims.

Finally, environmental change often endangers in the first instance "only" things that according to most strands of Western ethical thought, have no moral standing in their own right. Moral significance, as philosophers say, has traditionally been reserved for human beings (Johnson 1991). Most people are shocked by the mistreatment of other people and damage to their property. But reactions are much more confused—sometimes to the point of indifference—when the damage concerns nonsentient creatures, plants, ecosystems, and geophysical processes, especially if they are of no obvious economic utility.

Time and again in the twentieth century, there have been early warning signs of impending environmental and health problems that could be used as a basis for precautionary measures. Before there was scientific consensus, before there was a public outcry, "weak signals" of these problems were detectable (Faucheux and O'Connor 2000). These signals could be found in the odd scientific report, workplace health problems, and mobilizations by a few NGOs. In some cases, precautionary prevention guided policy and serious problems were mitigated. In others, timely preventive action was stalled and serious hazards were allowed to compromise public health and environmental well-being. The European Environment Agency (2001) has compiled a study of fourteen such cases. Overfishing caused the Newfoundland cod fisheries to collapse, in spite of assurances by fisheries scientists that careful fishery management had allowed the cod populations to rebuild. Nontoxic and nonflammable, chlorofluorocarbons were chosen for widespread use in aerosols and refrigerators beginning around 1950. Their ability to degrade the atmospheric ozone was hypothesized in seminal scientific papers in 1974. Later computer models of the phenomenon were more reassuring; only small long-term reductions of ozone were foreseen. Concern temporarily abated—until there were direct scientific observations in 1985 of a growing "ozone hole" over Antarctica. Only then was an international agreement to phase out CFCs reached.

Most alarmingly, there is global warming. The first scientific reports of climate change date back to the 1950s. The evidence became increasingly convincing in the mid-1980s. In 1985, studies of glacial ice cores showed that the surface temperature of the earth varied directly with the concentration of carbon dioxide in the atmosphere. But it was not until 1997, in the Kyoto Protocol, that the first international convention to limit greenhouse gas emissions was signed. Industrial nations pledged to reduce their emissions of greenhouse gases by 5.2 percent relative to 1990. President George W. Bush largely negated the direct value of the protocol by refusing to commit the United States—the world's largest emitter of greenhouse gases. He pleaded that the scientific evidence of human-caused global warming was still "uncertain." Even if the protocol was fully implemented, however, current estimates predict that it would reduce global warming by only .28°C or less. Meanwhile, projections of greenhouse gas emissions to 2020 show continued growth, not decline (Organisation for Economic Cooperation and Development 2001, 156–160). A study by the Intergovernmental Panel on Climate Change (2001) foresees an average warming of 1.4°C to 5.8°C (2.5°F to 10.8°F) by 2050. Should the higher estimates materialize, the consequences will be catastrophic for billions of people. Parts of the earth will become simply uninhabitable. Oceans will flood coastal areas. Water supplies will decrease severely in the hottest areas. Extreme weather events will become more common. Global agricultural productivity will decline. There will be increased mortality from tropical diseases.

The world enters the twenty-first century more or less aware of unprecedentedly serious environmental problems, yet largely unable to generate sustained, concerted action to avoid the potentially serious consequences. Reactions come too late or are on too small a scale to forestall severe damage.

What is needed, therefore, is to take account of past errors, and draw lessons from the successes and failures in anticipatory risk management. The precautionary principle is this new imperative in its most general form. Where we face serious, long-term, and uncertain threats, we take special account of the possible shortcomings of our conventional ways of managing risk. We realize there is good reason to tilt risk management in favor of prevention and preservation. The precautionary principle guides us toward new rules and institutions that help us achieve what the more conventional management of risks could not reliably do.

In a sense, we imitate the sailor Ulysses. In book 12 of the *Odyssey*, Homer describes how Ulysses knew that his ship would pass the island of the sirens. He had been warned that their seductive songs would tempt him to bring his ship close to the rocky shore. If he heard them, his voyage would end in a fatal shipwreck. Ulysses also understood his own weakness: if he tried to resist, he would probably fail. Neither his own will nor his navigational skills—both of which were adequate to more ordinary situations—would suffice to reach his goal of sailing safely past the island. So he chose a special, preventive strategy. He had himself tied to the mast, while his sailors stuffed their ears with wax. It worked. Although he was indeed entranced by the sirens' call, the precautions he had taken allowed him to avoid disaster. Likewise, the precautionary principle helps us resist the temptation to believe that every technological risk is worth taking or that we will be able to repair whatever damage we do to our surroundings. That temptation is a siren's song.

Against the Precautionary Principle: The Virtues of Science-Based Risk Management

Critics of the precautionary principle reply that we already have the tools that we need to manage the new risks. These tools are summed up in the expression "science-based risk assessment." This framework, they say, not the precautionary principle, provides a rational way of coping with contemporary health and environmental risks.

Science-based risk management rests on the belief that there are four essential conditions for rationally assessing and managing risk.

1. Generally, a technology or practice should be regulated only if there is scientific evidence of its causal connection to an identified problem. Regulation must not be based on hearsay, speculation, or unfounded fear.

2. Studies of the problem must be objective—influenced as little as possible by people's emotions or the preferences of special interests. The quantification of observations and a reliance on scientific methods of verification are our best guarantee of objectivity.

3. Risk-management decisions should be cost-effective. We live in a world of scarce resources. Regulatory efforts devoted to one area necessarily divert resources from others. Rationally allocating social resources requires giving priority to those regulatory measures that bring the greatest net social benefits (for example, the largest number of lives saved or cancers prevented) per dollar spent. Thus, a comparative approach must be applied to the whole range of policy options, not just to the risks or benefits of options taken in isolation.

4. Ranking options consistently requires measuring them on a common scale. In rational policymaking, the claim that option A is superior to option B is not merely a policymaker's ideological preference or the outcome of intense lobbying efforts. Establishing priorities requires commensuration. One must devise common measures for goods (money or life-expectancy gains) so that as much as possible, quantified risks can be

put on a single, ordinal scale. Then it becomes possible to say that option A is superior to option B, because A yields a larger quantity of the measured good than B.

Critics charge that the precautionary principle violates such protocols. It does so, first, by opening the regulatory door to unfounded and even entirely speculative risks. "The mere *possibility* that use of a particular technology might kill off the human race is sufficient to prevent that technology being used or at least to limit its use severely," complains Julian Morris (2000a, 6). The underlying logic of precaution, he continues, is not rational and scientific but theological. According to the famous argument of Blaise Pascal, the probability that God exists may be small and the "costs" (in terms of sinful pleasures foregone) of living a Christian life may seem large. Nonetheless, the potentially infinite benefit (eternal bliss) that one stands to gain if one has faith necessarily outweighs whatever goods one might get by leading an ungodly life. It is better to bet on God's existence, advised Pascal, than against it. Similarly, proponents of precaution contend that: the chances of a technology causing a disaster may be small, but the magnitude of the potential catastrophe mandates taking preventive action now. It is better to act as if the catastrophe might occur than not to take precautions. Morris's point is that such an argument is far too easy: proponents of precaution need only *imagine* a catastrophic consequence proceeding from some technology in order to justify draconian regulation. Do we want to prohibit everything that somebody might regard as dangerous?

Critics worry that the precautionary principle could block a great deal of desirable technological innovation. John Graham (2002, n.p.) puts precaution to the test with the following thought experiment: "Imagine it is 1850 and a decision is made that any technological innovation cannot be adopted unless and until it is proven to be completely safe by the proponents of innovation. Under this scenario, what would have happened to electricity, the internal combustion engine, plastics, pharmaceuticals, the computer, the Internet, the cellular phone, and so forth?" No inventor could have guaranteed the safety of those products. Had such innovations been stalled, however, we would have lost out on inestimable benefits that we take for granted in today's society. Nor would we ever have learned how to control such adverse effects as they turned out to have.

In effect, argues political scientist Aaron Wildavsky (2000), the precautionary principle amounts to adopting a doctrine of "trial without error" in place of "trial and error" in risk management. Since it is so difficult to rule out the possibility of irreversible effects, the only sure way to prevent a potential catastrophe is to conduct no trials at all. Wildavsky might find support for this conclusion from experience in certain European countries. Not only has the commercial cultivation of GM crops been stopped but even limited, controlled experiments with them are uprooted by anti-GMO activists. In France in 2004, half of all open-field experiments with transgenic crops were destroyed by protesters (Le Puy-de-Dôme 2005). The precautionary principle can be used as a pretext for negating the very principle of free research (Ewald and Lecourt 2001).

Yet conducting no trials, say precaution's opponents, denies us the opportunity to learn about the phenomenon, correct sources of risk where they occur, and gain advantages from the improved technology. With respect to chemical regulation, for example, Wildavsky (2000) reminds us that while mistakes have been made, the chemical industry has gotten useful feedback about the effects of various toxic substances. The awareness that certain pesticides harmed bees or that some herbicides burned plants led to research to develop safer substitute products. Only when products are used extensively do we learn their most significant characteristics and give people the opportunity to modify them to the best advantage. Indeed, the most reliable way of reducing risk on the whole may well be to allow competition, so that innovators who find new ways to reduce risk can bring their improved products to market (Morris 2000a, 12). When we hear people voice fears of impending catastophe, we would do well to remember that this trial-and-error approach has brought people a high degree of health security. "The United States and other Western democracies have the healthiest people in the history of the world," notes Wildavsky (1995, 432).

The problem of overreaction to imagined dangers is only one facet of a much larger problem in any discussion of rational risk assessment, say precaution's opponents. Sociologists who study risk perception find that public attitudes toward risk are rife with unfounded belief, misunderstanding, contradiction, and ill-conceived solutions. Cass Sunstein (2002) marshals evidence to demonstrate that people's risk perceptions correlate poorly with scientific studies showing which risks are most probable and have the most serious consequences. People fixate on risks for which there is a vivid, relatively recent example (for instance, the Three Mile Island nuclear accident), or ones that correspond to their "intuitive toxicology" (say, a supposition that "artificial" substances are more dangerous than "natural" ones) or that other people are already talking about. Such social psychological phenomena disguise the real costs of risk reduction. As a result, voters end up pushing policymakers to spend vast sums to combat minor risks, all the while ignoring much more substantial and probable ones. One study suggests that if regulatory funding were better targeted, we could save sixty thousand more lives per year—at no additional cost (Tengs and Graham 1996). In rational policymaking, argue advocates of science-based risk management, what matters is not that people happen to fear a catastrophe but that we have evidence showing the probability of severe consequences and quantifying the number of lives that might be lost or damaged.

Opponents of the precautionary principle also fear that it will lead to massive overregulation of private enterprise. It invites new levels of politicization into the risk-assessment process. Officials in agencies like the EPA or the USDA will determine whether and how all sorts of products can be marketed. They will not make those decisions in a vacuum. Representatives of industry, trade organizations, and labor unions prowl the halls of the regulatory bureaucracy. Interest groups exert enormous pressure to make sure that policy favors their preferred outcomes. So as the precautionary principle brings yet more decisions under government purview, interest groups will see to it that decisions are shaped as a function of what benefits or hurts them: profits reduced or increased; jobs lost or protected. Economic reasoning even tells us to expect individual industries to use the precautionary principle against each other in order to gain competitive advantages over rivals. An innovative firm could find its new product line blocked by a court injunction when a competitor charges that the new product carries some uncertain, as-yet-unproven risk. Politicians are sure to join in the free-for-all. On a precautionary pretext, they will attempt to exclude some products from international commerce. In fact, though, they will simply be protecting industries important to their constituents.

Precaution's critics are even more suspicious of pressure groups that cast themselves as representatives of the public good. When an environmentalist organization such as Greenpeace campaigns against GMOs, charge the critics, it advances a particular and highly contentious political agenda. "Small numbers of vocal activists [tell us how they] want the rest of us to live our lives" (Miller and Conko 2001, 38). They want us to live with less technology and less commercial activity. In this view, the precautionary principle is little more than the vehicle of an ideological agenda.

According to those who are precaution skeptical, the best way to avoid rampant politicization is to adopt science-based risk assessment across the board. When there are regulatory disputes, all parties should be required to provide evidence from reputable scientists regarding the extent of the danger. That evidence should settle the question of whether there is genuine danger or not. The WTO agreement on the Application of Sanitary and Phytosanitary (SPS) measures shows how trade disputes are rightly handled. Without dispute-resolution procedures, innumerable cultural and economic differences between countries are liable to disrupt food trade (see Echols 1998). Americans have few qualms about eating beef from cattle raised on growth hormones (90 percent of U.S. beef is produced this way). Europeans want nothing to do with such meat. The French pride themselves on making pungent cheeses with unpasteurized milk. The USDA finds such cheeses unsafe and unfit for import. Allowable levels of food irradiation (to control insects on tropical fruit) are higher in the United States than in some European countries. The United States allows using chlorine compounds in cleaning chicken coops. Europe forbids it.

Does each country then allow products to be imported only if they are safe according to its own national standards? If so, trade diminishes, economies slow down, and consumers pay higher prices. In order to keep different standards from blocking commerce, parties to the SPS accord agree that their disputes will be settled by the use of "scientific principles" (Phillips 2001, 40–41). To prohibit trade in a foodstuff, it is no longer sufficient for a country unilaterally to declare it unsafe. That country must provide convincing scientific evidence of the product's harmfulness. The evidence is then reviewed by an external, arbitrating body—the WTO's dispute-resolution panel. Europe's dispute with the United States over hormone-fed beef showed how this works. The United States objected to Europe's import ban. Both sides submitted their evidence. The WTO panel reviewed the scientific evidence—and ruled that the Europeans' claims were unfounded. In fact, the EU's own scientific report on the safety of growth hormones discovered no evidence of significant harm. So Europe's ban on such products was in violation of the SPS agreement (Majone 2002). Sound science stepped in to correct a "precautionary" policy that in fact was just the result of politicians catering to irrational consumer beliefs (Miller and Conko 2001, 29). Precaution's critics argue that sound science is the only alternative to subjective, policitized risk assessment.

The deepest objection to the precautionary principle is methodological: the precautionary principle focuses on risks in isolation. According to defenders of science-based risk management, rational policy compares all the risks and benefits, and chooses the course of action that leads to the best consequences on the whole. The precautionary principle, in contrast, tells us to examine a particular product—for example, an environmentally persistent toxic chemical—and decide whether that product might carry too much risk. If so, its use is banned or greatly restricted. This approach methodically blinds us to the full range of risks that we face. Eliminating one risk may well increase another or deprive us of benefits that outweigh the risk itself.

One of the critics' favorite examples concerns the case of the environmentally persistent pesticide DDT (Sunstein 2005, 51; Wildavsky 1995, 55–80). While its power to control mosquitoes led to dramatic reductions in mortality from malaria in many tropical countries, concerns about its cumulative effects on wildlife caused many countries to discontinue its use in the mid-1960s. Malaria then resurged. Sri Lanka (Ceylon) went from having fewer than 20 cases of malaria in the last year of spraying (1963) to 2.5 million cases in 1969 (Goklany 2000, 191–192). Now it makes no sense to ban a product in the name of reducing risk if, in fact, forgoing that product worsens other risks. What matters in rational policymaking is not the losses expected in an isolated worst-case scenario. What matters is the expected *overall* loss or benefit from a policy (Majone 2002). Surveying the costs of precautionary action in relation to DDT, global warming, and GMOs, economist Indur Goklany (2000, 221) concludes that "by slowing economic growth and/or increasing energy prices, [precautionary] regimes could, in the final analysis, decrease overall access to food which could lower health status and increase death and disease in the poorer segments of society, especially in the developing world."

According to its defenders, the primary virtue of science-based risk assessment is that it helps avoid such irrational outcomes. They insist, however, that the alternative to the precautionary principle is not being antiprecautionary. It is to be scientific and pragmatic. Once we realize that the precautionary principle itself can cause harm to public health and the environment, we see that at the very least, it has to be supplemented with other criteria that allow these considerations to be factored into decisions. Goklany (2001, 89) proposes a framework with "a set of hierarchical criteria that can be used to rank the various threats that are increased or reduced by the policy under consideration based on the nature, magnitude, immediacy, uncertainty and persistence of each threat, and the extent to which it can be alleviated." This framework obliges decision makers to consider *all* the effects of a policy, giving special emphasis to effects on human health and mortality.

Thus, critics of the precautionary principle do not rule out precautionary measures entirely. They acknowledge that there may be cases where uncertainty combined with the magnitude and severity of a risk makes taking preventive steps the most prudent course of action. What they oppose is the idea that as a general rule, we should block a technological development or a social practice that might entail risk until we know it is absolutely safe.

Rebuttal: Antiprecautionary Fallacies

Goklany's analysis shows how slippery the case against the precautionary principle can be. Critics often seem to accept the logic of precaution in some circumstances. Then they immediately attach a host of conditions and considerations that effectively reject exactly what makes precaution a special form of risk management.

Goklany (2001, 9) claims to develop a "precautionary framework." The first standard he applies in implementing it is "the human mortality criterion": "the threat of death to any human being, no matter how lowly that human being may be, outweighs similar threats to members of other species. . . . In general, other nonmortal threats to human health should take precedence over threats to the environment." Effectively, the human mortality criterion does away with the precautionary principle—and then attempts to steal its identity. Contrary to Goklany's insinuation, the precautionary principle entails no presumption in favor of either the environment or human mortality. The point of the principle is that the chain of causation from the environment to deleterious effects on humans is often long—and plagued with uncertainties.

Giving *automatic* precedence to consequences for human beings, as Goklany proposes, is precisely the sort of thought pattern that may lead us to take extremely dangerous risks. James Lovelock (1995, 106–107,

111–112) has argued, for example, that we need to take special care of continental shelves and coastal wetlands because it is in these regions that microorganisms recycle elements such as sulphur and iodine in ways that help life reproduce on a planetary scale. Lovelock warns against turning coastal areas into monocultural kelp farms that might disrupt these processes. It is by no means clear that the human mortality criterion would respond to such concerns. Undoubtedly, some coastal human communities would be more prosperous if they could farm kelp. It might even be the case that their prosperity would allow them to save human lives—say, by building hospitals or offering less dangerous occupations to local workers. Weighing human lives against microorganisms, the human mortality criterion would then seem to favor coastal farming. It is an open invitation to downplay environmental concerns whenever an argument can be made that any human being might be threatened. If Lovelock's hypothesis is right, however, the consequences of generalizing such practices could be catastrophic.

Another criterion for a so-called precautionary framework is "immediacy": "all else being equal, more immediate threats should be given priority over threats that could occur later" (Goklany 2001, 9). Note the slippery "all else being equal." Precautionary situations are by definition those in which all else is *not* equal. Long-term threats are often unequal to immediate ones because we are less certain that they will happen. Just because we are better able to measure some threats now does not mean that future threats mediated by environmental degradation are necessarily less significant. But the bigger problem with the immediacy criterion is that it amounts to a denial of the whole strategy of precaution. The purpose of the precautionary principle is to help us address threats that are *not immediate*—ones in which the onset of harms may be delayed for decades. In democratic systems, immediate threats usually generate their own political reactions. It is long-term, deferred threats that require new and specialized attention. Calling the immediacy criterion precautionary is like amending the popularized Hippocratic injunction ("First, do no harm") to make it say, "Do harm only when circumstances call for it." It is not a minor amendment. It completely overturns the rationale and obligations of the principle.

The dodginess of the antiprecautionary position comes through in even the most meticulously argued case for science-based cost-benefit analysis. In *Risk and Reason,* Cass Sunstein (2002) proffers a seemingly modest defense of science-based cost-benefit analysis in all sorts of risk regulation. His discussion of discounting future benefits and costs is a good example of how to defend science-based risk regulation without adopting a directive as unnuanced as Goklany's immediacy criterion. Sunstein is aware of the evidence that in general, people tend to value more highly near-term benefits and costs than the same outcomes in the longer term.[3] This causes a problem for the environmentally concerned cost-benefit analyst. It suggests that allowing preferences today to dictate policy affecting people's future welfare will lead to irrational results: short-term benefits will systematically outweigh long-term well-being, as if people in the future were worth less than present-day consumers.

Yet a thoroughgoing defender of cost-benefit analysis—but not Sunstein—might actually embrace this implication. For two reasons, it might make sense to discount future values. First, standard economic theory explains why today's money is worth more than tomorrow's. A dollar today can be invested and turned to productive use. Even if one were guaranteed to receive a dollar in one year, it would be worth less than a present dollar because the present dollar, sensibly invested, will earn additional value in the course of that year. Conversely, this means that future costs and benefits must be discounted because, dollar for dollar, they are worth less than near-term costs and benefits. Second, the present is more certain than the future. Rational people are willing to pay more for goods that are certain. In fact, risk analysts sometimes combine these reasons into a general rationale for opposing precautionary action. They contend that investments in today's technologies lay the foundation for an environmentally safer future (think: GMOs that reduce pesticide usage) and that future people will be technologically better able to take care of themselves (thanks to our investments). So we should not assume that costs we leave to them will be as expensive for them to handle as they would be for us. Today's uncertainties will generally be resolved in their favor. Appropriately discounted, long-term policy consequences can therefore be evaluated in cost-benefit terms. In regard to global warming, for example, Bjorn Lomborg (2001, 318) has adduced an economic analysis of this sort to show that "it will be far more expensive to cut carbon dioxide emission radically than to pay the costs of adaptation to the increased temperatures."

Sunstein (2002, 122–123, 224–228) has doubts about pushing cost-benefit analysis this far. He is sensitive to the uncertainties of fact that go into such calculations. Sunstein denies that all costs and benefits can be translated into monetary values. He insists on distinguishing between latent harms that occur in a person's lifetime (which that person may be in a position to discount rationally) and harms to future generations. Choosing discount rates for the value of harm to future generations requires making assumptions about economic growth that are highly disputable. He questions the moral status of people's time preference for the present. At the same time, Sunstein worries that giving future generations equal moral standing with the present one could condemn us to intolerable levels of self-denial. While he favors quantification and consistency wherever possible, his dialectic ends only by asking that in difficult cases, regulatory agencies make sure that their choices are "articulated and reasonable" (228). The modesty of Sunstein's argument overall consists in claiming only that "cost-benefit analysis should be seen as a simple pragmatic tool, designed to promote a better appreciation of the consequences of regulation" (xiv).

If only the argument remained at that level. Then a proponent of precaution might have relatively little to criticize. After all, precaution, too, is about well-articulated and reasonable choices. But the thrust of Sunstein's work is less modest—and less friendly to precaution—than it initially appears.

Risk and Reason amasses social scientific evidence to demonstrate the endemic irrationality of public attitudes toward risk. Sunstein finds that when the public and experts disagree about risks, "experts are generally right and ordinary people are generally wrong" (55). When he finally comes to the precautionary principle, Sunstein categorizes it among approaches to environmental protection that are "unhelpful, sometimes even ludicrous" (100). In particular, he charges that the principle is self-contradictory: "If the precautionary principle argues against any action that carries a small risk of significant harm, then we should be reluctant to spend a lot of money to reduce risks because those expenditures themselves carry risks. . . . The precautionary principle, taken for all that it is worth, is literally paralyzing. It bans every imaginable step, including inaction itself" (104).

One of the most common fallacies in critiques of the precautionary principle consists in the following gambit: precautionary situations (where risk is not well understood) are lumped together with situations where risks are relatively well understood. Then precaution is made to appear preposterous, because in situations where risk is understood, cost-benefit calculations appear rational. This is what happens in Sunstein's argument. Before taking up the precautionary principle, his case for the superiority of cost-benefit analysis cites examples where there are abundant actuarial data: shark attacks, the risk of skin cancer from sunbathing, and deaths from motor vehicle accidents. That is all well and good, but it is beside the point for the precautionary principle. The precautionary principle is precisely for cases of serious potential danger where risks are poorly understood. The real question is, What do we do *then*?

Sunstein has trouble admitting that such cases even exist. Sometimes, he seems to suggest, they do. "Where a risk would be very high," he says (104), "and when we can reduce or eliminate it with cash, it makes sense to endorse the precautionary principle" (2002, 109). For once, the precautionary principle is not so ludicrous after all. In the next breath, this admission vanishes: "A competent cost-benefit analysis takes good account of the precautionary principle by asking regulators to attend to low-probability risks of significant harms. . . . Cost-benefit analysis incorporates all risks, on all sides of the equation" (104). This assertion, with its talk of low-probability risks in the assessment equation, effectively denies the existence of precautionary situations. For the purposes of dismissing the precautionary principle, Sunstein writes as if all risks were calculable enough to be subject to cost-benefit analysis.

Then the argument slides around one more time. Sunstein is too environmentally sensitive to go along with Wildavsky's (1995, 433) assumption that species and human societies are generally "resilient" enough to adapt to new environmental challenges. Sunstein seems to admit that some ecosystems just might be so vulnerable that human-created shocks could provoke enormous damages. Now in view of such a possibility, how do we proceed? Does any special logic prevail? Yes—and no. No, not really: Sunstein (2002, 105) suggests that in deciding whether to take special precautions, "everything depends on the facts," because "resilience is a matter of degree." As the European Environment Agency (2001, 169) points out, however, in precautionary situations we are dealing not with facts but with "uncertainty," or even worse, ignorance. We are in a domain of "inevitable surprises or unpredicted effects. . . . By their nature, complex, cumulative, synergistic or indirect effects . . . have traditionally been inadequately addressed in regulatory appraisal." Sunstein's recourse to the "facts" is an attempt to bring precautionary situations back within the ambit of that traditional model.

Then again, yes: Sunstein admits that cost-benefit analysis cannot supply the answers in certain cases. We face hard choices where "political judgment" is necessary (Sunstein 2002, 105). Fine. But on what grounds? What goes into that judgment? What *principles* are involved? It cannot be the principle that public policy should maximize social welfare, because the quantifying preconditions for applying such a principle are unmet. Nor can it be the democratic principle that the people should decide. According to Sunstein, ordinary people are too irrational to make good decisions. And the scientists disagree. So now what? What logic should guide decision makers? How do they—or we—think about this situation? That is what the precautionary principle is for.

Perhaps out of a newfound awareness of this gap in his argument Sunstein followed up *Risk and Reason* three years later with an essay focused on the precautionary principle. While repeating most of reasoning of his earlier work, he filled in the missing response. "When citizens face catastrophic risks to which probabilities cannot be assigned," he declares, "it makes sense for them to adopt an Anti-Catastrophe principle." According to this principle,

> if regulators are operating under conditions of uncertainty, they might well do best . . . [by] identifying the worst-case scenarios and choosing the approach that eliminates the worst of these. It follows that if aggressive measures are justified to reduce the risks associated with global warming, one reason is that those risks are potentially catastrophic and existing science does not enable us to assign probabilities to the worst-case scenarios. (Sunstein 2005, 109)

As he affirms, this is a "reconstruction" of the precautionary principle.

In comparison to Wildavsky's wholesale rejection of the precautionary principle, this is progress. A respected U.S. authority on risk management explicitly makes room for precaution in his analysis (although, chastely, he insists on renaming it). Sunstein's reconstructed precaution endorses ideas like using "rough, general categories of probability" rather than falsely precise measures to estimate potential threats; he sees the wisdom in gradually implementing policies rather than proceeding "on the basis of a principle of 'Act, then learn'" (117). These are the sorts of recommendations that defenders of the precautionary principle routinely make. Sunstein even agrees that a "weak" form of the precautionary principle, of the sort adopted at Rio in 1992, is unobjectionable (18, 23, 24).

Yet the ambiguities of his earlier work recur in this one. His reconstruction surrounds the anticatastrophe principle with so many qualifications drawn from science-based risk assessment and cost-benefit analysis that in the end, the departure from those preferred methods is barely noticeable. Sunstein (2005, 112) stipulates that decision makers must still weigh the likely consequences of any proposed anticatastrophe measures (for example, increases in unemployment and poverty caused by efforts to limit greenhouse gas emissions). They must be "closely attentive to the idea of cost-effectiveness" (115). Sunstein (116) doubts that the irreversibility of environmental damages constitutes a sufficient reason for precautionary action. Before action can be justified, he emphasizes, the potential damage must rise to "a certain level of magnitude." Then, when deciding whether an outcome qualifies as catastrophic, "it is appropriate to weigh both probability and magnitude." (117)

Again, it is those quantitative measures that are so often lacking in relation to new risks. Take GMO assessment. It is a powerful indication that we are not in the domain of traditional risk management when insurers refuse to cover the potential damages from transgenic crops, claiming that too little is known about their effects for them to calculate coverage (Underwriters 2003). So it would be interesting to know whether Sunstein believes GMO regulation falls under the anticatastrophe principle or not. It is peculiar to find him mentioning GMOs only in passing since the controversies surrounding them have done so much to publicize the precautionary principle. Still, Sunstein is not shy about bringing GMOs into his general argument about public irrationality. He associates fears of them with a "false belief in the benevolence of nature" (Sunstein 2005, 44–45, 51). He refers to their potential benefits. Nothing he says suggests that he sees them as potentially dangerous. Sunstein leaves the impression that there is no reason to regulate GMOs in a precautionary way. Yet at no point does he review any of the scientific controversies discussed in my first chapter. This is an odd way of proceeding in an argument about relating risks more consistently to "the facts" as established by experts. Like Goklany, Sunstein utters the word precaution, but his heart is not in it.

His heart is elsewhere. It is in the defense of a cost-benefit state. Sunstein (2002, 4–5) lauds "a genuine revolution" that requires governments to regulate only "after making an effort to quantify and balance both benefits and costs." This revolution applies to the regulation of "arsenic in the water and ozone in the air, . . . global warming and . . . genetically modified food, . . . cellular telephones and airline safety." That list says it all: there are no new risks. GM foods and airline safety are on the same plane, so to speak. Matters of immense scale, cumulative harm, latent effects, irreversibility, potential interference with critical ecological cycles, troubling scientific uncertainty, and moral imperceptibility have no essential bearing on the type of analysis used in risk assessment. All risks fit within a single framework.

Critics of the precautionary principle are committed to a form of "comprehensive rationality"—to methods of risk assessment in which "all important considerations will have been identified, tabulated, and weighed in a manner that leads to the identification of a first-best social outcome" (Kysar 2004, 8–9). No matter how much Sunstein tries to moderate his expectations regarding quantitative risk assessment, he cannot resist the attraction of comprehensive rationality. This is what causes him to waver so much on precaution. On the one hand, he cannot deny that certain environmental dangers could have characteristics that cause them to escape the net of science-based risk management. On the other hand, everything else in his argument aims to convince readers that cost-benefit analysis is superior to any special rule like the precautionary principle. In a cost-benefit state, the commitment to a *methodology* seems to take precedence over the acknowledgment of troubling new realities. In an age of global environmental risks, that is a luxury we cannot always afford.

A Panoply of Precautionary Measures

There is one other important aspect of the precautionary principle that its critics shortchange. The critics ignore the extensive work of activists and scholars devoted to showing the variety of ways that precaution should be implemented. Too often critics assume that precaution means either "Whatever it is you're doing, you've got to stop" (Christine Todd Whitman, quoted in Federal News Service 2001) or "Ban every imaginable step" (Sunstein, 2002, 104). They reduce precaution to prohibition. Now any principle can be made to appear absurd if it is interpreted reductively enough. Take the "polluter pays principle," for example. This principle of EU law stipulates that those whose activities or behavior contribute to environmental damage should pay the costs of prevention and repair. That sounds reasonable enough—and it is. Yet if that principle is interpreted so strictly that it means people must *invariably* be charged for *every* environmental change they cause, in *exact proportion* to the degree of harm, it is clearly unreasonable. It would be administratively cumbersome in the extreme, impossibly costly to enforce, broadly destructive of employment, and corrosive of individual freedom. But the principle is reasonable if it is understood as mandating laws forbidding various types of environmental degradation (thereby forcing those who would cause such degradation to absorb the costs of preventing it); if it allows for pollution permit systems; if it requires those engaged in environment-transforming activities to anticipate the consequences of their activities for others; and if it includes narrow exceptions for special hardship cases.

Likewise, precaution should be understood to imply a broad range of possible measures—measures calibrated to the degree of uncertainty and the seriousness of the consequences that are feared. The burgeoning literature on implementing the precautionary principle brings out the following types of policies.

• Precaution can mean setting up research programs whose purpose is to gather further information about the risk and test successive hypotheses about it (Kourilsky 2002, 57–59; Ewald, Gollier, and Sadeleer 2001, 48–49). Precisely because a risk is poorly understood, there is reason for society to demand more in the way of scientific investigation. The task would be to widen the range of hypotheses concerning the risk-producing activity: how it might spread, how its effects would play out in more diverse environmental circumstances, what its longer-term consequences might be, what effects it might have on a wider array of organisms, and so forth. Precaution would also go into choosing how experimentation took place: in confined laboratories or the open air, and with what sorts of safeguards.

• Precaution can mean that long-term environmental and health monitoring should be instituted (European Environment Agency 2001, 170–173). Precaution suggests *continuing* vigilance. Monitoring should be "holistic": "a range of ecosystem variables should be [monitored] and linked to sustainability indicators that can provide early warnings and feedback" (Deville and Harding 1997, 50). It is not just a matter of testing a potentially risky process once and, having discovered no grounds for immediate alarm, treating it as if it were entirely innocuous. If doubts remain, it makes sense to have labeling and traceability requirements (Kourilsky 2002, 66). In that way, if unanticipated problems occur later, it remains possible to investigate whether the monitored activity is responsible. If necessary, appropriate remedial actions can then be taken. Giving pride of place to reversible policies is a hallmark of precautionary action.

• Precaution can mean deliberately orchestrating multidisciplinary expertise (Harding and Fisher 1999, 290–298). Perceiving environmental problems, especially in their early stages, requires comparing evidence gathered in diverse disciplines—biology, ecology, soil chemistry, hydrology, and workplace safety studies. Often specialists in such disciplines are only vaguely aware of each other's work, and their differing research protocols may make data comparison difficult. Deliberately multiplying the types of expertise brought to bear in evaluating complex patterns of health and environmental consequences as well as organizing networks for cross-checking information are precautionary measures (Tickner 2003b, 11). Transdisciplinary problem-solving aims at the early detection of research blind spots and revealing contestable assumptions.

• Precaution can mean reinforcing the independence of regulatory bodies. The point is to ensure against government agencies developing a too-cozy relationship with the industries they oversee such that they end up downplaying precaution. Reinforced independence can be accomplished by requiring regulators to disclose their financial and research links to the industries they are regulating, and creating internal ethics committees and codes to govern remuneration (Ewald, Gollier, Sadeleer 2001, 49). Freedom of information requirements, too, can help prevent bias by opening the regulatory process to public commentary and diversifying the range of groups with access to regulators. In public law, precaution can mean establishing a duty for government agencies, manufacturers, and users to make public information about their activities: ongoing experiments, safety protocols, observed anomalies, accidents, and safety breaches (O'Brien 2000, 122; Lascoumes 1997, 136; Noiville 2002, 38).

• Precaution can mean systematically favoring environmentally "clean" technologies. One such approach is called alternatives assessment. As Mary O'Brien (1999, 208) explains, this approach "consists of publicly examining a full range of alternatives to a potentially damaging human activity or social arrangement." The case for alternatives assessment begins by noting facile value assumptions, false precision, and unequal power relations that are often hidden in cost-benefit analyses. Alternatives assessment seeks to mitigate such biases by obliging decision makers to consider *all* reasonable choices in relation to an activity with environmental effects, not just whether a proposed activity is "safe enough" or acceptable in cost-benefit terms. Alternatives assessment requires making special efforts to consider practices that are likely to have the least adverse impact. The evaluation process should take seriously the "no action" alternative, asking whether an activity is simply too dangerous or is unneeded (Tickner, Raffensperger, and Myers 1999). In a similar vein, precaution is associated with rules requiring the adoption of "best available control technology" (BAT) to reduce environmental degradation (O'Riordan and Jordan 1995, 193; Applegate 2000, 436–437). Both approaches suggest that where there is a potential, avoidable risk, precaution gives the advantage to policies that reduce the overall impact on the environment (Bodansky 1994, 217).

- Precaution can mean building in larger safety margins, devising backup safety systems, and putting emergency plans into place.

- Finally, in cases of the most potentially serious and uncertain risks, precaution *can* mean banning a technology or strictly minimizing its use. Even in these cases, however, it is not just a matter of "stopping what you're doing." Precaution might require that, and still a product or process might be phased out with greater or lesser speed. Particularly vulnerable populations may get precautionary protection first. Or local exceptions to a precautionary prohibition may be allowed. If precautionary alarms had been sounded about the pesticide DDT, and yet if a precautionary ban would have meant that thousands of people would die in certain tropical countries because no adequate substitute for mosquito control could be found, then perhaps for those regions, for a time, an exception to a precautionary ban might be arranged. Making a temporary, localized exception to the principle does not mean that the principle itself should be overturned. Precaution could still dictate that the use of the pesticide be avoided in every less dire circumstance. It could still dictate that alternative methods of pest control be favored and that publicly funded research be oriented in that direction. And precaution could still dictate that where exceptions are made, their effects be carefully monitored and indiscriminate usage be prohibited.

All entries except the last one suppose that action in relation to the suspected technology or process goes forward. Precaution is not tantamount to systematic renunciation, prohibition, stalling, and stonewalling. Far from it. Precaution implies research, experimentation, phased introduction, traceable usage, and redundant safety measures.

Once we see the critics' own ambiguities and understand the range of measures available to precautionary policymakers, it is all that much easier to answer the remaining charges against the precautionary principle.

Does the precautionary principle require decision makers to consider risks in isolation, without regard to the opportunity costs and adverse consequences of precautionary regulations? Certainly no more than science-based risk assessment does. Under that regulatory regime, when a given risk-creating activity is brought forward, risk assessors presume that *that* activity must be allowed to proceed unless probable harm can be demonstrated. It is enough if that activity or technology—in isolation—cannot be proven dangerous in itself. O'Brien (2000, 81) provides a startling example of what this means in practice: "The Federal Insecticide, Fungicide and Rodenticide Act precludes consideration of alternatives (e.g., that more benign alternatives exist) when registering a pesticide for sale and use in the United States. . . . In other words, registration of a carcinogenic pesticide cannot legally be denied on the basis that less murderous pesticides exist." Taking each pesticide in isolation, risk assessment cannot consider the total load of carcinogens in the environment. There is growing suspicion that industrial chemicals have contributed to a cancer explosion in the last twenty years (Epstein 2002; Belpomme 2003)—even though environmental and bodily complexity prevent tracing all the causal pathways with certainty. So there is substantial reason to create a presumption in favor of preserving environmental characteristics intact, where reasonable alternatives to potentially dangerous products exist. A concern for cumulative environmental impacts argues for developing a range of alternatives, and then ranking them in relation to the degrees and types of environmental consequences. This is what the precautionary principle calls for—while science-based risk assessment does not.

Does a principled approach to risk assessment force policymakers into a regulatory straitjacket, requiring them to ignore real-world complexities like the difference between likely and unlikely catastrophes or the fact that regulation itself may have undesirable consequences? Not at all. Theorists of precaution generally propose graduating precautionary measures from the least restrictive (further research and monitoring), to moderately restrictive (alternatives assessment, BAT regulations), to the most restrictive (requiring larger safety margins or outright prohibition) (Deville and Harding 1997, 25–42). Likewise, the scientific uncertainty of risks could be put on a scale, running from a simple conjecture, to a well-supported hypothesis backed up by empirical evidence and scientific modeling, to a proven danger whose existence is accepted by the scientific community. Then, selecting which measures to use in any particular case can be thought of as a matter of rough proportionality (Godard 2001b, 97). The greater the seriousness of the potential risk and the less advanced the state of the scientific knowledge about it, the further along the scale of measures one might choose.

Does precaution divert attention from the potentially negative consequences of precaution itself? By no means. If some strict precautionary measure might itself cause great harm (for instance, banning a pesticide allows a disease to run rampant), there are strong reasons for trying to find a way to allow the activity to proceed (Deville and Harding 1997, 44). It may be wise to move back down the scale of precautionary measures a step or two. A commitment to precaution does not exclude consideration of any possible consequence of a policy choice. It demands a *complex judgment.* What makes this judgment so different from risk assessment is that it takes place under a general guideline favoring prevention and the search for alternatives to environment-damaging practices rather than arguing for an "acceptable level" of risk. Moreover, it never forces decision makers to pretend that they can quantify, make commensurate, and maximize benefits when, in truth, the conditions for such operations are unavailable. Finally, thinking of precaution as a matter of action along a graduated scale has the advantage of bringing the elements of judgment out into the open and making them subject to debate, rather than burying them in methodologies understandable only by experts.

Science or Precaution? A Misleading Dichotomy

Critics say that the precautionary principle is antiscientific. To this charge there are two responses. First, there is good reason to say, with Andrew Stirling (2000, 91), that precaution can reasonably be perceived as *more* scientific than the traditional approach, where alternatives are ignored and there is misplaced confidence in the existing state of knowledge. Precaution favors an "extended science," with additional transparency in argumentation, acknowledged uncertainties, and an openness to the ongoing revision of knowledge. It is also about *better* science—science that is transdisciplinary and holistic, attentive to ecological complexity; science whose research program retains greater independence from social and economic pressures (Levins 2003; Harding and Fisher 1999, 293–294; Barrett and Raffensperger 1999).

Second, there is nothing laudably "scientific" about "science-based risk management" if it yields *false* information. The public record abounds with examples where officials, pointing to scientific data, have given safety assurances that later turned out to be wrong (European Environment Agency 2001). How can this happen? Fallaciously, regulators have been known to interpret the absence of proof of harm as the proof of the absence of harm. On occasion, the same agency both promotes and regulates an industry, causing it to err on the side of industrial interests. Sometimes, regulators are responding to political superiors who have ideological reasons to pick and choose the evidence on which they rely. At times, the scientific data used by regulators are shot through with bias because they have been collected and interpreted almost entirely by the interested parties themselves. Or what are called scientific data turn out to be nothing more than speculative extrapolations based on a computer model. Or a regulatory agency consults only a narrow range of relevant scientific fields in coming to its assessment. Claims that risk assessment is science based should not be accepted at face value. They need to be critically assessed in a broadly inclusive political process.

It should be recognized, finally, that there is nothing scientific about the nonprecautionary belief that the earth is always resilient enough to recover from humanly created disturbances. That is not a testable hypothesis in a scientific sense. It is a worldview—almost a matter of faith.[4] Of course, a precautionary perspective that sees the world as finite and fragile is not scientific, either. Both sides are gambling that events will bear out their worldview, without anyone being able to run a controlled experiment to see if one is right and the other is wrong. The difference is that the precautionary perspective calls for proceeding with special care, imaginatively diversifying the scientific investigations about potential environmental impacts. Then, if ecosystems begin to show evidence of being as fragile as feared, we can still reverse course and return to something close to the situation that existed before we allowed the risk to spread. In contrast, when nonprecautionary policymakers give the green light to an irreversible course of action with potential world-altering consequences, we simply have to hope for the best. How ironic that critics say precautionary reasoning is theological, when it is nonprecautionary policy that stakes everything on faith.

As one approaches policy debates over environmental risk, it is best to be aware that the term scientific sometimes serves as little more than a rhetorical device designed to give certain political preferences the mantle of rational superiority to alternatives. It is breathtaking to read Washington policy analysts make a categorical assertion that Europe's process-based regulation of GMOs is "unscientific" (Miller and Conko 2000, 89). The European approach, after all, is backed up by prestigious scientific committees and renowned scientists. As seen in the previous chapter, there are good, scientific, empirically grounded reasons to suspect that gene splicing is inherently susceptible to generating unexpected and potentially irreversible consequences, both for the organisms produced and the environment. The European decision to regulate all organisms created by the process of genetic engineering may be debatable, but it is not unscientific. Not so long ago, even U.S. commentators would probably have recognized this, because the United States has its own precautionary traditions. Whether its more recent emphasis on science-based risk management puts it inevitably on a collision course with those working for an international consensus on the precautionary principle is the topic to which I now turn.

3

Comparing Precaution in the United States and Europe

The strikingly different fate of GMOs on the two sides of the Atlantic seems to rest on starkly contrasting philosophies of risk management. "Precaution Is for Europeans" (2003) runs a headline in the *New York Times*. The implication is: for Europeans—and *not for Americans*. As "the conventional wisdom" would have it, "Europe . . . seeks proactively to regulate risks, while the US opposes the precautionary principle and waits more circumspectly for evidence of actual harm before regulating" (Wiener and Rogers 2002, 318). Science-based risk assessment is that circumspection made into policy.

The conventional wisdom is not entirely wrong, but neither does it tell the whole story. It is true that since 2001, the administration of George W. Bush has campaigned consistently against the precautionary principle. Yet precaution has deeper roots in the United States than is sometimes imagined. By the mid-1970s, U.S. law and legal reasoning incorporated many defining elements of precautionary reasoning, and applied them across a range of health and environmental issues. It is even the case that Europeans have often picked up on this reasoning and reformed their own regulatory practices as a result. Any assessment of the principle's prospects as a basis for consensus in international environmental regulation must take account of how the logic of precaution evolved in the regulatory environment of the United States. While the regulatory climate has certainly changed since the 1970s, there is no deep-seated U.S. hostility to the very notion of precaution. Indeed, the principle has made headway here since about 1998.

The conventional wisdom does not tell the whole story on the European side, either. For it is undeniable that European enthusiasm for the precautionary principle is in part a reaction to the regulatory failures that European countries suffered in the 1980s and 1990s. The scandal surrounding mad cow disease in particular made people extremely sensitive to the practices of industrialized agriculture that forced supposedly unnatural violations of species boundaries. So it may seem that Europe's current precautionary stance is more a contingent reaction to recent events than a result of carefully thought-out policy.

There remains, however, an important element of truth in the conventional wisdom. Since the early 1970s, Europeans have been at the forefront of efforts to turn precaution into a principle—something that precaution has never been in U.S. law. Under certain circumstances, precaution cannot be reduced to a mere policy option or a demand for a higher degree of risk aversion in general. The European history of the precautionary principle shows how precaution acquired special moral significance. The precautionary principle is not meant to replace science-based risk assessment across the board but to indicate that risk assessment does have limits—and when these limits are reached, special obligations ensue. In addition, making precaution principled signifies an aspiration to devise an internationally acceptable rule for handling risks falling in that category. Making precaution more than a preference, though, entails coming to a common understanding of the scope of its application, situating it in relation to other social values (such as efficiency), and subjecting the judgments that it invites to tests of fairness, transparency, and consistency.

It is the growing international legitimacy of precaution in this principled sense that has stirred precaution's U.S. opponents to active resistance.

How Deep Is the U.S. Opposition to Precaution?

Since coming to office, the administration of George W. Bush has taken the lead in opposing policies inspired by the precautionary principle. In April 2001, Bush unilaterally withdrew the United States from negotiations on climate change in the framework of the Kyoto Protocol. The administration also pushed away any commitment in favor of the Cartagena Protocol on Biodiversity, of which Articles 10.6 and 11.8 take up the precautionary principle explicitly.[1] This protocol applies to the international use or transfer of GMOs, requiring exporting countries to evaluate their risks and allowing importing countries to refuse imports even in the "absence of scientific certainty . . . concerning the extent of their unfavorable effects" (Convention on Biological Diversity 2000). At the Johannesburg summit in September 2002, U.S. representatives opposed any mention of the precautionary principle (Green Fades 2002), just as they had done in the WTO talks in Doha in November 2001. This antiprecautionary stance finds its most determined expression in relation to the regulation of and trade in GMOs. In May 2003, the administration's foreign trade representative, Robert Zoellick, announced that the United States was going to take the EU before the WTO's dispute resolution body in order to challenge the precautionary grounds for its GMO regulations.

These positions are not just circumstantial reactions in favor of particular U.S. interests. They form part of a concerted campaign against the precautionary principle itself. For Ann Veneman (U.S. secretary of agriculture from 2001 to 2004) fostering trade depends on "the adoption of science-based systems, as opposed to opportunistic ones, such as the precautionary principle" (State Department Transcript 2002). Addressing European ideas directly, John D. Graham (2002), an administrator in the Office of Information and Regulatory Affairs of the Office of Management and Budget, criticizes an "extreme" policy, according to which "any technological innovation cannot be adopted unless and until it is proven to be completely safe by the proponents of the innovation." Graham concludes that the U.S. government supports "precautionary approaches to risk management but we do not recognize any universal precautionary principle. We consider it to be a mythical concept, perhaps like a unicorn."

Anyone listening to this drumbeat of criticism can be forgiven for adopting the conventional wisdom. The United States appears reflexively antiprecautionary. In fact, arguably, not just this or that administration but the political culture of the United States itself casts precautionary regulation in a suspicious light. That most famous nineteenth-century observer of U.S. political life, Alexis de Tocqueville ([1835] 1969, 463), noted that the inhabitants of the New World wanted to see science advance rapidly so that its practical applications could be turned "immediately" into ways of "getting wealth more quickly . . . [and] of diminishing the costs of production." The modern predilection for short-term profit exerts constant pressure against precautionary oversight.

Moreover, the legal framework of administrative decision making as it has developed in the United States in the twentieth century also works against precaution. Comparative risk expert Sheila Jasanoff (2000, 72) remarks that while Europeans talk of precaution, "risk . . . is the term heavily favored in U.S. legislation and public policy." Risk, she continues,

> is actuarial in spirit. One can (indeed, one often must) insure oneself against various kinds of risks for which actuarial data are available, such as fires, floods . . . or automobile accidents. When used in environmental decision making, risk retains the connotation of something that can be clearly defined and quantified, hence managed. It is a relative concept that risks can always be offset against benefits, and risk-based laws often explicitly prescribe that the benefits of policy action (which are, in turn, quantified) should outweigh the risks.

The discourse of risk assessment in the U.S. idiom favors quantification, commensuration, comparison, and careful measures of efficiency. Typically, the aim of U.S. health and environmental policy is to *manage* risk, not to avoid or hold it to a minimum (Applegate 2000, 435).

Yet as Jasanoff (2003) would be the first to point out, the precautionary idea actually has well-developed roots in the United States. It is important to realize this, if only to set the historical record straight. In addition, reviewing the role of the United States in developing precautionary standards helps dispel pessimism about the principle's prospects as an international norm of environmental risk regulation that might eventually win U.S. acceptance.

It is true that the "precautionary principle" has no official status within U.S. federal law. But that by no means implies a systematic absence of precaution in U.S. approaches to health and environmental regulation. In fact, knowledgeable European commentators often credit U.S. precedent with inspiring "precautionary" regulatory reforms in Europe (see Ewald, Gollier, and Sadeleer 2001, 52, 56; Noiville 2003; Kourilsky 2002, 105, 110). In the past decade, Europeans have followed the lead of the United States in trying to create more independent regulatory bodies—ones that are less subject to pressure from politicians and economic interests. Outside of the United States, regulatory and "promotional functions" are often housed in the same ministry (Jasanoff 2000, 73). European health and food safety scandals in the 1980s and 1990s (discussed below) exposed the vulnerabilities of such a system. The British parliamentary committee that studied the mad cow scandal complained of the bias introduced by the political control of the composition of scientific advisory committees, the pressure exerted on civil servants, and the reluctance of politicians to make regulatory decisions that might damage nationally important industries (Phillips, Bridgeman, and Ferguson-Smith 2000). To counter such problems, the EU assembled a new European Food Authority, modeled partly on the USDA.[2] Henceforth, risk assessment would flow from "scientific advice . . . based on the principle of excellence, independence and transparency," thus avoiding "opinions . . . guided by interests other than scientific rigour" (Lafond 2001, 7). Regulatory institutions must be designed so that risk evaluators can form judgments based on the evidence before them, not based on extraneous considerations of the potential economic or political repercussions of regulation.

Precaution, however, pertains not just to the independent evaluation of existing evidence. More distinctively, it is a matter of how uncertainties regarding evidence are handled. In this respect, too, U.S. regulatory practice has played a crucial role in the evolution of the precautionary idea. Whether or not the word precaution is used, one can say that the precautionary idea in risk regulation is at work whenever authorities take early preventive measures to forestall a potential, irreversible danger, even though causal links in the chain leading to that danger have not yet been firmly scientifically established. Such an approach is apparent in the FDA (2000) report "Precaution in U.S. Food Safety Decisionmaking." The report emphasizes how "risk assessment procedures include . . . conservative assumptions about uncertainty"—assumptions requiring more safety than is proven necessary by scientific studies. It asserts that the FDA may employ "precaution in risk management" to assure food safety "when the risk assessment indicates significant uncertainty in the probability of the risk management options to achieve an acceptable level of risk." Similarly, the marketing of pharmaceuticals in the United States is governed by precautionary reasoning (Vogel and Bensedrine 2002, 18). In an approximate way, the adjective precautionary can be applied to any preventive measure that builds in a large safety margin, or that leaves administrators with a space of judgment such that they can take early and effective action, independently of their ability to establish a need to do so by reference to authoritative quantitative evidence.

Working from this broad conception of precaution, political scientist David Vogel (2003) notes that "a precautionary approach underlay American food safety regulation," insofar as companies were required to "establish the safety of a process or an additive prior to approval." The Delaney Amendment of 1958, which prohibited the marketing of any food product containing a potentially carcinogenic additive, is often cited as an example of U.S.-style precaution (Jasanoff 2003, 231; Bodansky 1994, 210; Applegate 2000, 421). Sponsors of food additives are "required to make an affirmative showing of safety; if this showing falls short, there is no approval even if there is no affirmative showing of risk" (FDA 2000, 6). U.S. tort law holds food processors to standards of "strict liability." The absence of actual knowledge of a product's harmfulness does not constitute a legal defense in such a regime. Moreover, risk-assessment procedures are made to include numerous conservative assumptions (for example, uncertainty factors for different sensitivities of population subgroups and incompleteness in the database). These effectively operationalize a precautionary approach. Where new technologies might cause serious, irreversible damage to substantial human interests, uncertainties in the scientific record are not allowed to forestall regulatory action.

Similar reasoning crossed over into U.S. federal environmental law decades before it became the norm in Europe. The National Environmental Protection Act of 1969 clearly articulates the state's precautionary duties. To protect future generations, the act requires that "accidental and undesirable consequences" of human actions be *avoided*—not just made subject to legal penalties if they occur (Applegate 2000, 421). Federal administrators examine any project that might have an impact on the environment before it is undertaken. In the Clean Air Act (1970 and 1977), an "ample margin of safety" is applied to potentially dangerous substances. The Clean Water Act (1972) mentions the goal of "zero emissions." These laws embody a precautionary logic insofar as they require a level of safety that goes significantly beyond what is justified by scientific evidence alone. The Endangered Species Act (1973) enjoins federal agencies from undertaking any "irreversible or irretrievable commitment of resources" that might foreclose "reasonable and prudent alternative measures" to save a species (*U.S. Code* 16, §§1533–1539).

In subsequent decades, U.S. environmental law took a quasiprecautionary turn, especially in regard to regulating sources of toxic chemical pollutants. Like the precautionary principle, the policy of pollution *prevention* rests on a recognition that certain sources of environmental risk "are invisible and otherwise . . . difficult to detect, and . . . may affect health and cause environmental damage at trace concentrations, although the degree of uncertainty [concerning their effects] tends to be very high" (Gottlieb 1995, 19). Regulatory action is deemed justified nonetheless. The Toxic Substances Control Act (TSCA) of 1976 gave the EPA the authority to require the phaseout of certain toxic substances as well as to control the production, importation, and marketing of chemicals found to pose an "unreasonable risk" (Mazurek, Gottlieb, and Roque 1995, 61). Where earlier legislation such as the Clean Water and Clean Air Acts applied to the *release* of certain substances, the TSCA moved a step back in the pollution chain, regulating the *production* of toxics. In a related vein, the Toxics Release inventory was established in 1987. This obliged industries to report emissions of 329 specified toxic chemicals, thus enhancing the opportunities for citizen groups to pressure manufacturers to reduce forms of pollution that correlate with suspicious patterns of illness in the population. Congress passed the Pollution Prevention Act in 1990. This act aimed at the source reduction of toxics—that is, at diminishing the amount of hazardous substances released into the environment (Mazurek, Gottlieb, and Roque 1995, 73). In all these cases, laws favoring pollution prevention resemble precaution insofar as they call for anticipatory environmental action.

Equally worthy of mention in a history of U.S. precaution are judicial decisions in which some of the laws mentioned above are given an explicitly precautionary reading. Interpreting the Clean Air Act in 1976, a federal appeals court held that

> where a statute is precautionary in nature, the evidence difficult to come by, uncertain, or conflicting because it is on the frontiers of scientific knowledge, the regulations designed to protect the public health and the decision that of an expert administrator, we will not demand rigorous step-by-step proof of cause and effect. Such proof may be impossible to obtain if the precautionary purpose of the statute is to be served. (*Ethyl Corp. v. EPA* 541 F.2d1 [DC Cir.1976])

Likewise, in 1975 a federal appeals court ruled in favor of EPA regulations on asbestos fibers in mine ore effluent, even though there was as yet no evidence concerning health hazards from waterborne (as opposed to airborne) asbestos. There was "some health risk," the court wrote, so it was appropriate to take a "precautionary and preventive measure to protect the public health."[3] The U.S. Supreme Court read the Endangered Species Act as aiming at a sort of "institutionalized caution" in respect to development projects that might lead to irreversible damage to a whole species (*Tennessee Valley Authority v. Hill,* 437 U.S. 153 [1978]).

Finally, the Great Lakes Water Quality Agreement is one of the clearest examples of precautionary action in the history of U.S. environmental policy. This agreement, signed between the United States and Canada, has decreed a goal of phasing out all persistent toxics in the Great Lakes ecosystem. The precautionary nature of this goal was acknowledged when the binational commission charged with overseeing this agreement held in 1992 that persistent toxics must be eliminated "whether or not unassailable scientific proof of acute or chronic damage is universally accepted" (quoted in Tickner, Raffensperger, and Myers 1999).

From the laws and court cases cited above, one can infer three essential features of precautionary action that are embedded in U.S. law. First, it is recognized that there are risks for which a strategy of anticipatory action is more reasonable than after-the-fact liability or cleanup. Second, a strong case can be made for such anticipatory action where there is a danger of especially serious and/or irreversible consequences. Finally, in cases of this sort, the absence of firm, quantitative, scientifically validated evidence regarding the danger's probability of occurrence or the causal mechanisms involved in producing it does not justify deferring preventive measures. Precautionary elements like these have been pervasive enough in U.S. regulatory practice to lead James Cameron (1999, 250)—one of the first to write on the precautionary principle in English—to assert that "no country has so fully adopted the essence of the precautionary principle in domestic law as the United States."

That assertion calls, however, for two important qualifications. First, no *principle* actually motivated this series of regulatory approaches. Thus, while the National Environmental Policy Act seems precautionary—it mandates forward-looking impact assessments of proposed environmental alterations—it creates no obligation on anyone's part to mitigate any dangers that might be discovered. Nor is the existence of the TSCA evidence of a true commitment to preventing uncertain environmental risks. The EPA has generally avoided giving the TSCA high priority and has been deferential to industry's confidentiality claims (refusals to divulge information about production processes on the grounds that they involve commercial secrets). It is reported that in the first fifteen years after the TSCA was passed, the EPA used its "broad authority to restrict the use of toxic chemicals . . . against only five substances" (Mazurek, Gottlieb, and Roque 1995, 61). In fact, by 1990 the EPA had considered only 386 chemicals for *testing*, out of some 70,000 on the market. This contrasts to the explicitly precautionary chemicals policy proposed by the EU in 2001. The Registration, Evaluation, and Authorization of Chemicals system will require industry to use new safety standards in testing the over 30,000 chemicals that have been put on the market since 1981. Not surprisingly, Bush administration officials geared up to oppose this policy soon after it was put forward (EPA, Industry 2002).

So, however cautiously the U.S. government has treated some risks at some points in recent history, precaution is, at most, "a preference" (Applegate 2000, 439) or an "approach" (Graham 2004) in U.S. law. This means that from time to time, precautionary logic is persuasive to legislators, judges, and administrators. It is then applied on a case-by-case basis, with little concern for consistency in comparable cases and no systematic attempt to justify it. A precautionary approach was evident when Canada discovered a single mad cow in one of its herds. George W. Bush's Department of Agriculture immediately suspended all beef imports from Canada—without waiting for scientific studies on the extent of the danger, and without weighing the risks versus the benefits of the ban (Canada Stunned 2003). The precautionary *approach* makes judgment a matter of official discretion. Discretion means that considerations such as market efficiency and utilitarian optimization can easily overrule precaution (Applegate 2000, 429). A precautionary approach refuses to acknowledge the existence of certain risks whose seriousness gives them a different moral status from those involved in situations of more limited danger.

Second, recent decades have seen persistent efforts to make the U.S. regulatory regime less precautionary than it was in the 1970s. A 1980 decision by the U.S. Supreme Court marked a turning point (Jasanoff 2003, 234–236; Bodansky 1994, 204). The case of *Industrial Union Department, AFL-CIO v. American Petroleum Institute* turned on whether the Occupational Safety and Health Administration had to demonstrate a "significant risk" before it could regulate a toxic substance (here: benzene) in the workplace. The Court majority held that regulators had to provide quantitative evidence justifying their standards; otherwise, the Court reasoned, government agencies might choose to regulate any of "thousands" of suspected carcinogens, thus imposing "enormous costs that might produce little, if any, discernible benefits" (448 U.S. 607 [1980]). The intention was to limit the right of standard-setting agencies to make qualitative judgments about potential dangers when the evidence was scant or ambiguous. This decision made quantitative risk assessment essentially obligatory for all U.S. agencies involved in health regulation. Executive Orders from presidents Reagan, Bush, and Clinton essentially followed suit: all major rules proposed by federal agencies were to be preceded by a cost-benefit analysis and were only supposed to go forward if the benefits exceeded the costs (Sunstein 2002, 20–21). Congress reduced the scope of the Delaney amendment in 1996 so that it no longer applied to pesticide residues in foods.[4] Over the same period, the United States has foresworn the leadership role that it once played in promoting international environmental agreements (Paarlberg 1999). That earlier leadership role was evident, for example, in the phase out of CFCs. The United States prohibited the use of CFCs as aerosol propellants in 1977—a decade before the links between CFCs and ozone depletion were well established. Cautious reasoning of that sort has not been allowed to determine U.S. policy with respect to greenhouse gas emissions or GMOs.

The absence of an articulated precautionary principle in U.S. law, or in its political discourse more generally, has made it difficult to mount resistance to these changes—or even to perceive them as a shift in emphasis within a regulatory regime. U.S. precaution has always been ad hoc and discretionary. Policy gets shaped through incremental adjustments, the gradual building of precedent, and a pragmatic balancing of competing considerations. Since there is no principled expectation in favor of precaution, ad hoc, discretionary policies that are non-precautionary in nature seem consistent with the regulatory regime.

At the same time, however, it cannot be said that recent nonprecautionary developments signal a definitive rejection of precautionary reasoning. Most of the statutes and judicial decisions mentioned earlier remain on the books. Precautionary assumptions—ones that deliberately overestimate the risk from pollution where human and environmental health are concerned—continue to guide risk assessments by the EPA (General Accounting Office 2000). There are examples extending from the 1980s all the way up to the present showing that a precautionary logic continues to have a place in U.S. regulatory practice (Wiener and Rogers 2002; Jasanoff 2000). When all of these precedents are taken into account, it is impossible to affirm the "conventional wisdom" that pits a precautionary Europe against a risk-taking United States.

Is European Precaution Really Principled?

Perhaps, though, a closer look at European risk management would reveal that its precautionary measures are not really principled either. Comparing a wide range of perceived dangers, Jonathan Wiener and Michael Rogers (2002, 322–23) observe:

> Europe appears to be more precautionary than the US about such risks as GMOs, hormones in beef, toxic substances, phthalates, climate change, gun and antitrust/competition policy. The US appears to be more precautionary than Europe about such risks as new drug approval, the ban on CFCs in aerosol spray cans and the ban on supersonic transport to protect the stratospheric ozone layer, nuclear energy, lead in gasoline, particulate air pollution, highway safety, teenage drinking, cigarette smoking, mad cow disease in blood donations, potentially violent youths, "right to know" information disclosure requirements, and missile defences.

That observation leads them to conclude that precaution depends on "the context of the particular case" and not on some "overarching national regulatory posture" (342).

Such a conclusion has the merit of reminding us how difficult it is to develop valid, cross-national generalizations about the objects of regulatory concern. In different countries, perceptions of risk vary considerably and the range of regulatory response is even wider. Factors that help account for the international variability of regulatory outcomes are legion. There are differences in political structure—for example, the presence or absence of environmental parties in parliaments as well as diverse ways of incorporating technical expertise in decision making (Jasanoff 2000, 73). Culturally rooted dispositions in regard to certain products (for instance, a country's favorite foods) play a role (Echols 1998). The ease or difficulty of bringing liability lawsuits affects the felt urgency of regulatory reform.[5] The availability or not of judicial review in the countries' legal traditions shapes politicians' willingness to undertake precise regulatory commitments (Wiener and Rogers 2002, 240). The relative power of particular interest groups in different nations' economies creates varying degrees of enthusiasm for regulatory measures that might put an important industry at a competitive disadvantage in international trade.

The factor that seems to play the largest role in determining whether certain risks become matters of regulatory concern is their ability to remind the public of a disaster or regulatory failure of recent occurrence. Comparative risk specialist David Vogel (2003) argues that for both the United States and Europe, this phenomenon helps explain the emergence of precautionary-type regulations at different points in time. If Americans demanded more stringent regulation starting in the late 1960s, it was in the wake of their exposure to the thalidomide scandal (1962), Rachel Carson's *Silent Spring*

(1962), Ralph Nader's *Unsafe at Any Speed* (1965), Love Canal (1977), and Three Mile Island (1979). Regulatory reforms took place in the 1970s and 1980s and authorities regained the public's confidence. In the absence of any major public health crisis in the 1990s, there has been no groundswell of support for new types of precautionary legislation.

Over approximately the same period, recounts Vogel, Europe went from a relatively low level of regulatory initiative to a state of high alert. A series of regulatory scandals and breakdowns in the 1980s and 1990s undermined the credibility of health and environmental authorities, leading to calls for heightened regulatory vigilance. The Chernobyl nuclear accident spread a radioactive cloud over Europe in 1986. Notoriously (and ludicrously) French authorities claimed that meteorologic conditions had stopped the cloud at the French border. That same year, a major chemical fire at the Sandoz factory dangerously polluted the Rhine River. Again, that same year, the first cases of an entirely new cattle disease were officially acknowledged in Britain. Nothing did more damage to the reputation of European regulatory systems than the crisis that grew out of the spread of mad cow disease.

Bovine spongiform encephalitis (BSE) resembles another brain-wasting animal disease with which scientists had long been familiar: sheep scrapie. So it took less than a year to arrive at the hypothesis that the two diseases were linked. How might cows contract a disease hitherto confined to sheep? Sheep—including infected ones—were ground and reprocessed into the feed designed to give extra protein to cattle. Yet, even as scientists grew more certain that this link explained the disease, numerous questions remained unanswered. What was the specific pathogen involved? What parts of the cow were infected? Were there risks for human beings in eating infected cows? Ten years passed between the first hypothesis of the cause of the disease and the British government's announcement in March 1996 that eating infected beef could indeed cause a similar fatal illness in human beings—new variant Creutzfeldt-Jakob (NVCJ) disease.

Between 1986 and 1996, the British Ministry of Agriculture repeatedly used the uncertainties surrounding the disease as a pretext to avoid taking decisive preventive steps, out of fear that such measures might damage the British beef industry. In 1987 and 1988, the meat of infected animals remained on sale for human consumption. Up through 1990, British authorities balked at accepting new slaughtering methods that might minimize the likelihood of infected organs contaminating meat. In 1990, the minister of agriculture told the House of Commons that there was "clear scientific evidence that British beef is perfectly safe" (Hansard quoted in Zwanenberg and Millstone 2001, 161). Although Britain ceased using ruminant protein in ruminant feed in 1988, contaminated feed continued to be used for nonruminants (for example, pigs and poultry), and Britain continued to export the feed to other European countries. Cows in whom the disease might still be incubating continued to be exported through 1989. BSE thus spread into Europe's free internal market. Not until 1994 did the European Commission ban feeding ruminant animals with meat and bonemeal. Not until 1996, when the British announced evidence that BSE had caused NVCJ disease in humans, did the commission ban British meat for commerce in the EU.[6]

Because NVCJ is a disease with a long incubation period, it is difficult to predict what the final human cost of these policy errors will be. Estimates of new cases of NVCJ that might occur in the future range between one hundred and one million (Collinge 1999).

Unsurprisingly, Europe's regulatory failures stirred cries for reform and greater caution. GMOs were the first targets of this heightened sensitivity. The first shipment of transgenic crops to Europe arrived only seven months after Britain's devastating announcement that eating infected beef could induce NVCJ. Small wonder, then, that GMOs were greeted with the label "mad soybeans." Scientists insist that mad cow disease and genetic engineering are entirely separate issues (Houdebine 2000, 105–114). But a series of troubling resemblances caught the public imagination. In both cases, the drive for intensified, industrialized production determined how food was being treated, the significance of species boundaries was denied, and government officials claimed that the scientific evidence was sufficient to assure the public of the safety of the resulting foodstuffs. That Europeans demanded greater "precaution" in handling GMOs than had been exercised in relation to British beef thus seems like a perfect example of a contingent reaction to a policy failure. Like Americans in the 1970s, traumatized Europeans wanted enhanced regulatory protection in the 1990s.

Such a reading, however, seriously understates the significance of the precautionary principle in European thinking. It makes the precautionary principle appear, once again, as a mere approach. Now we use precaution (when the public demands it), and now we don't (once the crisis has past.)

Yet the European reaction to GMOs in 1996 was not just a crisis response. Chapter 1 showed how Germany's precautionary biotechnology policies of the 1980s became the basis for Europe-wide regulations in the early 1990s. The EU had adopted the precautionary principle as a founding principle of community environmental law in 1992, and when GMOs arrived, many member states were still in the process of transposing the principle into national law. The continuity of this history demonstrates a consistently deepening commitment, arising out of a set of reflections about the state of the world. What principled precaution means, and the case for proceeding in a principled fashion, emerges from three key moments in its European development.

First, scholars usually trace the European roots of the precautionary principle to the Vorsorgeprinzip that was written into German environmental law in the 1970s (Ewald, Gollier, and Sadeleer 2001; O'Riordan and Jordan 1995; Bourg and Schlegel 2001). The precautionary principle has appeared in German policymaking regarding acid rain and justifications for energy tax policies designed to reduce the consumption of fossil fuels (Boehmer-Christiansen 1994, 49). *Vorsorge* means foresight or anticipation, with overtones of deliberate planning. In one of its earliest applications, German air-quality legislation called for using state-of-the-art technologies—rather than proportioning pollution control requirements to predictable environmental damages. Likewise, lawmakers were advised that the complexity of the North Sea ecosystem made it too difficult to trace cause-effect relationships between specific pollutants and environmental damage. Precaution dictated generalized preventive measures, especially reducing the emissions of hazardous substances at the source by using the best available technology (von Moltke 1988, 59). By 1984, Vorsorge was understood to call for "the early detection of dangers to health and environment" as well as "acting when conclusively ascertained understanding by science is not yet available" (Boehmer-Christiansen 1994, 37). "Proof of damage is not required . . . when irreversibility is feared," added the authors of the 1984 West German government report on the protection of air quality.

These ideas resemble those that make up the "precautionary ideal" in the United States—except that in Germany, Vorsorge immediately had the force of a moral requirement *(Gebot)*. The Vorsorgeprinzip is not a government command. It serves instead as "a philosophical principle and tool of persuasion to justify the setting of ambitious environmental targets" (Boehmer-Christiansen 1994, 55). Appeals to Vorsorge tend to appear early in the policymaking process, where its function is persuasive, not punitive. It creates a normative orientation for policy across a wide range of issues, such that a foresightful duty of environmental care obtains even where the scientific evidence of harm is not yet dispositive. Vorsorge favors the general implementation of "best practice" in relation to a potential environmental problem, not deciding on what measures to take by balancing predictable benefits and known costs.

Indeed, Germany added the Vorsorgeprinzip to four other fundamental principles of environmental policy in 1976 precisely in order to counterbalance tendencies within the policy process to make economic feasibility the decisive test of policy desirability. German guidelines speak of an "imperative to minimize risks."[7] *Minimizing* contrasts to *optimizing*. Optimizing would suggest quantifying as much as possible the costs and benefits of alternative environmental protection measures, then choosing the one that brought the greatest net benefits. Minimizing, on the other hand, foregoes balancing in favor of reducing potentially damaging practices as much as possible. A precautionary strategy makes sense in cases where the quantification is undependable, where optimization has a record of sanctioning lax environmental protection, or where irreversible damages are possible. It would doubtless be an exaggeration to say that the Vorsorgeprinzip requires that environmental protection measures be chosen entirely independently of their economic feasibility. Still, it calls for "doing more than is necessary by other criteria" (von Moltke 1988, 60).

The second source of principled precaution is the thought of philosopher Hans Jonas, particularly his 1979 book, *Das Prinzip Verantwortung* (literally, "the responsibility *principle,*" but translated as *The Imperative of Responsibility*). It is a significant index of the difference between European and U.S. precaution that European historical accounts almost always mention Jonas's work while English language treatments usually ignore it.[8] I work to correct that oversight in chapter 4. What is crucial in the present context is that Jonas presents the issue of preventive environmental action in terms of a new *ethical principle*.

A new principle is needed, Jonas argues, because humankind's technological power has created an ethical gap. In the past, humanity was effectively part of nature and had to suffer its power. Nature served as a limit to our activities and it managed to recover its balance after human intervention. But now our technologies allow us to transform the whole world—with the potential for life-threatening environmental side effects. Because of this unprecedented power, our traditional ethics, which were designed to order relations between people (and not between people and nature) no longer suffice. A new ethic is needed, Jonas contends, one that emphasizes not our *rights* to action but rather our *responsibilities* toward others, especially future generations. Uncertainty about the extent of potential future catastrophes does not exonerate us from responsibility. Should "uncertainty . . . be our permanent fate," Jonas (1984, 191) maintains, we must deduce from that certain *"moral consequences."* As Jonas reasons, when it is a matter of serious, global dangers for which the scientific evidence is too undeveloped to allow us to calculate probabilities, we need only imagine the possible effects of our choices. The mere possibility of a consequence disastrous for the future of humanity justifies forbearance (Jonas 1984, 25–38).

More explicitly than had ever been done before, Jonas made the case that decision making in relation to potentially catastrophic risks carries with it moral responsibilities of such weight that only a principle, not pragmatic balancing, is appropriate. That sort of reasoning has gained wide currency in Europe. Jonasian echoes are unmistakable in the words of a European Commission spokesperson, who defends precautionary chemical testing: "If there is scientific uncertainty as to the nature of a risk . . . , those in public office charged with protecting the public health . . . have a *duty* to respond and not wait until their fears are realized, until the worst is happening" (Government, Chemical Industry 2003).

The third distinctive feature of European precaution consists in state-led efforts—ongoing since the late 1990s—to shape a statement of principle that fits the range of serious risks encountered in technological societies.[9] Individually and collectively, European countries have sought to sharpen the definition of the precautionary principle and structure its implementation. Their goal has been to enhance its acceptability as a general rule governing risk management at an international level.

Delimiting the field of the principle's application has been at the heart of these efforts. When is precaution called for? The 1987 Ministerial Declaration of the Second International Conference on the North Sea (when precaution made its first explicit appearance in an international treaty) stated that a precautionary approach "may require action to control inputs of [the most dangerous] substances [into the North Sea] even before a causal link has been established by absolutely clear scientific evidence." The declaration targeted "polluting emissions of substances that are persistent, toxic, and liable to bioaccumulate."[10] Precaution was deemed appropriate in relation to pollutants whose characteristics made them particularly likely to create long-term problems in a complex, geographically extensive ecosystem. It was recognized that the complexity of the system and the delayed manifestation of consequences made acquiring "absolutely clear scientific evidence" problematic.

Subsequent formulations have not always followed that precedent of explaining the conditions of precautionary action. The precautionary principle was included by name in the 1992 Treaty of the European Union (Maastricht Treaty). Unfortunately, no further definition was offered.[11] The intention, apparently, was the broad one of favoring a preventive rather than a reactive approach to environmental policy (Weale 1992, 80). In such a context, precaution can be made to apply to almost anything. In France since 1995, fear of GMOs along with regulatory failures such as the spread of mad cow disease and the marketing of chicken containing the notorious pollutant dioxin have made the precautionary principle almost a household word. It is encountered weekly, if not nightly, on newscasts and in the daily papers. But the meaning of household words can be as untidy as our households. When the authorities were caught unprepared to handle the traffic jams of winter vacationers returning to Paris, they were criticized in the name of the precautionary principle; precautionary measures were urged against a school director suspected of being a Scientologist (Bourg and Whiteside 2003, 166).

There is a certain logic in such appeals. It is always possible to call for greater caution in the face of a risk. After some undesired consequence materializes, one often wishes that preventive measures had been taken earlier. Yet the history of the precautionary principle shows that it was not conceived simply to codify increased risk aversion across the whole range of risks. It originated in attempts to deal with environmental problems like pollution in the North Sea, where ecosystem complexities made it impossible to predict the long-term effects of discharges (Sadeleer 2001a, 549).

Nowhere has the debate over the principle's appropriate field of application been pushed further than in France. In 2002, the French government appointed the so-called Coppens Commission to develop language—including precautionary language—for a "Charter for the Environment" to be added to the Constitution. The most divisive issue facing the commission was whether to make precaution an approach or a principle. Significantly, the defenders of principled precaution (the position that prevailed) argued in terms of its appropriateness in handling "a new category of risks." These risks, they explained, "are not accidental, but rather are gradual or delayed [in manifesting their effects]; they cannot be separated from accumulative processes that occur over a relatively long period" (Ministère de l'Écologie et du Développement Durable 2003, 43). The case for precaution rises to the level of principled action especially for "delayed, global risks" that are "serious, because they concern ecosystems that condition the reproduction of the conditions of our existence, and irreversible, because they involve mechanisms and systems marked by great inertia" (Bourg and Whiteside 2003, 160).

Such reflections help distinguish precaution from general risk aversion in the face of uncertainty. They call attention to characteristics of environmental systems that in twentieth-century experience, have repeatedly made conventional, science-based risk assessment underestimate their vulnerabilities. These factors include the existence of initially unsuspected interconnections between phenomena; the systems' tendency to displace, preserve, and concentrate chemicals; their inertia; and their susceptibility to dramatic change once certain thresholds are crossed. Uncertainty plagues these risks precisely because of the characteristics that make them so environmentally problematic. While this reasoning follows up on Jonas's concern about new risks that flow from our unprecedented power to affect the global environment, it does not limit itself to situations endangering the entire future of humanity.

Keeping Precaution Reasonable

One might still object that European statements of principle hardly answer all of the questions about when precaution is required. Is the potential disappearance of a single species of fish sufficiently "serious" to justify a precautionary response? (Just any species? The snail darter?) Does *every* persistent chemical fall under precautionary suspicion or just the ones for which there is already *some* evidence of potential harmfulness? Is an environmental change really "irreversible" if a remedy can be found for its harmful effects (for example, a medical treatment is discovered that protects against the cancerogenic effects of long-term exposure to a pollutant)? Precaution's defenders generally admit that ambiguities remain regarding how serious potential damages have to be in order to trigger the precautionary principle, how much scientific evidence is necessary in order to make the existence of a threat plausible, and what measures are appropriate in response (Godard 1997a; Sadeleer 2001b).

No concise statement of principle is going to resolve all cases. The meaning of characteristics such as serious or irreversible will have to be subject to further legislative and jurisprudential clarifications. In that respect, however, the precautionary principle is hardly different from any other orienting principle of government action. Committing to "equal opportunity employment" or "cost-effective" regulation leaves open innumerable details of definition, scope of application, appropriate forms of measurement, procedures of implementation, and arbitration with competing values. Open-endedness hardly means that such principles are vacuous—much less "mythical."

Moreover, it is possible to adjust precaution in ways that are responsive to critics' concerns, without giving up on its principled character. One such adjustment would bring certain economically inflected criteria into its definition. The Rio Declaration of 1992, for example, states that precaution means not "postponing *cost-effective* measures to prevent environmental degradation." France followed this lead in the so-called Barnier Law (1995). Its version of the precautionary principle holds that "the lack of certainty . . . must not delay the adoption of *effective and proportionate measures* that aim to prevent a risk of serious and irreversible damage to the environment." In effect, such wording heeds critics who complain that a principled commitment to precaution is too costly. One reason to favor a precautionary approach, they might say, is to avoid making administrators apply precautionary measures to cases where the chances of environmental damage seem particularly far-fetched or the expense of such measures will be particularly burdensome. Including the language of proportionality in the precautionary principle is designed to accommodate this critique, while preserving the principle's moral force.

Not all defenders of precaution are happy with a version of the principle that includes economically inflected criteria. In their seminal article on the precautionary principle, James Cameron and Julie Abouchar (1991, 6) claimed that the Vorsorgeprinzip cannot count as truly precautionary because German law "marries precaution to economic considerations." They argued that such considerations have been used to justify the nonimplementation of precautionary standards.[12] Past regulatory failures like Britain's mad cow debacle have occurred when administrators failed to take precautionary measures for fear of hobbling an industry or slowing the economy. Building a requirement of cost-effectiveness into the precautionary principle seems to subvert its purpose. That purpose, some contend, is to articulate a logic distinct from quantitative risk assessment and normatively superior to it. "Proportionality," too, contradicts the very logic of precaution, asserts philosopher Jean-Pierre Dupuy. Precaution applies where environmental effects are poorly understood. GMOs, for example, may be innocuous—or they may have as-yet-unforeseen, irreversible, negative consequences for the global food supply and the environment. What is a proportionate policy in relation to an unknown danger? Proportional to what? Doesn't the proportionality of precautions depend entirely on whether catastrophic consequences occur—which is precisely what we do not know (Dupuy 2002, 103–104)?

Not necessarily. Legitimate social concerns about cost and proportionality can be taken into account without setting them up to trump precautionary reasoning. In the EU, cost-benefit estimates are allowed to influence the choice of measures used in precautionary action, but not to determine whether precautionary action is taken in the first place (Christoforou 2003, 249). More generally, cost concerns can be brought into a risk-management process that is *structured as a whole* to achieve precautionary effects. Insofar as figures are available at all, measures of cost-effectiveness, for example, have a place in *deliberations* over risk at certain stages in the evaluation process—not to determine the outcome but to inform the deliberators' judgment. For precautionary reasons discussed earlier, the deliberative body should be composed in a way that fosters its independence from outside economic pressures. Then, independent risk assessors are in a position to *decide* how pertinent the cost figures are. Deliberators can judge that certain figures are persuasive because of the care that went into gathering them and the soundness of the methodology used in their compilation. In other cases, however, the deliberators may find reasons to discount them. They may ascertain that in this or that case, quantitative assessments were one-sided, overoptimistic, or simply speculative. They may decide to reject them because they discover biases in their sources. At all events, the figures become *part of* a precautionary evaluation, not superior to it.

Precaution's principled status can be further secured by adding rules to ensure the fairness of its application. Among U.S. critics, accusations that the precautionary principle is nothing more than a pretext for protectionism are common currency (EU Fear-Mongers 2002; Kilama 2003). The unfolding of the GMO controversy illustrates how such charges undermine attempts to find a precautionary regulatory consensus at an international level. On the U.S. side, Republican Senator Jim Talent of Missouri charged that "there is no reason other than market protection not to permit biotech product into Europe" (U.S. Takes Aim 2003, A1). George W. Bush has accused the Europeans of having "blocked all new bio-crops because of unfounded, unscientific fears" (U.S. Takes Aim 2003, A1).

When encountering such charges, a healthy reaction is to remember that the word science hardly ensures that a policy is free from commercial favoritism. In what looks like the exact opposite of precautionary politics, the USDA specifically forbade an American slaughterhouse from testing for mad cow disease (Barred from Testing 2004). The government claimed there was "no scientific justification" for such testing. Do not miss the irony: the government appealed to science to justify *not* undertaking scientific tests. It was not special concern for consumer health that motivated this policy. The USDA was responding to pressure from the largest meatpacking companies. The industry feared that if one distributor could apply a "BSE-free" label to its beef, consumers would start to question the safety of any meat that was not so labeled. The companies worried that market pressure would eventually force all of them to adopt expensive testing programs. And so in the name of science, the government stepped in. In the case of GMOs, Europeans sometimes argue that the supposed scientific grounding for U.S. policy is really only a stratagem used to protect America's lead in the field of agricultural biotechnology (Whiteside 2003b, 84). Charges of commercial favoritism can be exchanged all too easily. Each side impugns the motives of the other, with little attempt to examine the factual basis of their charges or their consistency. Founded or not, such accusations inflame emotions and stall effective action.

To allay concerns that precautionary regulation could mask protectionist impulses, the European Commission issued a communication in February 2000 that spelled out the conditions for a "Recourse to the

Precautionary Principle." In addition to requiring proportional measures and comparative examination of the benefits and burdens of proposed courses of action, the commission elaborated on two criteria designed to promote fairness: The criteria of nondiscrimination and coherence. Nondiscrimination means that "comparable situations are not treated differently. . . . Precautionary measures should apply so as to attain an equivalent level of protection, regardless of geographical origin or the nature of production." Coherence entails a commitment to ensuring that new precautionary measures are comparable in type as well as the scope of application to measures already taken in equivalent areas where scientific data are more certain (Commission européenne 2000). The commission's criteria make explicit what is implicit in the concept of a principle: all parties who accept a normative rule agree to submit their claims to procedures of debate that check their accuracy. Arbitrariness is limited by requiring appeals to evidence, testing for consistency, and setting standards for impartial testimony.[13] Missing from the commission's list, however, are any requirements of transparency and publicity. I will argue for these in chapter 5.

Precaution and Free Trade: Opposing Principles?

Ideas such as those embodied in the European Commission communication or France's Environmental Charter attempt to reconcile the precautionary principle with the practices of liberalized international trade. The question raised by such efforts is whether the precautionary principle is only a circumscribed exception to "free trade" or it constitutes a far-reaching, environmentally inflected reinterpretation of the very conditions of international commerce. Recurrent, unresolved disputes between Europe and the United States in the 1990s tip the balance in favor of the latter view.

The precautionary principle emerges at the intersection of two of the most powerful "globalizing" trends at work in the world today. In the words of international relations theorist David Held (2002, 60–61), "globalization" refers in one sense to the "growing magnitude of networks and flows of trade, investment, finance, culture and so on." In another sense, it alludes to "the deepening impact of global interactions and processes," including environmental ones. The precautionary principle is clearly a reaction to the second sense of globalization. The number of treaties invoking the principle attests to the growing international awareness that ostensibly local actions such as dumping wastes into the ocean or propagating GM crops actually affect environmental conditions across vast areas—in some cases, around the globe. Only concerted action on a global scale can protect common goods like species diversity and climate stability. At the same time, the globalization of trade and finance in the 1980s and 1990s means that to an unprecedented degree, national borders have become permeable to investment capital, manufacturing, and goods. In the United States, presidents from Reagan to Clinton championed free trade agreements. In Europe, the Single European Act of 1986 knitted members of the European Community into a more integrated trading bloc. At the level of international commerce generally, passage from the General Agreement on Trades and Tariffs to the WTO created a more comprehensive system for monitoring the implementation of trade agreements as well as a new system of arbitration to resolve disputes. These developments mean that barriers of all sorts—tariffs, import quotas, arbitrary product specifications used to prohibit the sale of goods, subsidies to favored industries—have recently been dismantled in favor of so-called free trade. Trade liberalization is supposed to promote greater efficiency in the use of resources, greater consumer choice, and more rapid economic development.

These two forms of globalization often pull policymakers in opposite directions. Free trade requires that countries open their borders to products manufactured elsewhere. But then if there is a breakdown in the originating country's product-safety system, importing countries may find their own safety and environmental standards compromised. This is exactly what happened with the mad cow scandal: infected British beef spread into Europe's food distribution system. The solution would seem to be to allow countries to refuse entry to dangerous products. That solution, however, raises troubling questions for defenders of free trade. Who determines what is dangerous? How dangerous? How is "dangerous" distinguished from "unwanted" (because some domestic constituency is determined to hang on to its profits or jobs)? Such concerns explain why one so often hears that environmental and safety measures are a pretext for protectionism pure and simple. Furthermore, trade liberalization implies easing the movement of capital, not just products. Businesses move geographically in search of conditions most advantageous to production. Under such conditions, governments can be tempted to compete for business by offering comparatively lax environmental standards. One solution might be for environmentally responsible governments to put tariffs on products imported from the laxest countries, if not to ban them entirely. Again, free trade would suffer.

The point of international environmental agreements is to overcome these tensions by means of mutually acceptable standards, principles, and procedures. In the 1960s and 1970s, the European Community worked to harmonize the national standards of member countries so that concerns about food additives, pesticides, plant diseases, and so forth would no longer impede the movement of foodstuffs. In a similar vein, the United Nations set up the Codex Alimentarius Commission to develop international standards for food safety. In its 1994 SPS agreement, the WTO encouraged the adoption of these standards for the worldwide food trade and required any state wishing to restrict imports according to more stringent standards to demonstrate a scientific basis for doing so (Pollack and Shaffer 2001, 157–160). In principle, one can have both free trade and environmental protection, provided that all parties to trade submit themselves to a common set of norms for environmental protection (Victor 2000, 158–160).

The spread of the precautionary principle in international treaties can be seen in this light. As Steven Bernstein (2002, 3) contends, since the 1980s, "sustainable development [has become] the dominant conceptual framework for responses to international environmental problems." Since development cannot be sustainable if development-supporting ecosystems are permanently damaged, such damage must be scrupulously avoided (Zuindeau 1997, 197). In essence, the precautionary principle, in the elaborated form that has gradually taken shape in Europe, is a new, candidate norm for international agreement. It responds to the question, How shall competitive nations with divergent trade interests proceed in situations where there is a possibility that proposed technologies or practices may cause serious, irreversible damage to people and the environment, and yet in which scientific uncertainties make it impossible to determine the probability of such an eventuality? Shall they come to no agreement at all and therefore each set their own standards? Nonagreement is clearly unsatisfactory if the actions of some nations impose grave dangers on all. Shall they then agree to regulate the technology or practice, but only if it fails the tests of science-based risk assessment? That response, however, overstates the capabilities of science-based risk assessment to furnish timely and accurate predictions of impacts in many situations of environmental complexity. The incorporation of the precautionary principle into agreements like the Rio Declaration and the Treaty on the European Union suggests the emergence of a growing international consensus that taking precautionary measures is the more reasonable course in such situations. According to this reasoning, the precautionary principle is a component of "liberal environmentalism." It is one clause in a much larger, liberal international settlement. That settlement itself places environmental protection within a broader set of commitments to preserve state sovereignty over resources, promote free trade and economic growth, and favor market instruments (as opposed to direct state regulation) as a means to achieve environmental ends (Bernstein 2002, 4).

Yet such reasoning itself understates the degree to which the precautionary principle challenges the premises of liberal environmentalism. Seeing this challenge is crucial to understanding why the United States and Europe have so often been at loggerheads in recent years. One reason to think the precautionary principle might be at odds with liberal environmentalism is that liberal arrangements seem incapable of actually preventing severe ecological problems. Bernstein (2002, 3)—who is not overtly critical of the liberal environmental settlement—nonetheless notes that it "may be vastly inadequate to significantly forestall, let alone stop or reverse, current trends in greenhouse gas emissions that lead to climate change." Now concluding that existing measures may be "vastly inadequate" to prevent enormous, long-term damage affecting billions of people is not a minor criticism of liberal arrangements. It is precisely such concern that motivates many defenders of the precautionary principle. They want a new and more stringent standard of environmental care because the liberal compromise offers insufficient protection against potential catastrophes. In that case, the precautionary principle is not part of liberal environmentalism. It becomes a superior norm. When it is rightly invoked, liberal trade policies must give way.

The philosophical clash between liberal environmentalism and the precautionary principle is even more strongly highlighted when scientific uncertainty is taken into account. Nicholas de Sadeleer (2001b, 91) expresses well just how central science has been to modern concepts of legality and responsibility:

> Since the beginning of modern times, positive law has been connected with scientific certainty: In order to be allowed to deviate from the principle of the free circulation of goods, national regulations must prove with certainty that a risk is present; to get damage reparations, the victim must demonstrate the existence of a causal link between the damage suffered and the event . . . ; permission to sell a product or a new technology can only be denied if an alleged risk is proven. This assumes not only continual recourse to scientific expertise but also that these experts be able to offer . . . completely reliable answers.

The reliability and universality of scientific understanding are supposed to cut through the innumerable subjective reasons that individuals and states use to protect their own interests. Claims based on economic advantage, prestige considerations, and cultural differences are all tested according to scientific protocols designed to guarantee objectivity. This is what underlies the U.S. government's position in favor of science-based risk assessment. The United States will agree to restraints on trade, even to its own disadvantage at times, but only on one condition: there must be good, scientifically established reasons that justify the other party's policies. But to the extent that the precautionary principle validates scientific *uncertainty* as a reason to restrain trade, it shakes the foundations of international agreements. Where uncertainty afflicts risk assessment, agreement has to be reached in a new way. All parties seek out a set of morally grounded rules and procedures that they recognize as reasonable to adopt in the face of serious potential harm. Once more, the precautionary principle appears not to extend the liberal environmental settlement but to challenge it at its core.

The controversy over GMOs bares yet another stumbling block on the route toward international consensus. Liberal trade agreements rest on a distinction between products and the processes used in creating them (Godard 2001a, 55–56). Importing countries may legitimately assess products for their intrinsic safety and healthfulness. But the WTO generally forbids countries from erecting import barriers because of objections about the production processes that created the good. In practice this means that with few exceptions, importing countries may not refuse products just because they deem workers in the exporting country to be underpaid or they condemn the environmental damage the production causes there. The distinction between products and processes facilitates free trade by disallowing far-reaching, subjective, political judgments that might otherwise interfere with the exchange of goods.

As the GMO case demonstrates, there can be precautionary reasons to challenge the product/process distinction. European regulatory systems subject the process of gene splicing to precautionary scrutiny because of uncertainties regarding engineers' abilities to control the traits that are transferred and understand how these new organisms will behave in the environment. In order to treat GM crops with precaution, it is necessary to apply preventive measures along the entire chain of production: from laboratories that develop seeds, to open-air field experiments, to crops and their surroundings, to separate facilities for transporting and stocking foodstuffs, to appropriately labeled products that end up on supermarket shelves. A breakdown at any point in this regulatory chain can give rise to claims that precaution has not been observed—and therefore that commerce in these goods can be legitimately interrupted. The precautionary principle requires supplying not only regulators but also consumers with the information they need in order to spot potential anomalies and side effects at any point in the production process. In effect, the precautionary principle encourages individuals and states to think of themselves not only as competitive, self-interest-maximizing consumers (as in the liberal model) but as *citizens* whose vigilance protects the common good. In fact, that orientation toward a citizenship perspective can be considered a fourth point of conflict between the model of liberal environmentalism and the precautionary principle. Chapter 5 examines that conflict in detail.

These conflicts go deeper than disagreements over the merits of a few products or risk-assessment methods. They call into question many commonly held "liberal" assumptions about the relationship between free trade generally and the common well-being, the possibility of discovering truths that provide objective and politically neutral grounds of consensus, and the relative importance of consumer and citizenship roles in the individual's life. In other words, the precautionary principle does much more than ratchet up widely held expectations of how to handle environmental risk. It raises profound philosophical questions about the very nature of good governance. Some of these are as old as political theory itself. Others are startlingly new. These questions merit examination in their own right.

4

Precautionary Theory: Science, Uncertainty, and Political Authority

How do we protect ourselves against our own ignorance? That question has troubled political philosophers ever since Socrates wandered the streets of Athens and probed the confident assertions of the opinion makers of his day. He tried to show them that their unexamined views about such matters as the nature of piety and the value of political rhetoric endangered their souls and threatened to undermine the very possibility of a good life in the city as a whole. Much of the subsequent history of Western ethics is a series of ruminations on and proposed remedies to this all-too-common predicament of human life: we aspire to virtue and yet frequently descend into vice.

The precautionary principle responds to a predicament that is just as dramatic but much less familiar. It aims at long-term, often invisible dangers that prior ages could scarcely have conceived. In the sparsely populated, technologically undeveloped world that existed before the Industrial Revolution, who could have predicted that humanity, collectively, would soon have the power to change the climate by altering the chemical composition of the atmosphere, or to alter the distribution of flora and fauna across the face of the whole planet? In a world populated mainly by peasants, struggling to keep the land productive by tilling in their night soil, what imaginative leap would it take to conceive of communities that accept creating nuclear waste so toxic that elementary safety requires sequestering it from the environment for tens of thousands of years? Who could have dreamed that people would be able to reconfigure radically the genetic structure of all life-forms—including themselves?

If our environmental predicament is unprecedented, so too is the political theory needed to grasp it. The precautionary principle, in particular, is not just a guideline added to a long list of risk-management procedures—as if someone scribbled one more safety-enhancing rule on the "In Case of Fire" instructions posted on the hotel room door. Its defense involves challenging assumptions that have guided political thought since its origins in ancient Greece. The principle highlights two of the most underexamined questions of modern political thought. First, how can human communities take responsibility for the biophysical surroundings on which the existence of life depends? Second, given the democratic aspirations of most contemporary societies, how much deference does science deserve in the policymaking process?

In the last few decades, a number of thinkers have begun to tackle these questions, in the process offering a philosophical grounding for the precautionary principle. Most noted among them is the German philosopher Hans Jonas, as discussed in chapter 3. Jonas's "imperative of responsibility" describes a future-oriented attitude of care and caution with respect to a nature endangered by humankind's technological power. The most distinctive competing line of justification for the precautionary principle is offered by the French sociologist of science Bruno Latour. A comparison of the ideas of these two thinkers demonstrates that Jonas is the closer to inspiring today's defenders of the precautionary principle. Latour nonetheless does the signal service of suggesting how to think about precaution without deferring entirely to scientific authority.

A Unique Predicament

Why does the precautionary principle need special philosophical justification? It's just common sense, one might think. "Better safe than sorry." "An ounce of prevention is worth a pound of cure." Isn't the precautionary principle just a dressed-up version of homely advice that has been around for ages?

One should beware reducing precaution to folk wisdom. Precautionary situations fit poorly into established patterns of thought. Even the thinkers who are most highly reputed for their reflections on overcoming social disorder and injustice made assumptions that obscure the nature of today's environmental problems.

- Traditionally, political theory has aimed at problems with substantial temporal immediacy. Theorists addressed themselves to members of a (potential) community who had much to gain or lose in the short term, depending on whether they organized themselves according to the vision of an improved political-social order that the theorist proposed. Niccolò Machiavelli's prince was supposed to deliver the Italians from the humiliation and depredations of foreign invaders. Obedience to Thomas Hobbes's sovereign promised relief from civil war. But experience with environmental problems such DDT pollution, dioxin, and radioactive waste disposal shows that processes of bioaccumulation occur over decades before eventually causing cancer or reproductive failures. We take these risks carelessly in part because they involve a displacement toward the future of the hardship, expense, or sense of loss that they may eventually cause. Our environmental predicament necessitates a newly prospective orientation—one that systematically searches out future effects of changes that we introduce into the environment and that requires preventive action on the part of many who will never feel the consequences of their efforts.

• Traditionally, theorists of popular government have argued that the people, even if they are not "wise," know when they are in distress. Although they lack the cobbler's technical knowledge of how to make good shoes, ordinary people know when the shoe pinches, as Aristotle once pointed out. Yet in regard to environmental problems, individuals do not easily perceive gradual increases in the incidence of disease or the slow deterioration of ecosystems—even when they are victims of them. The perception of environmental problems often requires scientific mediation. At the same time, we cannot afford to let science simply dictate our choices. In part this is because of uncertainties in scientific observation. It is also because nonenvironmental values continue to deserve consideration. Civil liberties and democratic participation, for example, are not to be automatically overridden because of the perception of environmental risks. So our environmental predicament necessitates reconceiving the relationship between popular participation, scientific advice, and political decision making.

• Traditionally, political theorists have idealized geographically limited polities. Political unity has been for people sharing a language, a religion, or a culture. Or it has been hypothesized as the result of a "social contract" that brings a finite number of individuals under a set of common laws and institutions. Ethics were designed primarily to order relations between "neighbors" (Jonas 1984, 4–5). Distant peoples were hardly a matter of ethical concern. The idea that there are problems whose scale demands worldwide cooperation, however, is quite recent. Our environmental predicament necessitates inventing principles and institutions of unprecedented scope: ones in which citizens of every nation can see their interests served.

· Traditionally, Western ethics has reserved moral concern for beings who are rational, and who can, as members of the community, participate in formulating its rules and knowingly obey them (Ferry 1995, 3–18). Correspondingly, antisocial behavior usually involves deliberately or negligently imposing some tangible harm on another person. Yet important environmental "evils" do not fit that model. Global warming and some types of pollution (for example, fertilizer runoff causing algal blooms in estuaries) become problems only through processes of accumulation or in synergistic combination with other environmental factors. No one seems directly or individually responsible. Moreover, if causing or allowing a species to disappear is considered an evil, it seems that environmental issues concern not just the human good but the good of nonhuman creatures. So environmental concern seems to call forth a new ethics to take account of new, complex conditions of responsibility.

· Traditionally, "nature" has stood for a fixed, immutable order external to humans and subject to their will in limited ways. To philosophers of antiquity, nature appeared as a set of repetitive cycles against whose background human communities attempted to build their more lasting structures (Arendt 1959, 84–85). In modern philosophy, altering nature, especially taking away its ability to do harm to human interests, has been a more prominent theme. Most famously, René Descartes looked forward to an era when scientific knowledge would make humankind the "master and possessor" of the earth. In a related perspective, Francis Bacon imagined a utopia in which science and technology allowed society finally to control factors like weather and the productivity of plants. For Karl Marx, revolutionary improvements in technology and social organization were on course to end "the reign of necessity" in human affairs. But these modern ideas presume, too, that nature has a constancy that no human intervention can fundamentally change. Scientific studies in the past century have brought to the fore probable limits in the self-replenishability of many ecosystems. At the same time, scientists have often had to admit the uncertainty of their findings, as if to confess that they could not see nature as objectively as once had been thought. Under such conditions, a more uncertain, more fragile nature obliges us to reconceive the role of scientific expertise in promoting social progress.

Of course, these sources of perplexity do not mean that every idea from past political theories must now be tossed in the trash bin of history. Since the 1960s, the literature of environmental political theory has burgeoned. In it, theorists typically draw on traditional concepts of justice, rights, and representation, while attempting to extend or modify their meaning by applying them to a new context. The problem is that conceptual tools devised centuries ago to regulate problems *within* human communities apply imperfectly—sometimes very imperfectly—to problems that arise at the interface of humanity and nature. Often, our inherited political vocabulary rests on notions of human agency that implicitly deny the moral seriousness of the very problems that environmentalists wish to decry. Words can fail to translate what is radically new in the sources of environmental concern.

This is the case with one of the most frequently cited traditional concepts in the literature on precaution. A number of authors have proposed Aristotle's notion of *phronesis* (variously translated as prudence, practical wisdom, or intelligence) as a precursor of precaution (Ewald, Gollier, and Sadeleer 2001, 43; Bourg and Schlegel 2001, 146). Phronesis, says Aristotle (*Nicomachean Ethics* 1143b25), is the "science of what is just, fine and good for a human being." Like precaution, phronesis involves applying intelligence to complex situations, refusing both to let things take their course or to allow immediate emotional reactions to dictate the path of action. In the words of one commentator, phronesis is a "disposition to deliberate well . . . so as to attain the best, ultimate and most comprehensive ends open to man" (Sullivan 1977, 83). It seeks the "right proportion" and aims especially at preserving the conditions of collective well-being (Delannoi 2000, 12–13). Crucially for those drawn to parallels between prudence and precaution, Aristotelian phronesis requires skill in gathering empirical knowledge and experience in making judgments about it. Prudent action has to be calibrated intelligently to the circumstances. Faced with danger, the prudent person, says Aristotle, avoids both cringing fear and brash heroics. The courageous "mean" praised by Aristotle consists in conduct that allows people to protect themselves and others from danger, when all factors are taken into account. Some circumstances require more boldness, and others require more caution.

According to those who link precaution and phronesis, the modern devaluation of prudence set the stage for nonprecautionary approaches to technological risk. The ancestor of science-based risk assessment, says Gil Delannoi (2000, 12), is "the Cartesian and Baconian project . . . [which] brought about the idea of unlimited progress based on science and technology. . . . Technical progress would . . . be certain to limit the risks inherent in the human condition." Hobbes carried this attitude into political philosophy proper. He explicitly relegated prudence to the rank of a derivative and inferior form of knowledge. In its place, he set up the ideal of a positive science of human nature. Methodical application of scientific analysis would bring greater certainty to human affairs than the ancients had ever known. Peace and material betterment for all would be the result.

Periodically, a philosophical voice has sounded a note of caution in the face of such confident forecasts. In the eighteenth century, Giambattista Vico expressed his unease with the modern mind. That mind uses mathematized science and logical rigor to attain a supposedly determinate, universal knowledge of causes and effects (Pons 1995). But, he warned, the human world is shot through with contingency; social interaction generates causes too numerous to be sorted out scientifically. Against science Vico pitted "baroque prudence." Through prudence, intelligence recognizes the limits of its own penchant for systematization and methodically controlled experience (Salomon 1999, 11). And that, one might argue, is exactly the function of the precautionary principle.

Nonetheless, this parallel between prudence and precaution must not be taken too far. Aristotelian prudence relates primarily to the way one handles one's *own* emotions and impulses in concrete situations. Prudence is a form of intelligence that integrates ordinary experience extraordinarily well; it is highly practiced in making judgments that help prevent a life ruined by vices like cowardice or gluttony. It is oriented inward. Precaution, in contrast, essentially aims to prevent harmful effects on ecosystems and distant others. It is bound up with situations that might hardly engage the emotions at all, were it not for scientifically grounded anticipations of danger. So precaution starts from the methodical, specialized knowledge that Vico saw as diametrically opposed to prudence. Equally distinctive is the fact that precaution responds to uncertainties in that specialized knowledge. Precaution gets its meaning in relation to the fantastic power that technoscience has given us over the world, and in its inability to predict or remedy all of its effects. Prudence, in contrast, concerns the judicious handling of "the recurrent, typical situations of private and public life." It is not a matter of "remote planning" (Jonas 1984, 5). So even if the precautionary principle can be said to owe something to the spirit of prudence, the unprecedented problematic to which it is addressed nonetheless demands novel efforts at philosophical comprehension.

Jonas: Philosopher of Precaution

The precautionary principle lacks a "true philosophical pedigree," sighs Latour (2000a, 339). If that observation is close to the mark, it still slights the role of one famous philosopher: Jonas and his 1979 work, *Das Prinzip Verantwortung*. But Jonas's thought has had a peculiar fate. Most who mention Jonas's influence hasten to distance themselves from his ideas. In fact, however, Jonas's reasoning is more crucial to the precautionary principle's philosophical pedigree than many want to admit.

For Jonas, a new human predicament took shape in the twentieth century. The "unintended dynamics of technical civilization" and its "exponential acceleration" now confronts us with "the apocalypse of the 'too much,' with exhaustion, pollution, and desolation of the planet" (Jonas 1984, 202). The effects of modern technology are cumulative and so, in their most serious manifestations, endanger future generations (7). These dangers do not, though, generally prompt communities to make timely self-regulating responses. Quite the contrary: "Experience has taught us that developments set in motion by technological acts with short-term aims tend to make themselves independent, that is, to gather their own compulsive dynamics and automotive momentum by which they become not only . . . irreversible, but also forward-pushing" (32). Technological change is self-propelling. This situation is all the more disconcerting because the very scale of changes unleashed by our technologies makes their effects far surpass our predictive knowledge. If our technologies are so powerful that they can cause massive, irreversible effects, and if, once introduced, they tend to develop their own, barely controllable dynamic, then, deduces Jonas, we have a heightened duty of "vigilance over the beginnings" of those technologies. Only at the beginning do we have a chance of affecting the course of change.

Transgenic crops offer a fine example of how a new technology becomes subject to "compulsive dynamics." The claims about their potential to improve agricultural practices notwithstanding, transgenic crops are not like a new technique of crop rotation or organic farming. Producing a transgenic plant requires an enormous investment in research and development. Companies that develop GMOs expect a solid return on that investment. To that end, they have to insist on patenting their products. This means that farmers using these products must sign contracts not to reuse the seeds from year to year, as has been the traditional practice (Teitel and Wilson 1999, 76). Legal compulsion thus underwrites the new agricultural biotechnology. Moreover, today's GMOs are designed to be integrated with other products (like the herbicide Roundup) commercialized by the same company that developed them (Lepage and Guery 2001, 27). Farmers growing these GMOs are not just purchasing a seed; they are buying a crop-management system. Essentially, the current generation of GMOs is designed to serve the model of large-scale, industrialized monoculture (Seralini 2000, 97). This is true, even as multinational biotech firms penetrate markets around the world and persuade foreign aid organizations to spread GMO cultivation in lesser developed countries (Brunel 2002, 29). To the extent that the GMO crop-management system lowers the costs of production, competitors find themselves at a disadvantage and are eventually forced to adopt this model as well. Meanwhile, lobbyists for biotech companies find partners in the halls of government. The industry shapes its own regulatory environment. The U.S. decision not to test GMOs with anything like the care applied to new medicines was essential to launching these products. With a low profit margin, the economic viability of these crops requires shielding them from lengthy, expensive testing (Seralini 2000, 88–89). Regulation is conceived *from the start* as much a matter of public relations as of public safety. Politicians have been happy to do what is necessary to favor biotechnology, as they see electoral advantage in creating jobs in a new industry and boosting their country's exports.

In the space of a couple of decades, these compulsive dynamics are set to transform world agriculture. This process is taking its course with remarkably little oversight or reflection, at least outside of Europe. Politics as usual and economics as usual dictate the conditions under which this powerful technology is applied. Surely Jonas (1984, 19) is right to remind us, however, that "[the questions raised by the philanthropic gift of science] must be dealt with ethically and by principle and not merely by the pressure of interests."

What principle? Jonas (37) proposes the imperative of responsibility: "Never must the existence or the essence of man as a whole be made a stake in the hazards of action." This, he says, is an "unqualified command." In cases where it applies, "caution becomes the core of moral action" (38). If a choice carries some "apocalyptic potential," even small, then we must give that possibility much greater weight in our reasoning (34). Jonas labels his reasoning a "heuristic of fear." Fear arises not because we are actually in the threatening situation but because we can summon it imaginatively for morally salutary purposes. Fear pertains especially to the conditions that future generations will have to endure. It is not so much fear for one's own lot as for the well-being of others. It is an *altruistic* fear (Larrère and Larrère 1997, 244).

It is the political application of this moral reasoning that has cost Jonas so much influence among defenders of the precautionary principle. In the course of an argument pitting his "imperative of responsibility" against "the principle of hope," as set forth by the utopian Marxist Ernst Bloch, Jonas ends up arguing that protecting future generations will probably require an authoritarian form of government. The problem, he alleges, is that people in democratic societies are addicted to the pleasures of mass consumption. They are therefore most unlikely to impose on themselves the necessary discipline (Jonas 1984, 149). "Only a maximum of politically imposed social discipline," Jonas (142) maintains, "can ensure the subordination of present advantage to the long-term exigencies of the future." It will require great power to put the brakes on the compulsive dynamic of technological progress. So "the coming severity of a politics of responsible abnegation, [makes] democracy (in which the interests of the day necessarily hold the stage) . . . at least temporarily unsuited. . . . [O]ur present comparative weighing is, reluctantly, between different forms of 'tyranny'" (151).

Jonas never fills in the details of what he means by a responsible tyranny. He seems to have in mind a regime in which a political elite consults scientific advisers about nature's objective limits and the technologies that threaten to exceed them. It would then be up to that elite to impose the necessary social discipline. Jonas thus joins a handful of ecoauthoritarians who believe that the logic of our environmental predicament leads unavoidably to solutions involving concentrated power, an increased reliance on expertise, and coercion (see Barry 1999, 194–202; Dryzek 1997, 31–33).

This conclusion has drawn intense fire (Larrère and Larrère 1997, 244; Godard 2000, 139–140; Lecourt 1990, 169–170; Bourg and Schlegel 2001, 167; Ferry 1995, 76–78; Bourg 1996, 57–78). Jonas's conclusion is a philosopher's deduction—and not necessarily a convincing one. His pessimism about people's willingness to support precautionary measures derives from no actual studies of people's responses to environmental risk. Since 1979, when Jonas published *The Imperative of Responsibility*, social theorists such as Ulrich Beck (discussed in chapter 5) and Anthony Giddens have studied the emergence of a "risk society" that provides an attitudinal foundation for a democratized form of precautionary politics. The precautionary principle is open to a much more democratic interpretation than anything Jonas envisaged. Nor does Jonas bother to cite any examples of tyrannies that have lived up to their ideals. Although he acknowledges the shortcomings of authoritarian regimes, he still must be criticized for underestimating their irrationalities. He imagines benevolent dictators dosing out only environmentally necessary constraints. He is not overly worried about the record of corruption that goes with the concentration of power without accountability. His authority would apparently decide, without popular consultation, what level of consumption constitutes a "tolerable subsistence for the world's population" (Jonas 1984, 187). Jonas seems untroubled by the potential for terrible abuse of this degree of political authority. Legally defining "subsistence" would mean having the power of life and death over populations on the most massive scale. In the Soviet Union in the 1930s and China in the 1950s, undemocratic leaders wielded such power with horrific effect, at the cost of tens of millions of human lives.

One must also suppose that Jonas's regime would have to implement a surveillance system to ensure that mandated constraints were obeyed. Research would have to be controlled, industry prevented from commercializing forbidden products, and consumers prohibited from engaging in environmentally damaging behavior. Dissidence that challenged the elite's judgment could hardly be encouraged. In the absence of checks and balances as well as critical challenges, this system would likely cut decision makers off from accurate information about the environment rather than guarantee their access to it. It is worth remembering how Soviet planners constantly received information from below indicating that industries were meeting their production quotas, when in fact the economy was in severe disarray. Jonas's prescriptions are based on one of the most fundamental errors one can make in social theory: he compares how real, existing democratic regimes *do* work (very imperfectly) with how an ideal, completely untested, regime *should* work. Compared with the record of actual authoritarian regimes, however, democracies—with all their flaws—show unmistakable advantages.

Whatever his errors, Jonas offers no general ideological defense of tyrannical regimes. His conclusions are based entirely on an estimate of its supposedly greater ability to avert environmental catastrophe—an estimate that is, in principle, empirical. A showing to the contrary would be sufficient to reverse his judgment, as is evident from his clearly stated preference for democratic liberties (Jonas 1984, 149). It is also hard to deny that, if certain dynamics intrinsic to democratic societies—unquenchable mass consumption, a penchant for endless debate, and a vulnerability to pressure group politics—made them unable actually to avert a global-scale catastrophe, that failure would weigh heavily in an assessment of the merits of such a regime in today's world. Rather than dismiss Jonas because of his authoritarian conclusions, we do better to examine the philosophical presuppositions that underlie them. Identifying and criticizing those presuppositions helps open paths to alternative ways of framing precautionary ideas.

Jonas's argument is driven in an authoritarian direction by his understanding of the nature of nature. This is true on two levels. On one level, Jonas argues that it is from *nature itself* that we must deduce our moral responsibility to protect nature. Our environmental predicament originates partly, he charges, from wrongly seeing nature as composed only of purposeless matter. We see oceans just as immense sinks, trees as fortuitously accessible mines of fiber, and animals as instinct-driven products of a mechanistic process of evolution. These things have no intrinsic goals, so they have no claim on our moral concern. They are just things. We may use them as we please. But, objects Jonas (1984, 74), "nature evinces at least one determinate purpose—life itself." Nature consists of interrelated, goal-directed processes of all sorts: birds building nests for the purpose of sheltering their young, cats hunting mice for the purpose of stilling their hunger, and bees and flowers coexisting symbiotically for the purpose of their mutual nourishment and reproduction. For Jonas (69–70), it is as if nature itself *wanted* things to come forth, exist, develop, and become richer and more varied. This coming forth solicits our moral concern. We already have experience with this sort of moral reaction. When we see the coming forth of an infant, we understand naturally our responsibility for helping this fragile being to live. Likewise, Jonas (90) reasons, we must respond to the purposes inherent in all of nature's life-giving processes by taking care of them, by acting on their behalf.

This way of framing nature contributes to Jonas's authoritarian conclusions by setting up a strict hierarchy of values: nature's goals take precedence over objectives set by mere human will. Nature has authority over humanity. In fact, Jonas's model for this authority is one of the oldest in the history of political thought: the authority of parents over their children (98). Jonas chooses this model not only because it helps us understand a "natural" feeling of responsibility but also because it fits the nonreciprocal character that responsibility must take in regard to nature. Nature, like children, can neither articulate its needs nor discern those of others. Just as parents rule children for their own good, so people must govern nature. Much modern political theory, in contrast, rejects paternalism as a model of governance. Most famously, in his *Two Treatises of Government,* John Locke contended that paternal rule, applied to competent adults, is fatal to liberty. It dispenses with the need to consult the governed about their views. It encourages arbitrary, indeed tyrannical, behavior on the part of rulers. Moderns usually argue that responsibility is created between equals by exchanging promises: promises between entrepreneurs create the responsibility to fulfill business contracts, and promises between citizens and their political representatives create reciprocal responsibilities of obedience and good governance. But nature cannot make promises in this way. So if we have responsibilities to it, a noncontractual model of obligation appears necessary. Jonas's argument for purpose in nature leads him to a paternalistic model of governance, in spite of its antidemocratic implications.

On a second level, it is the *facticity* of nature that underwrites Jonas's political conclusions. Jonas assumes that comprehending our ecological crisis, and designing measures to deal with it, is essentially a matter for technical experts. When Jonas (6) warns of "the critical vulnerability of nature to man's technological intervention," he formulates his lessons in terms of an external, objective reality. Although he concedes that this reality is impossible to grasp in its totality, he believes those trained in the natural sciences are in the best position to discover the limits of its capacity to endure technologically inflicted damage. It is they who have brought forth the "fairly recent and upsetting discovery" that the "countless and delicate balances" of "spaceship Earth" can be disrupted by human activity (188). Jonas (189) expects "the chemist, the geologist, the meteorologist," along with various policy experts, to pool their knowledge in order to constitute a "global environmental science" that will indicate "how much [human intervention] *nature* can stand." In regard to their views, "the philosopher has nothing to say, only to listen." For the population at large, that posture of listening becomes simply obeying. The natural sciences are hard for most people to understand, and anyway, the public is disinclined to limit its ecologically destructive practices voluntarily. So again, ecoauthoritarianism follows neatly from Jonas's reasoning about the nature of nature.

Latour and Democratizing Science: Precaution without Nature?

What if Jonas's view of nature were incorrect? What if nature never had the facticity he attributes to it? What if nature were, instead, the product of complex interrelations always involving far-reaching networks of humans and things not human? What if the ethical pull that we feel from nature came not from nature-in-itself but from the fact that nature has always been something that took shape in relation to human values and activities? Questions such as these raise the possibility of grounding the precautionary principle in a philosophy that unlike Jonas's, is highly receptive to democratic concerns. Such a philosophy is proposed by Latour. According to the authors of one widely read study of the precautionary principle, Latour is "the philosopher who has best expressed the political situation that has given rise to the precautionary principle" (Ewald, Gollier, and Sadeleer 2001, 42; see also Godard 2001b, 96; Joly et al. 2000, 171).

Latour maintains that the precautionary principle flows from a revised understanding of what constitutes "rational" action in relation to science-based areas of public policy. The now-outdated "positivist" version of such action went like this: "The experts are brought together, the relevant information gathered, the issues aired, then action follows as a direct result. . . . Once the decision has been made, vigilance is no longer necessary, except in the details of its application" (Latour 2000a, 341). The new situation comes from the realization that experts do not agree and that the decision to take risks is essentially a political one. "Henceforth, public life must get used to cohabiting, not with scientists who settle controversies through the indisputable certainty of their views, but with researchers characterized precisely by the uncertainty and controversial nature of their provisional results" (Latour 2000b). Unable to predict all the effects of the processes it lets loose into the environment, contemporary science has, in effect, turned the world into a laboratory. Still, it is a laboratory that we all inhabit. The products of science affect the quality of life in a "common world." As such, its "experiments" must be exposed to wider debate. Thus "what the precautionary principle clamors for loud and clear is that, by breaking the link between expert knowledge and action, we finally unleash the forces of inquiry that will allow us to maximize vigilance, puzzlement, and risk-taking all at once, in regard to questions that heretofore had been withdrawn from discussion" (Latour 2000a, 346). The precautionary principle incites us to debate about what risks we really want to take and under what conditions. For Latour, the precautionary principle is essentially a means of bringing science in line with democracy. Its function is to make the polity more alert and open up discussion concerning the effects of technological innovation.

Latour's provocative formulations call forth numerous questions. Is he trying to justify the political regulation of every facet of scientific research and technological innovation? Is he saying that scientific understandings of the world are no better than the views of ordinary people? If so, isn't that a dangerously antiprecautionary position (since most early warnings about possible environmental threats come from scientific studies)? If not, just what is the meaning of "breaking the link between expert knowledge and action"—and what makes such a proposal precautionary? Finding answers to these questions requires delving into Latour's version of the "reality of science studies."

Since the early 1980s, Latour has been prolifically publishing works in the sociology of science that subvert widely held beliefs about the ability of science to discover objective nature (Whiteside 2002, 127–140). The reality of science, argues Latour, is that it does not consist simply of a vast corps of impartial observers using rigorous methods of empirical inquiry and verification to establish the truth about how nature operates. In fact, science is and always has been a highly *political* process. Political, in this context, means that scientists use techniques of persuasion—rhetorical appeals and deliberately staged demonstrations—to win the consent of key actors who will help them make their hypotheses credible. They assemble networks of like-minded scientists, resources, interest groups, and highly contrived experiments that together, give their views the solidity of fact.

For example, Latour describes how Frédéric Joliot in the 1930s sought to demonstrate the feasibility of controlled fission in a nuclear reactor. The success of his efforts depended on far more than inducing neutrons to split uranium isotopes. Joliot needed the interested support of a mining company to supply him with radioactive ore; he relied on the advice of a colleague who understood the advantages of "heavy water" in moderating nuclear reactions. In the tense political environment just before the outbreak of World War II, Joliot drew support from the French minister of armaments to get access to a quantity of Norwegian-produced heavy water. Nuclear reactions thus became bound up with projects for national defense. Latour (1999a, 89–90) concludes this story with the following startling meditation:

> Having gained his laboratory, [Joliot] had to go and negotiate *with the neutrons themselves*. Was it one thing to persuade a minister to provide a stock of graphite, and quite another to persuade a neutron to slow down enough to hit a uranium atom so as to provide three more neutrons? Yes and no. For Joliot, it wasn't very different. In the morning he dealt with the neutrons and in the afternoon he dealt with the minister. The more time passed, the more these two problems became one: if too many neutrons escaped from the copper vessel and lowered the output of the reaction, the minister might lose patience. For Joliot, containing the minister and the neutrons in the same project, keeping them acting and keeping them under discipline, were not really distinct tasks. *He needed them both.*

On this view, science does not offer privileged access to the truth. It is riddled with contingencies. The minister's impatience becomes a factor in the process of discovery. Science does not constitute a realm of knowledge distinct from and superior to every less methodical form of inquiry. Its accomplishments are inseparable from such factors as commercial interests, the personal convictions of scientists, and international rivalries. Latour's reality of science studies involve following all the entanglements of people and things that go into producing generally accepted claims about how nature operates. In so doing, he claims to dissolve the distinction between nature and society. When that distinction collapses, so too do claims that the polity should defer to experts whose knowledge of nature makes them uniquely competent to help society progress.

The distinction between nature and society, Latour (1991, 20) at first argued, is an artifact of "the modern constitution." In force essentially since the seventeenth century, the modern constitution creates a strict distinction between scientific and political representation. Political representation is grounded in the will of the people and originates in a social contract. Scientific representation designates the process by which scientists speak for things. Scientists describe their properties and their interrelations. The modern constitution exists in the form of a tacit commitment that runs through the institutions of modern societies: politicians do not poke their noses into laboratories and decide what is, or is not, true about nature; and scientists, qua scientists, have no privileged access to the will of the people and so cannot decide what goals the polity should pursue (Latour 1991, 43). While that constitution never accurately described what took place in the world, Latour contends, moderns' belief in it accelerated scientific research by giving scientists a free hand to pursue their experiments—whatever the consequences.

By the late twentieth century, however, something had exposed the modern constitution to view and made it outdated. With the help of engineers and entrepreneurs, science had unleashed ever greater numbers of "hybrids" into the world. Hybrids are phenomena like climate change, GM plants, or endangered species whose movements are tracked by satellite. Partly the result of human action, and partly of matter and processes that transcend human control, hybrids cannot be classified as strictly natural or social. The hypothesis of Latour's, *We Have Never Been Modern,* is that hybrid phenomena have now become so prolific that we can no longer treat them as marginal (1991, 180; also 1994, 103). Their undeniable and sometimes troubling existence now obliges us to abandon the modern constitution. A nonmodern constitution would acknowledge the complicated processes by which humans and nonhumans are entangled, and would subject hybrids to political scrutiny. The germs of Latour's view of the precautionary principle are already implicit in this analysis insofar as he associates precaution with new institutions aiming to end the conceptual separation of scientific and political decision making. In 1991, Latour proposed a "parliament of things" in which all those who make up the networks constituting hybrids have an opportunity to debate their desirability. Still, Latour had not yet adopted the language of precaution. Latour (1991, 194) suggested only that more democracy might slow down "the mad proliferation of hybrids."

His subsequent works have pushed the philosophical quarrel over nature and society from modernity back into antiquity. Simultaneously, he has come to see our inability to grasp our environmental predicament in even more deeply political terms. It is not just the chance separation of nature and society that prevents us from perceiving the processes associating humans and nonhumans. It is a distrust of democracy itself. In *Pandora's Hope,*

Latour (1999a, 13) argues that at least since Plato wrote in the fourth century BCE, philosophers have emphasized the objectivity of nature (and the special rationality of those disciplined enough to grasp it) because they have seen only one frightening alternative: "mob rule." Philosophers assert that without some objective measure of truth, everything becomes subjective. The opinion of "the crowd" then counts as much as the views of the expert. And since the crowd is ignorant and always more numerous, it is to be feared that "if reason does not rule, then mere force will take over" (Latour 1999a, 10). Today's critics of the precautionary principle brandish the same threat. They warn that the precautionary principle invites "political" technology assessments rather than "rational" ones; they worry that regulators will respond to the crowd's passions rather than to what experts know about nature. For Latour, these charges are part of a rhetorical stratagem that has nothing to do with trying to understand the entanglements through which science really produces its knowledge claims. It has everything to do with elites who wish to protect their positions as the sole arbiters of the truth about nature.

Once this ruse is exposed for what it is, the path is cleared to philosophize, finally, about how much more extensive networks of people and things can be brought systematically into the processes that decide the composition of their common world. In *The Politics of Nature,* Latour describes new political forms that would "bring the sciences into democracy." He sketches out the responsibilities of two legislative bodies whose function, together, is to give humans and nonhumans adequate representation. The balanced roles of these houses constitute a new way of conceiving the separation of powers (Latour 1999b, 242). The upper house would be responsible for "taking account" of what exists. It is a place for debate about how to detect phenomena and make them visible. While provoking inquiry concerning the appearance of unexpected phenomena, it searches out "reliable witnesses" and "credible spokesmen" (Latour 1999b, 158). Many of these would be scientists, certainly, but they might also be members of consumer associations or wildlife protection groups, and so forth. In effect, the upper house considers who should serve on a "jury" that will examine how the phenomena in question affect other constituents of the polity. The lower house would see to the orderly arranging of the polity as a whole. Its central question is, Can we live together?—where "we" is people and all the nonhuman phenomena with which they become entangled. Debates in the lower house project scenarios of what the common world may be like as its constituents change. The crucial role of politicians, says Latour (1999b, 198), is to keep alive "a certain sense of danger originating from the things excluded" by the existing order. It is the business of the lower house, then, to establish hierarchies and priorities. Hierarchy implies that in some cases, the house will decide that certain hybrids may be too troublesome to allow into the common world. These will be declared "enemies" and then expelled (Latour 1999b, 239).

Latour will add: none of this is to say that scientific understandings of nature will simply become a matter of voting or that judgments about environmental risks will be reduced to electoral machinations. Science retains its specificity. Its ingenious, meticulously arranged experiments create more extensive and intensive connections with things than people have in ordinary experience (Latour 1999a, 97). Experimental results, mathematized and reduced to complex formulas, show how "mute" things answer our questions (Latour 2000c, 115–116). Scientists make things speak to us. They give them a voice that we can hear in our assemblies. What they do not do, however, is establish certainties that might legitimate making their understanding of environmental risks override judgments made in a more inclusive political process.

Latour's way of conceiving the process of constituting a common world prevents anyone from claiming certainty as the grounds for taking action. What characterizes political ecology as such is that "it slips from certainties about the production of risk-less objects (based on a clear separation of things and people) to uncertainty over the relationships whose unexpected consequences threaten to disrupt" the community's plans (Latour 1999b, 41). Decades of controversy over whether global warming is occurring and whether, if so, it is humanly caused, have given us the spectacle of innumerable experts contradicting each other. Various interests groups—indeed, whole nations—take positions on the question as a function of whether it will help or hinder the interests of their members. At no point is the question resolved by the discovery of what nature really is, definitively. "Ecological crises," asserts Latour (1999b, 35), "appear . . . as *crises of objectivity.*" In Latour's proposed parliament of things, this analysis of the crisis is institutionalized. The existence of dangers is deliberately subjected to debate from every quarter. Based on this view, "political ecology does not seek to *protect* nature. On the contrary, it seeks to take charge of a even larger diversity of entities and destinies, in a more complete and more intermixed way" (Latour 1999b, 37).

This "taking charge" *is* Latour's interpretation of the precautionary principle. That is, the precautionary principle is not one particular rule or even an overarching directive to guide risk-management policy. Precaution signifies a wholesale rethinking of institutions such that our "risky attachments" to things become a matter of general debate and legislation. For Latour (2000a, 343), "the precautionary principle has no other meaning than to welcome, finally, issues with a scientific basis into democracy."

No less than Jonas, then, Latour believes that the instability of nature in relation to our newfound technological powers challenges premises that have guided philosophical inquiry since the earliest days of Western thought. A new philosophy of nature is in order. But in Latour's case, it would be better to say: this is a new philosophy *without "nature"* (Latour 1999b, 42). For our predicament, as Latour sees it, is not that our socially produced technologies make us run up against the limits of nature's capacity for self-renewal. It is that our very concepts of nature and society make us unable to perceive the complex, political processes by which things are brought into the world. This failure of perception then derails thinking about which of our creations we really want to live with. Precaution, in contrast, takes shape in a reorganized community that decides democratically, after extensive and regularized efforts at exploration and experimentation, how various associations of human and nonhumans can live together on one earth (Latour 1999b, 68).

Precaution = Uncertainty + Fear

Current environmental controversies show that Latour captures some features of precautionary reasoning missed by Jonas. First, Latour allows us to call into question virtually any human-nonhuman interaction that causes unease in the community. If today some communities worry about the environmental effects of GMOs or the dying away of local forests, it is not necessarily because these phenomena presage a global catastrophe. Yet that is what it takes to trigger Jonas's imperative of responsibility: a disaster that threatens all human life as such. Imagining catastrophe on that scale actually creates too restrictive a version of precaution. There are hardly any real-world situations to which this test applies. Why does Jonas set the bar so high? Probably because in the Kantian ethical tradition (in which Jonas is steeped), "moral" action is guided by absolute, unconditional principles. The moral good differs from the instrumental good by excluding trade-offs and consequentialist calculations. Murder is wrong not because it leads to bad consequences (which, after all, may or may not occur) but because it is wrong *period.* At the same time, as a critic of Immanuel Kant, Jonas is a consequentialist. Unlike Kant, Jonas would not say: let justice be done though the world may perish. For Jonas, the imperative of responsibility is precisely to prevent that terrible consequence. Yet consequentialism is usually thought to allow for considerable moral flexibility. So how can Jonas both hold to an absolute moral principle and be a consequentialist? His ingenious solution is to imagine a catastrophe that ends human life. This way of framing the argument automatically precludes any thought of taking the risk in order to gain compensating benefits. The worst-case scenario means there would be no one left to enjoy those benefits. Thus the case for unwavering adherence to principle is made. But it is made in such a way that it almost never applies. No critic of transgenic crops goes so far as to predict the apocalypse.

Latour's notion that we are constituting a common world is suggestive of a much broader array of precautionary concerns. Opponents of GMOs worry about the possible spread of "superweeds" and the loss of biodiversity, while GMO defenders tout the advantages of reducing pesticide use, increasing crop yields, and developing plants with special nutritional properties. Over both sides of the debate hover scientific uncertainties that may never be fully resolved. We simply cannot know all of the conditions under which GMOs will be cultivated across the world. We cannot predict with certainty how pollen carried far from its source may interact with thousands of species of soil bacteria and plants. "No one knows what an environment can do," insists Latour (1999b, 261). In addition, whether or not unanticipated effects will get reported and their causal connections validated depends on an enormous number of social and political factors. Coming to know that there is something to worry about is a complicated social process that cannot be taken for granted. What precaution calls for is not a moral rule à la Jonas—one that prescribes our obligations in advance of an inquiry—but as Latour suggests, monitoring, experimentation, procedures, and democratic debate.

There is also something seductive in Latour's contention that political ecology cannot be about "protecting nature"—as if nature had some clear identity to begin with. Arguments that we should "return to nature" always end up idealizing an environmental condition dissimilar from the present state, but by no means free of human influence. Certainly this is the case with every example involving agriculture. Every form of agriculture requires "artificial," humanized conditions, not "natural" ones. Latour's philosophy might therefore help us avoid fruitless debates about which practices are natural (and therefore presumptively better) and which are artificial. What we are really asking in relation to GMOs, for example, is not, Are they natural? It is, Are we willing to take the risk of living with them, once we have faced up to as many of their advantages, potential dangers, and social repercussions as possible, even if there are uncertainties surrounding all the evidence we hear?

There is a question that must be asked regarding Latour's philosophy as well. Are there any limits at all to what humanity may decide to do to its environment? At times Latour seems so open to experimentation that the very notion of precaution disappears.[1] Here is one of Latour's (1999b, 262) conclusions: "No one has gotten from nature the right to decide the relative importance and hierarchy of the entities that make up the common world at a particular moment. No one knows, but all can carry out experiments—on the condition that they accept taking the path of trials, while obeying procedures that really avoid shortcuts." Whether that conclusion differs at all from a nonprecautionary position according to which we should just proceed by trial and error depends on what is meant by the "path of trials." Are those trials necessarily any more rigorous than those used in conventional risk assessment? It is hard to tell. When Latour takes up the problem of experimenting with GMOs, he does not emphasize the potential dangers that have motivated precautionary measures. Instead, he brings out how little we know about how genes will actually spread in the environment. Since we don't know, he concludes, we must experiment (Latour, Schwartz, and Charvolin 1991, 28–31, 43–54). Latour (2000a, 346) accepts the fact that such experiments effectively turn the world we inhabit into a laboratory. Precaution, as he sees it, is no barrier to that development. The precautionary principle is a "protocol" for proper laboratory procedures.

Important values are lost in this way of framing precaution. First, there is no way to express a desire not to live in a laboratory. That, however, is sometimes what people most want to say in their democratic deliberations. During a public debate on GMO field trials held in France in 2002, the most strongly voiced concern was the participants' opposition to the idea that scientists had the right to turn traditionally social areas—fields and undeveloped land that were considered part of a community's heritage—into laboratory-like venues where genes might spread hither and yon in ways no one could predict (Babusiaux et al. 2002, 16, 19). In the words of the president of France's Commission for Sustainable Development: "Even if GMOs manage to show all the good characteristics that have been promised, it will still be the case that the land has been transformed into an immense field for experimentation" (Testart 2001). The risks that people foresee concern not only their own health or livelihoods (which are often dependent on thriving local ecosystems). They also concern unwanted changes in the boundaries between what is considered of collective significance and what is subject to private manipulation. Latour's project of bringing the sciences into democracy might actually cut out some of the key concerns that emerge in democratic debate.

That is a paradoxical result to encounter in a philosophy that expresses so much confidence in the judgment of laypeople. It also indicates that Latour, unlike Jonas, does not take up the challenge of attuning political decision making to long-term environmental problems. Latour (1999a, 251) has a reply to those who distrust the people's judgment, especially in regard to the technical matters of environmental policy: "The demos is endowed with all the morality and all the reflexive knowledge it needs in order to behave itself." The people have skills, knacks, and pragmatic understandings—all that it needs to "brew itself toward a decision" (Latour 1999a, 247; cf. 231). That is more a statement of faith, however, than an answer to the theoretical predicament described earlier. To cite just one problem: Latour's populist formulations shed no new light on how to create institutions that take better account of the good of future generations. Even if the people are endowed with the wisdom to protect their own welfare, they have too often shown themselves shortsighted in regard to the welfare of those who come after them. Hunters and fishers gradually destroy entire species; car drivers add greenhouse gases to the atmosphere every day. The precautionary principle, as derived from Jonas, attempts to remedy failures of vision by newly emphasizing long-term moral responsibilities. Latour's parliament of things, on the other hand, only widens the representation of people and things, here and now. As such, there is nothing uniquely precautionary about its procedures.

There is a second and even more significant cost of accepting Latour's perspective. He is much less clear than Jonas about why taking precaution is necessary. Jonas says that we must take special precautions because we do not want to cause widespread death and ecosystem collapse in the future, or take the risk of destroying the conditions of a truly human life. There are apocalyptic dangers to fear. That is a high threshold for precaution, and many ambiguities remain about what Jonas means by a truly human life. It is nonetheless certain that important things are at stake. Thus, one understands why sacrifices might be justified to protect them. Now Latour too says we should be careful. We should follow protocols and avoid shortcuts. But why? What is at stake? What is endangered? Latour is not one to dwell on apocalyptic dangers; in fact, he seems downright skeptical of them (see Latour 1999b, 255). He writes occasionally of dangers and risks, without specifying what they might be. He says that the parliament may eventually declare something an enemy of the common world, but never explains the grounds on which such a judgment might be made.[2] Yet it is not just because a technology may introduce widespread change or unfamiliar combinations of things into our world that we take special precautions. It is because there are reasons to expect palpable harm to things human beings care deeply about: life, health, freedom, property, and aesthetic values. Latour's discussion tends to sweeten the case for precaution by omitting its potentially bitter emotional grounds. At any rate, he does not see any particularly novel *moral* aspect to the choices we must make (other than the fact that a wider range of actors should participate in the decision making).

These comparisons between Jonas and Latour suggest that the German thinker actually has the better grasp of the predicament that underlies the precautionary principle. The fundamental logic for precaution is this: the fear of serious consequences, combined with uncertainty about the conditions under which they might materialize, creates a moral obligation to take precautions. Precaution is found at the intersection of uncertainty and the risk of immense harm. This is the essential logic of precaution as adopted by most other environmental thinkers in the 1990s and afterward. Such theorists emphasize the need to make precaution principled (Sadeleer 2001a, 553; Ministère de l'Écologie et du Développement Durable 2003, 42–43). They underline our moral responsibility to protect future generations (Lepage and Guery 2001, 128–129; 137). They justify precaution by reference to potential catastrophes so serious that they call into question the very idea of technological progress (Bourg and Schlegel 2001, 79–81, 123). And they insist that a strategy of avoidance, not mitigation, must be implemented in regard to potentially irreversible environmental damage (Dobson 1996, 414). In all these ways, they follow in Jonas's footsteps—even if they keep their distance from his authoritarian conclusions.

Imagination and Scientific Study: Precaution as a Learning Process

They might still seek to disassociate themselves from Jonas, however, in one other respect. Many reject his "heuristic of fear" as too hypothetical a way to go about justifying precaution. The authors of one general introduction to the precautionary principle develop the relevant contrast.

> Jonas's vision is dominated by the idea that man has an excess of technological power, which must now be limited. The philosophy of precaution . . . is not so negative. It is not opposed to economic development. It does not advocate abstinence. It does not condemn technological power. . . . On the contrary, the philosophy of precaution is in truth an act of faith in science and technology . . . [because it hopes to make] economic activity progress in the direction of using new, clean, environmentally-friendly technologies (Ewald, Gollier, and Sadeleer 2001, 35–36).

For Dominique Bourg (1998, 55–57) as well, Jonas's highly speculative, fear-based reasoning leads to an "obtuse rejection of all innovation." The precautionary principle, contrariwise, leads to "reasonably circumscribed" measures based on scientific data. These authors emphasize that the precautionary principle dictates procedures for *going forward* in situations of uncertain risk, not for stopping a technology dead in its tracks (see also Godard 1997a, 60; Bourg and Schlegel 2001, 167–170).

One latter-day Jonasian understands this very well. Philosopher Jean-Pierre Dupuy rejects the precautionary principle as too dangerous because of its action orientation. Rather than convincing us to avoid certain dangerous technological choices, the precautionary principle actually reinforces the illusion of our times. It encourages us to believe that we can control technological risks, if only we strengthen our risk-management procedures with another layer of hypercautious security measures. The precautionary principle is part and parcel of the logic of *mastering* technological dangers, says Dupuy (2002, 103–104). Paradoxically, while defenders of precaution claim to see threats so unprecedented that they defy our best efforts at rational analysis, they end up demanding that precaution be made "reasonable" by adding to it requirements of scientific study and cost proportionality. The principle does nothing to rein in the dynamics of economies governed by market values that accelerate technological innovation. Yet this, for Dupuy (67), creates the conditions of unplanned, irreversible environmental damage. The problem is not that we do not *know* that there are disasters to come; it is that we do not really *believe* in them, according to Dupuy (141). Writing in the aftermath of the September 11 terrorist attacks on the World Trade Center, Dupuy reminds us that the worst outcomes are often the least anticipated ones, the ones no one would have thought likely—until they occur. We cannot protect ourselves by extrapolating forward from existing experience. Where we must really start, contends Dupuy (50), is by acknowledging that we are powerless to master our own power. We must instead—as Jonas advocated—project ourselves imaginatively into a future catastrophe and use that worst-case scenario to guide us in our present choices (84, 87). If we are to avoid the worst, we must unambiguously reject certain practices and technological choices that might provoke a disaster.

Dupuy's critique, unfortunately, proves too much. The problem with imagining worst-case scenarios is that at a purely conjectural level, an apocalypse can be associated with almost anything. Speculatively, a technology's catastrophic potential is limited only by the inventiveness of its detractors. One can imagine, say, some wayward GMO activating a hitherto unknown plant gene that causes the world's rice crop to wither. Mass famine would ensue. But then, one cannot restrict the pessimist's game to GMO opponents. GMO proponents can paint pictures of doom regarding the failure to exploit the technology's potential contributions to human welfare. Without them, they say, famines in the Third World are sure to get worse. As catastrophic scenarios multiply, they become less and less helpful in deciding what risks are worth taking.

Olivier Godard (1997b, 56) emphasizes that precaution calls not for imagining worst-case scenarios but for testing allegations of potential environmental dangers scientifically. The precautionary question is not, Who can imagine the worst outcome associated with this or that technological choice? The question is, What evidence do we have, what signals are we already receiving, that suggest a real potential for danger? And then, what experiments can we undertake, what series of gradual measures of implementation can we design, that will allow us to confirm or disconfirm the reality of that danger before it becomes widespread or irreversible?

In fact, this partially empirical approach is probably closer to Jonas's intentions than Dupuy's metaphysics of catastrophe. Jonas certainly believes that scientific evidence counts in deciding whether an imagined problem has any grounding in reality. He calls on the philosopher to listen to biologists, agronomists, chemists, economists, and others. Then Jonas (1984, 189) notes, "Unfortunately [the philosopher] cannot borrow firm results for his purposes from the present state of the art. All quantitative predictions and extrapolations, even in single disciplines, are at this time still uncertain, let alone their integration into the ecological whole. . . . Still, for various lines of progression one can indicate the kind of limits that lie in the nature of the case." Applying this way of thinking to the prospects for generating power by nuclear fusion, he mentions problems of thermal pollution, the biochemical fate of soil and water, and the planetary oxygen economy. Jonas (190–191) concludes: "So long as we have not attained certainty of prediction here, and especially in view of the likely irreversibility of some of the initiated processes . . . caution is the better part of bravery and surely a command of responsibility." His fears do not spring from pure imagination. They start from some scientifically developed information about potential problems and the prospects for their technical mastery.

Two nuances, both building on Jonas's reflections, help support a better focused interpretation of the precautionary principle. First, precaution is a reaction to our partial knowledge of environmental processes. Precaution is the most general norm in a hierarchy of norms that aims to translate environmental learning into policy. If a general stance of precaution is justified, it is because twentieth-century experience has revealed previously unsuspected sources of environmental degradation. Avoiding these problems requires learning our lesson and adapting our social institutions. Jonas's own references to cumulative, long-term, and irreversible environmental damages are evidence of these recently learned lessons. At the beginning of the twentieth century, "the assimilative approach" prevailed: it was widely assumed that the environment could absorb pollution without harmful effects (Cameron and Abouchar 1991, 2). By the latter half of the twentieth century, this assumption was severely challenged. It is no accident that the precautionary principle made its first appearance in an international treaty when the long-term effects of dumping in the North Sea began to be apparent. Excess nutrients were causing oxygen depletion and massive die-offs of organisms. Fish stocks were disappearing. These effects were difficult to monitor in the marine environment; partial measures of protection based on presumably safe levels of emissions were repeatedly proven wrong by the continued deterioration of the ecosystem (Hallers-Tjabbes 2003, 334–335). So in the 1987 London Declaration, the North Sea states adopted the "principle of precautionary action." This principle would be engaged whenever "there is reason to assume that certain damage or harmful effects on the living resources of the sea" could occur—even if "a causal link between emissions and effects" could not be established. More specifically, the signatories aimed at "reducing emissions of substances that are persistent, toxic and liable to bioaccumulate."

That use of categories is characteristically precautionary.[3] As Joel Tickner (2003a, 272) argues, "When evidence is limited and uncertain, information is most appropriately presented in terms of categories of evidence rather than continuous quantitative estimates of risk." This is because categories of evidence open up wider opportunities to evaluate how damage may occur, even before slowly developing harms become evident. Categories such as persistent, liable to bioaccumulate, and environmentally mobile do not themselves describe specific harms that result from an emission. But they summarize the twentieth-century experience with substances that turn out to be dangerous to human health and the environment. Even absent causal linkages proving that a harm will come about, one can anticipate dangers by being attentive to the "biologic plausibility" that a substance will "cause effects in one or more organic systems in humans (and not only a specific one or through a specific mechanism)" (Tickner 2003a, 272). Similarly, a transgenic organism can be categorized according to its potential for weediness. Its ability to propagate itself widely in an ecosystem can be taken as evidence of its ability to disrupt otherwise-stable species interactions. In each case, categories help span the gap between partial knowledge of how ecosystems and organisms behave, on the one hand, and the insufficiency of knowledge, here and now, about specific harms, on the other. What is present in Jonas's reflections, and missing from Latour's, is the idea that precaution builds on environmental social learning.

The second nuance is that uncertainty—which is fundamental to every defense of the precautionary principle—comes in different types and degrees. Andrew Stirling distinguishes four gradations.[4] "Risk" applies to cases where one can foresee all possible outcomes and attribute probabilities to each one. "Uncertainty" describes situations where the range of possible outcomes is understood, but it is not possible to assess their relative probabilities. "Ambiguity" is the term in cases where we do not understand the range of possible outcomes. Finally, where neither a full range of outcomes nor probabilities is known, "ignorance" prevails. Ignorance, particularly, calls for precaution because it leaves us open to unhappy surprises. Stirling (2000, 81) insists that "recent examples of major 'risks' caused by technologies, such as the loss of atmospheric ozone, chemically induced endocrine dysfunctions, BSE show that the problem lies not in determining the probabilities of effects but in anticipating the possibilities themselves. These were surprises." To be sure, anticipating surprises requires scientific grounding—as Jonas understood. Without a considerable understanding of atmospheric sciences and inorganic chemistry, who could even conceive that using highly inert CFCs as aerosol propellants might cause ozone depletion?

At the same time, the project of anticipating surprises helps recast the strategy of precaution. For there is a precautionary alternative to spinning catastrophic scenarios out of pure imagination and metaphysical argument. Precaution can be a matter of assembling fragmentary, incomplete, dispersed knowledge and critical perspectives in new ways. It commands that different sciences, with different methodologies and assumptions, be brought systematically into contact with one another. It commands, too, that persons outside the networks of professional scientists be given opportunities to question the necessarily partial judgments formed in those circumscribed milieus. It mandates renewed efforts to expose commercial interests that disguise themselves as impartial science. It demands opening up the process of risk assessment to qualitative concerns: the impact of technologies on cultural integrity, the equitable distribution of goods, and power relations in society. In a sense, these ideas recall Latour's proposal of bringing the sciences into democracy—except that they express an attempt to remain receptive to people's moral reluctance to embrace unbridled experimentalism. More directly, a democratic interpretation of the precautionary principle suggests how we might build on Jonas's imperative of responsibility while rejecting its authoritarian leanings.

5

Precaution and Democratic Deliberation

Here is an irony worth contemplating: today, Jonas's suspicion of democratized risk assessment is relayed not by the defenders of the precautionary principle but by its critics. Cass Sunstein (2002, 4–5) asserts that "the American regulatory state, and indeed regulatory states all over the globe, are becoming cost-benefit states"—ones that place "a high premium on technical expertise and sound science." Such states take pains to avoid policy blunders that result from responding to irrational public fears. They give "a major role . . . to more insulated officials who are in a better position to judge whether risks are real" (Sunstein 2005, 126). Sunstein celebrates U.S. technocracy.

Elsewhere in the world, calls for a democratic or "deliberative" interpretation of the precautionary principle have become a commonplace of the literature on the politics of risk. Many of the key precautionary lessons that emerge in the conclusion of the European Environment Agency report (2001, 169) on the precautionary principle "relate to the type, quality, processing and utilization of information set within the context of a more participative and democratic process." For the most prolific French specialist on the issue, economist Olivier Godard (2000, 132), the precautionary principle entails "the development of new forms of interaction between the public and regulatory authorities, so as gradually to lessen people's suspicion of how expertise is used and to allow a wide deliberation on the risk-taking to which the public can consent." Australian scholars Ronnie Harding and Elizabeth Fisher (1999) conclude their reader with a call to make the precautionary principle a "transdisciplinary, deliberative problem-solving process." The Wingspread Statement mentions applying the precautionary principle in ways that are "open, informed and democratic" (in Raffensperger and Tickner 1999, 354), thereby thrusting the participatory impulse into North American discussions of environmental risk.

Words like deliberative, participatory, democratic, and discursive signal a commitment to change the way that risk-regulation decision-making processes are handled in Western democracies today. Making such procedures more deliberative entails first that they be made broadly inclusive. A key premise of democratic thinking is that what affects all should be decided by all. Taking this premise into risk regulation means that questions normally seen as the province of experts and functionaries, lobbyists and politicians, must somehow be brought before the public at large for comment, debate, and in some cases, resolution. Moreover, champions of deliberation contend that democratic debate aims to serve not just the largest coalition of private interests but rather the public good. Serving the public good means considering all the ramifications of a policy, for all sectors of society, for the long as well as the short term. Getting at the public good requires free debate, in which deliberators try to persuade each other by the force of the better argument. Values, in this perspective, are seen not as fixed interests that individuals bring to the deliberation. They are views enlarged, perhaps even revised and harmonized, by discussion and reflection so that they respond to the reasonable concerns of fellow citizens (Sagoff 1988, 40–42). Deliberative democracy, I shall maintain, complements rather than supplants the competitive processes of pluralist democracy. Much more than pluralists, deliberative democrats are on the lookout for innovative forums that favor enlarged, participatory thinking.

The case for a deliberative interpretation of the precautionary principle is not meant to foreshadow some utopian future when the familiar institutions of pluralist democracies wither away. Representative institutions and interest-group competition are not only unavoidable in large, internally diverse nation-states but have some potential precautionary virtues of their own. But linking precaution to deliberative democracy is intended to imply that the processes that trigger and implement precautionary measures should include regularized forms of nonexpert citizen participation and collective judgment. The objective is to make citizen deliberation a formal part of the process, just as regulatory bodies systematically include scientific and economic advisers. If this conception of precaution is to be convincing, however, the case for it must be made in terms of its *efficacy*. That is, the case for a deliberative interpretation of the precautionary principle rests on the plausibility of its actually forestalling environmental dangers, not just on the desirability of more democracy in general.

Lay Participation in Risk Assessment: The Challenge of Precaution

What can nonexperts actually contribute to political processes surrounding risk detection and management? Being able to distinguish genuine dangers from alarmist fantasies and rumors of catastrophe is not normally thought of as the public's long suit. In fact, if we look even at the Rio formulation of the precautionary principle, its logic seems to lead in directions that do not favor wide public participation.

The Rio declaration mentions "threats of serious or irreversible damage" to the environment. The first challenge to public consultation is, as German sociologist Ulrich Beck (1992b, 52–53) puts it, that today's "threats to civilization only come to consciousness in scientized thought. These are the hazards that employ the language of chemical formulas, biological contexts and medical, diagnostic concepts." In this context, ordinary perception and common sense are devalued. "The degree, the extent and the symptoms of people's endangerment are *fundamentally dependent on external knowledge*. . . . Affected parties are becoming incompetent in matters of their own affliction." Detecting long-range environmental risks appears to demand competencies that the public does not have. Implementing the precautionary principle entails more intensive and focused research programs along with better monitoring of environmental phenomena—not, it would seem, more lay participation.

In the second place, since Rio, the precautionary principle has been the focus of more and more efforts to give it juridical formulation. It is a *rule* that is finding its place in a complex legal order. Increasingly, courts are called on to give it greater precision, and to relate it to preexisting rules governing responsibility in case of accidents and the right of citizens to sue public authorities. Judges are likely to take on the tasks of defining thresholds of risk that justify taking precautions (see Bechmann and Mansuy 2002). They will decide whether certain precautionary measures are too strict or too lax (Sadeleer 2001b). They may end up attributing responsibility in cases where inadequate precautions were taken (Radé 2000). Courts will also probably have to sort out how precaution fits with treaties that open markets to international trade. They will have to reconcile new, precautionary rules with the long-standing norms of due diligence that apply in manufacturing and commerce. If the precautionary principle imposes new obligations on researchers and manufacturers, the matter of deciding who pays for such measures will undoubtedly get disputed in courts of law.

The "juridification of uncertainty" (Scott and Vos 2002) works against participatory precaution. Pressure is growing to make the application of precautionary norms more predictable by screening out the influence of opinions that do not bear directly on environmental and health concerns. In the case of GM crops, for instance, some of the hostility that Europeans feel toward them has to do with protecting jobs on small farms and avoiding dependency on powerful multinational firms (Maréchal 1999). These sorts of issues are not directly precautionary, and yet it is difficult to get laypeople to set them aside in their judgments about acceptable risks. The legitimacy of the precautionary principle will be undermined if it comes to apply to just any fear that people happen to have in regard to new technologies. So protecting that legitimacy requires measures to limit the effect of ordinary citizens' unfocused social concerns in decision-making processes (Scott and Vos 2002, 278, 282–285).

Finally, the precautionary principle cannot be implemented without some concern for its economic impact (Kourilsky 2002, 60–61). The Rio declaration mentioned "cost-effective measures"—implying that some precautionary measures may be too expensive relative to the anticipated advantages. Heightened regulatory activity is inevitably costly. Precautionary measures may include things like additional research, labeling requirements, and creating new regulatory agencies. Economists and sociologists of risk will inevitably be called in. They will evaluate comparative risk levels and the efficiency of chosen regulatory measures. One can anticipate thousands of pages of densely written reports, filled with charts and equations. Precautionary policymaking is not going to be determined simply by counting noses—especially when those noses are attached to heads filled with untutored, unquantified intuitions about whether regulating some new technology is "worth it" or will "cost jobs." Taking account of the precautionary principle's economic impact sits uneasily with deliberative procedures in which citizens present their concerns directly as arguments.[1]

Given these deficiencies of popular opinion relative to risk assessment, how can so many authors argue that implementing the precautionary principle requires popular participation? Broadly speaking, there are two forms of justification, one based on the *preconditions* of legitimate decision making, and the other based on the positive environmental *consequences* to be anticipated from making risk assessment a more deliberative exercise. The latter justification, I shall contend, is the more fundamental one for precautionary purposes.

Harding and Fisher (1999, 292) announce the argument based on preconditions: "The first reason [why the application of the precautionary principle requires a deliberative process] is that in the absence of sufficient 'facts' on which to base a decision some other basis for decision-making is required. . . . The deliberative process is *the* legitimate basis for decision-making in a democracy."[2] Now that is not a self-evident conclusion. In the absence of sufficient facts, one might claim (as defenders of science-based risk regulation often do) that no public decision at all is required. Or one might insist on acquiring more facts by accelerating scientific research. An argument linking uncertainty and deliberation needs to be filled in with some more extensive social analysis that explains why those alternatives are inadequate to found legitimate policy. Such an analysis is behind Beck's (1995, 17) assertion that there is a "secret elective affinity between the ecologization and the democratization of society."

Beck's influential studies of risk society hold that industrialization has reached a point where it generates hazards beyond its ability to control. Increasingly, the topic of public debate shifts from familiar issues concerning the distribution of goods in the welfare state to conflicts over the distribution of "bads" (Beck 1996, 27–29). In a risk society, says Beck (1992b, 21), citizens perceive "the hidden face of progress": industrial civilization forces them to accept new and troubling types of risk. At the same time, he argues, factors like global economic competition and geographic mobility accelerate modernity's process of individualization. Detraditionalized individuals are simultaneously less inclined to sacrifice their well-being for collective goals and more determined to protect the quality of their own lives against potential dangers. In a world of pluralized lifestyles, individuals assert the values of "equality, freedom and self-expression promised by modernity, against the limitations, the functional imperatives and the fatalism of progress in industrial society" (Beck 1992b, 232). With increased reflectiveness, they come to challenge scientific assessments of technological risk. More and more frequently, one hears demands for more open, public debates about the potential negative consequences of innovation. Beck (1995, 16) foresees a day when "public experiential science . . . , accepted as legitimate knowledge and authorized to make decisions, would have the function of an 'open upper house of parliament.' It would have to ask 'How do we wish to live?' and it would have to hold the answers up as the standard for scientific plans and consequences." Daniel Cohn-Bendit (2000) neatly summarizes Beck's thesis by claiming that "a society aware of the risks that it runs, a 'risk society,' is a society in which the citizens reject blind confidence in the 'technicist institutions' that are supposed to know the common good better than anyone else."

Beck's case for precautionary deliberation starts from a background normative assumption that in general, legitimate policy derives from the will of the people. From this assumption, Beck criticizes the way that reliance on technical expertise is handled in contemporary democratic practice. Contemporary democracies usually allow for decision-making authority to be delegated to administrative agencies that solicit expert advice, provided that those agencies are ultimately responsible to democratically elected officials, and the scientific advice these officials get consists of something approaching factual certainty. The latter condition is supposed to mean that even as officials rely on expert advice, they still adhere to the people's will. The experts' factual information simply helps them carry out what the public really wants. But Beck emphasizes how, in many cases, scientific uncertainty is substantial. As a result, there is a legitimacy gap in the system: we-the-people delegate power to administrators only on the assumption that their function is merely to find the most effective ways to realize our objectives. Yet the scientific uncertainty means that administrators are left to make risk decisions without a firm factual foundation that would constrain their choices. They have decision-making power that escapes the ethical umbrella of democratic legitimacy. Under such conditions, contends Beck, power rightly reverts to the people. If there are risks whose magnitude cannot be calculated, it is the people's right to decide whether they really want to take them and under what conditions.

This is problematic as a justification for deliberative precaution. Its agenda is so broad that it risks undermining the specificity of the principle itself. Yes, the precautionary principle can be seen as a challenge to certain types of decisions made within the context of "technicist institutions." And it does rest on a certain skepticism that science is always adequate to the task of explaining natural phenomena that potentially generate risks. But citizens in risk societies worry about far more than health and environmental effects. As Beck describes them, citizens are concerned about job security, the injustice of unequal risk distribution, the loss of leisure time, and various forms of aesthetic deterioration. Deliberative precaution, on this interpretation, becomes a way of encouraging public debate about every possible consequence that a technology or social practice might have. The disadvantage of this interpretation is that it overshadows the hard-won environmental social learning embodied in the precautionary principle. From its earliest appearance in international treaties, the precautionary principle has targeted an unusual category of risk: risks that are serious in the sense of creating widespread, palpable harm to people, property, and ecosystems; problems that are long-term and irreversible. The case for precaution is that faced with the reality of this novel type of risk, we need new safeguards. Without consensus on the precautionary principle, nations delay preventive measures to forestall the risk. Thereby they impose the risk on everyone. The value of the precautionary principle depends on its ability to provide a new level of protection against such dangers. Its rationale is consequentialist. It looks to the good effects that will be gotten by adhering to the principle. Legitimacy-based arguments for deliberative precaution obscure this essential rationale.

Defenders of democratically legitimated risk assessment generally claim along the way that their proposals will, in fact, help us avoid unwanted technological risks. The problem is that the defenders move too quickly—and implausibly—to contend that the lay public has precaution-pertinent knowledge at its disposal. Consider Beck once again. He argues that the public awareness of environmental harm is increasing. In reference to environmental degradation generally, he claims that "the latency phase of risk threats is coming to an end." Previously invisible hazards are becoming visible in the form of dying forests, eroded monuments, and sea animals smeared with oil (Beck 1992b, 55). Such environmental issues have enough salience to provoke popular alarm and thus automatically motivate democratic forms of engagement. These are not necessarily the sorts of issues targeted by the precautionary principle, however. Oil spills and acid rain certainly merit regulatory attention. But they do not fall under the scope of a principle whose purpose is to justify action in the case of new technologies or collective practices where harmful effects have not yet been scientifically demonstrated—much less felt in the general population.

Beck offers a second argument to suggest the competence of laypeople in risk assessment. He contends that various "cultural sensitivities" can serve to trigger "political reflexivity" (Beck 1995, 15). In different cultures, people have special affection for certain landscapes or products. When these are perceived to deteriorate, nonscientized views react quickly. For cultural reasons, Germans care particularly about the health of their forests, while the French can be especially touchy about biotechnology innovations that threaten the distinctiveness of regionally produced foods (Bureau and Marrette 2000, 176–178). Arguments about cultural sensitivity do not, however, say anything very systematic about precaution in the face of new, global risks. Cultural factors can just as well cause environmental *insensitivity.* Somehow, Americans treasure wilderness areas, but their love of automobiles seems to overpower their fears of global warming. French public opinion remains wedded to nuclear power—while the problems of waste storage go unresolved. Cultural sensitivities seem randomly distributed and not particularly dependable in terms of evaluating risk.

A better, more focused argument is that since applying the precautionary principle may have far-reaching effects on people's lives—for example, the type of transportation they use or the availability of chemicals whose benefits they desire—their participation in precautionary decision making is essential (Dormont and Hermitte 1999, 56). Without it, those decisions will be resented as impositions and perhaps even undermined by noncompliance. This assertion concerns more than legitimacy. It suggests that the effectiveness of at least some anticipatory policies depends on people's acceptance of them. It appeals to the environmental consequences of inclusive political processes. Still, this reasoning does not go very far along the path of deliberative precaution. It seems to pertain more to the choice of precautionary measures than to the *discovery* of instances where precaution should be practiced. It does not yet offer a response to a defender of cost-benefit analysis who contends that the public acceptance of risk-reduction measures should be seen as a matter of more effective strategies of risk communication, not new forms of direct political participation (see Sunstein 2002, 264ff.).

The Consequences of Deliberative Precaution

The upshot of this critique of legitimacy-based arguments for deliberative precaution is this: the case for a deliberative interpretation of the precautionary principle needs to be made on the grounds that broader participation and deliberation play a crucial role in enhancing the principle's precautionary impact. That is, if there is a case for deliberative precaution, it must rest on demonstrating that nonexpert understandings can make some special contribution to the challenge of detecting and reacting to large-scale, latent, uncertain risks. Deliberation must connect to efficacy—to an ability *in fact* to help forestall grave dangers. How is that possible? Three consequentialist connections between deliberation and precautionary risk reduction are notable.

The first is that deliberation can constitute a stage in risk assessment that puts a check on the excessively action-oriented worldviews associated with particular professions and forms of expertise. Arranging risk-assessment procedures in ways that give greater discursive significance to questions about this action orientation helps expose potentially dangerous lacunae and risk-generating enthusiasms in expert views.

Consider the implicit action orientation of several forms of expertise. Economic studies of environmental problems are action-oriented in the sense that they are intended to identify and remove potential obstacles to economic change and development. Thus, if environmentally concerned citizens object to draining wetlands to build a shopping center, environmental economists will be brought in to evaluate the situation. Part of their job is to put prices on ecological services (for example, water filtration) that have no market price. The inclusion of such prices in impact analyses may or may not tip the balance in favor of conservation measures. What is not always noticed, however, is that the economic framing of the analysis has subtly redefined the environmental situation. "Ecological services" become goods made to compete with all other scarce goods in the economy. Action follows as soon as their value is outweighed by the aggregate value of other goods. The environmental goods are set to be traded off so that development can continue. But here's the rub: multiple, potentially false assumptions about the world and people's preferences go into such analyses. Cost projections may depend on rainfall extrapolations that turn out to be false because of climate change. The economic analysis may fail to notice that wetlands provide habitat for an endangered species. The tacit commitment to proceed with building the shopping center as soon as the benefits outweigh the costs may override a growing public sentiment in favor of sustainable development for future generations.

Similarly, risk analysis is action-oriented. Beck's critique shows how framing social choices in terms of risk is not a neutral description of a situation. It is part and parcel of an industrial-utilitarian order bent on facilitating production and consumption (Beck 1992a: 98; see also O'Brien 2000, 6). If a group opposes a technology or practice as "too risky," they will be told that all of the alternatives—including the status quo—carry risks as well. "A willingness to balance relative costs and benefits is inherent in the very adoption of the concept of 'risk' to describe one's situation," notes Langdon Winner (1986, 145). Looking at every choice as a risk is part and parcel of a worldview bent on maximizing social benefits. But here's another rub: some risks are novel, poorly understood, or can only be "calculated" by using highly controversial assumptions about the behavior of natural systems and people. Famously, the U.S. Nuclear Regulatory Commission's Rasmussen Report of 1975 determined that the probability of a severe accident at a nuclear power plant was only one in a billion per reactor year of operation. And then a reactor at Three Mile Island melted down four years later, due in large part to an unforeseen operator error.

Isn't research in the natural sciences different? Isn't it the function of the natural sciences to understand reality, not to change it? Not really. It is characteristic of the empirical sciences to conceive of nature as an object of possible technical control. Each hypothesis, each experiment, is designed with a view to better understanding and controlling natural phenomena. Knowledge of physical processes, gained by never-ending experimental research, underwrites great confidence in our ability to manipulate natural phenomena to our advantage.

In each case, experts bring to bear methods of analysis that on their own terms, admit no limits to action. Everything has an exchangeable cost, every action entails risk, and every natural phenomenon can in principle be understood, and then manipulated, using scientific methods. Their technical analyses presuppose the desirability of world-changing action. Moreover, experts suppose that in fairly short order we can acquire the knowledge required to decide when action can begin. Their action orientation constitutes a tacit commitment to proceed with world-changing measures, even though they may give a poor representation of certain aspects of reality.

The point, of course, is not that lay opinion understands the probabilities of nuclear accidents better than experts do. The point is that the experts' immersion in action-oriented systems is the source of overconfidence and contestable assumptions. To bring their lapses to light requires exposing experts to *action-questioning notions* that come from outside their frameworks. Such notions are the stuff of laypeople's nonprofessionalized, commonsense understandings of the world. Talk of the sacred, integrity, and inviolable rights is integral to everyday discourse. These concepts resist commensuration and trade-offs. When they are invoked, proposals for action encounter an obstacle.

Now it would be easy enough to respond that such action-questioning notions are never absolute. True enough. But their significance is usually embodied in special institutions and procedures through which action-oriented claims must pass. When action-oriented proposals run into individual rights, sacred burial grounds, and the like, their sponsors are constrained to make detours, answer questions, and face delays. They have to respond to different thresholds of evidence, convince specially constituted audiences, and plan for negative outcomes that they would prefer to downplay. Action must take a more difficult path—a path on which it can be delayed or even defeated.

Lay conceptions of nature should be understood in this way. They are not just romanticized or error-laden ideas destined to be replaced by more technically sophisticated understandings of the social and physical reality. As the sociologist Denis Duclos (1993, 67) maintains, "It is precisely what is non-reducible to concepts that suggests what is most 'natural' (non-cultural) in reality." Nature often corresponds to an intuition that every technically sophisticated view of reality is not a transparent window onto reality but a symbolic rendering of it. Behind every way of knowing nature, there is something more fundamental that is partially grasped by this way of knowing—and that partly escapes it. There is a real nature behind these occurrences. But it is a nature not yet revealed by today's action-oriented grids of understanding.

What happens when ordinary understandings of nature are overridden by professionalized ones is well illustrated by how Philippe Kourilsky (2002, 21–22)—general director of France's prestigious Pasteur Institute—analyzes the mad cow crisis: "Part of public opinion is convinced that the origin of the 'mad cow' problem is that industry implemented a feeding process that was contrary to the laws of nature. However, feeds made from both animal and vegetable matter have essentially the same composition, *provided that they are well prepared:* both are proteins and amino acids—the universal components of the living world, plants included." His point is that the people's intuitions about what is natural and unnatural have nothing to do with whether products really are safe. Biologists know—or should know—what the real composition of feeds are. The nature they deal with is composed of building blocks whose characteristics can be analyzed, and whose interactions can be understood and predicted. This understanding of nature sets up the world to be disassembled and reassembled, provided only that scientific creations are well prepared. Demanding that they be *well* prepared acknowledges that some procedures may not prepare things so well. Experiments sometimes will fail to yield the expected results or will reveal some hitherto unsuspected danger. But Kourilsky assumes the obstacles to be specifiable on scientific terms. More hypotheses, more experiments, are in order. Once the obstacles are identified and controlled, the world-altering action may proceed.

It is now believed that BSE is caused by a nonliving, misfolded protein (a "prion"). Up until the mid-1980s, food safety specialists assumed that feeding cows industrially processed sheep offal, even from sick sheep, posed no threat to cow or human health. Sheep tissue was, after all, only proteins and amino acids. That a nonliving, misfolded protein could induce further misfolding, survive at least some forms of processing, and jump various species barriers were not possibilities taken seriously by those who believed they already understood "essentially" the nature of the matter they dealt with. But here's yet another rub: they did not understand (Khachatourians 2001, 18–19). The matter that they were dealing with contained previously unsuspected components with behaviors that contradicted prevailing theory. Reductionist views of what nature is and what nature can do were partly responsible for imposing a grave risk on a wide population.

The precautionary principle is about avoiding serious damages that arise precisely out of that unexamined part of reality. An important precautionary function of widened deliberation is to increase the chances of non-action-oriented viewpoints being given genuine influence in risk-management decisions. The objective of a consequentialist, deliberative precaution is not to substitute popular feeling for expert judgment. It is to foster the growth of institutions in which experts' action-oriented concepts can be made responsive to other notions that leave more room for doubt about human mastery of the world, respect for life's complicated patterns, and considerations of wholesomeness and fittingness.

The precautionary effect of such arrangements is suggested by France's experiment with a "citizens' conference" in 1998. This event arranged for ordinary citizens and scientists to interact in a public arena, and citizens to deliberate about a reasonable policy to adopt with respect to transgenic crops. The event was, by many accounts, surprisingly successful. Scientists were forced to find a publicly comprehensible language to explain the stakes in the GMO debate; the citizens did not hesitate to interrupt and question the experts (Marris and Joly 1999). On occasion, the lay participants even challenged the experts' assurances of low risk and rejected assertions that transgenic modifications were essentially the same as natural genetic variation (La première conférence 1998). Often the scientists had to admit that the current knowledge about GMOs was insufficient to answer the citizens' questions. Meanwhile, media coverage amplified the effect. Adding a deliberative moment to this instance of risk assessment probably stiffened the government's resolve to abandon the use of antibiotic marker genes and require the labeling of GM foods (Bourg and Boy 2005, 94)—policies that its own expert advisers had not originally favored.

A second consequentialist reason to favor nonexpert public participation is to help assure that regulatory bodies actually function according to precautionary standards. Ideally, regulatory bodies are supposed to maintain their independence from the interested parties that they monitor and potentially discipline. But maintaining such independence is difficult in practice. The phenomenon of "regulatory capture"—in which regulators collaborate with and protect the industry they are supposed to oversee—is well documented in the social science literature on regulation. In some areas of high technology—this is particularly true in genetic engineering—almost all of the top experts have some links with the industry they regulate. They have had jobs, research grants, and consultative relations with the industry. Moreover, researchers necessarily become involved in the social values surrounding their fields of study. Thus, argues Philippe Roqueplo (1997, 46), "When he intervenes as an expert in a complex policy area, a scientist always functions, whether he knows it or not, as the advocate of a certain cause—especially since he believes that the stakes in the decision are high." Anyone who reads the popularizing works of scientists engaged in the debate over GMOs cannot help but be struck by the *social* vision surrounding the scientific arguments (see Gottweis 1998, 92, 147, 150). Those defending the safety of GMOs are not just making a judgment about the current state of scientific research. They are defending their laboratory's right to continue certain lines of experimentation. They are defending a world in which science contributes to social progress, as they see it.

In addition, the political authorities to which regulators report can easily end up regarding new technologies more in terms of their impact on employment or the country's balance of payment than on environmental health decades from now. Cases cited in the European Environment Agency report on the precautionary principle document the problem. The authors conclude that "one factor in the slow UK response to BSE was that the government regulatory body was responsible first to industry and only second to consumers. [Likewise, the history of asbestos regulation] provides a clear example of persistent obstruction and misinformation by vested interests and of drastic miscalculation in the wider regulatory process" (European Environment Agency 2001, 179). The problem of regulatory capture is, of course, a persistent one in modern representative democracies. There are no miracle solutions. Checks and balances, political oversight, legal accountability, and freedom of the press all have their place. The suggestion here, however, is that in precautionary situations, where scientific uncertainty is added to the mix, there is a strong case for opening regulatory processes to public scrutiny and organizing deliberative events that keep the *public* good—not the narrower perspective of organized interests and politicians responsive to them—at the forefront of attention.

A good example of this potential contribution comes from a recent report, *Public Perceptions of Agricultural Biotechnologies in Europe* (Marris et al. 2001). This sociological study compared what decision-making leaders thought were the grounds of public distrust of GMOs with what citizens *actually said* when they were questioned in discussion groups. The discrepancies between official expectations and public reasoning were striking. The leaders attributed public reticence to factors like scientific ignorance and an unrealistic desire for "zero risk." What the researchers found, however, was that most public concerns had to do with the adequacy of already-existing measures that had been taken to control risks. The citizens asked:

- Do the regulatory agencies actually have enough power and the funds to counterbalance the interests of the large firms that want to develop these products?

• What contingency plans exist in cases where unanticipated harmful effects occur?

• Can the rules imposed by the regulatory authorities really be applied effectively? (Marris et al. 2001, 63–70).

In all of these questions, what we hear is a healthy dose of skepticism regarding the real workings of the regulatory authorities. Citizen participation might help prevent some of the safety-reducing dysfunctions of regulatory politics. The challenge is to organize public participation and debate in ways that allow a wider group of stakeholders to interject questions about the quality and scope of scientific studies used in risk assessment (Levidow and Marris 2001, 355–356). Citizens might also be brought in to observe the functioning of regulatory bodies. There, they could verify that established procedures had been followed and, if necessary, question the good faith with which information had been shared (Godard 2000, 142). In a similar vein, Sanford Lewis (1999, 248) proposes "citizen oversight boards" that could be "empaneled to ascertain when available information triggers action requirements (e.g., restrictions, bans or phaseouts of substances or activities." Such third-party review of regulatory performance could help reinforce safety measures. And that is the point of the precautionary principle.

Third, in some cases, nonexpert knowledge can usefully complete expert knowledge in regard to understanding the complexity of social practices that generate risk. That is, democratically inclusive measures built into procedures for risk detection and management can have a precautionary effect to the extent that they increase the sensitivity of such procedures. Increased sensitivity means an earlier detection of potential problems, before they spread or become irreversible. It means that assumptions about how risks are handled can be examined, challenged, and modified by confrontation with lay experience. Brian Wynne's (1996) study of Cumbrian sheep farmers and environmental radioactivity is illustrative here. He recounts how, following the Chernobyl nuclear accident, expert analysis of the spread of contamination led to restrictions on sheep movements and sales. Yet the scientific studies on which policies were based overgeneralized the assumptions about soil composition in the affected area—assumptions that could be challenged even by farmers with local knowledge.[3] Radiation persisted in ways that contradicted the scientists' initially confident predictions. Local farmers' suspicions that some of the radioactivity originated from a nearby nuclear power plant forced a reexamination of the data and a discovery that Chernobyl could account for only 50 percent of the local contamination. The scientists assumed that sheep farmers could easily move flocks from the more contaminated hilltop grazing to the less contaminated valleys—an option that the farmers themselves knew to be unrealistic. "The benefit of attending to lay knowledge is its complementary character, its sometimes firmer grounding in real-world operational conditions" (European Environment Agency 2001, 177).

Pluralism and Participatory Democracy

The idea of widening the debate about technological options and their attendant risks straddles the ideals of deliberative and pluralist democracy. Deliberative democracy promotes direct citizen participation rather than representation. It depends on an ethos of seeking the common good, not just satisfying interests and accepting social compromise. It favors settings in which the better argument prevails, not mere numbers, economic power, or brute coercion.

In the United States and across Europe today, democracy is more pluralist than deliberative. In a pluralist democracy, people with shared interests form groups that try to shape policy in their favor by means of electoral mobilization, lobbying, and legal maneuvering, within the context of representative assemblies. As John Dryzek (1997, 100) explains, "Political rationality [under such conditions] means that all actors have to be mollified, pretty much in proportion to their ability to create difficulties for government officials, irrespective of whether they are motivated by conceptions of the public interest or more selfish material interests." Decisions in pluralist democracies are reached by arranging trade-offs among interest groups, manipulating—often suppressing or distorting—information, and yielding to scarcely veiled threats of electoral retaliation or denial of services. Like sausage making, these methods are not particularly appetizing to watch, but for most purposes they may yield a palatable enough product.

In relation to precautionary situations, however, their implications are more disturbing. Short-term electoral advantage comes to the fore in pluralist decision making, not the long-term environmental consequences. Political mobilization usually occurs around visible problems affecting clearly identifiable victims, seldom around invisible, slowly accumulating dangers. Politicians respond to domestic constituencies, not to people around the globe who may suffer far more of the consequences of large-scale ecological disruption. Pluralism bears some direct responsibility for the nonprecautionary character of contemporary politics.

Nonetheless, even on their own terms, pluralist democracies can be reformed so that they combine some aspects of deliberation and precautionary decision making. For instance, they can adopt procedures and practices that encourage wider rather than narrower participation. Pluralist democracies can create political structures promoting greater foresight, not less. They can create a legal context that is more rather than less supportive of groups willing to challenge business as usual. To the extent that they "do more" in each of these ways, pluralist democracies can be made to lean toward a more deliberative ideal. Consider several such possibilities in more detail.

One way of doing more is to create a standing parliamentary commission or some array of permanent advisory bodies whose mission is to engage in prospective analysis of environmental risks and counsel legislators on how to mitigate them (Mironesco 1998). From 1972 to 1995, the U.S. Congress received reports on issues like climate change and genetic engineering from the Office of Technology Assessment. This office was a sort of in-house think tank designed to give Congress a source of unbiased technical expertise. It sought to clarify the options that the legislators faced, not to advocate for a particular solution. Inspired partly by this model, France created the Parliamentary Office for the Evaluation of Scientific and Technological Choices in 1983. Composed of equal numbers of senators and representatives, this body mainly holds private hearings with expert advisers. Occasionally, however, it also puts together public hearings, as it did in 1990 concerning the exploitation of natural resources in the Antarctic (Le Déaut 1999, 159–161). Since such agencies have an explicitly future-oriented mission, they are capable of making legislators discuss problems that might occur far beyond the electoral cycles that they can anticipate during their careers. Also, to the extent that reports and hearings raise public awareness of looming environmental problems, they have a quasideliberative function. A more aware public can react, debate, initiate litigation, and apply pressure to legislators.

A second means of opening pluralist democracy to precautionary deliberation is by favoring alternatives assessment over cost-benefit analysis. As an action-oriented mode of evaluation, cost-benefit analysis is by its very nature seeking permission to proceed with some activity, provided that the potential damages are "acceptable" on balance. Alternatives assessment, in contrast, is a mode of evaluation whose fundamental principle is that it is not acceptable to harm humans or nonhumans if there are reasonable alternatives (O'Brien 2000, 6–7). In relation to an activity with environmental effects, it requires consideration of all reasonable choices, including especially those likely to have the least adverse impact. An alternatives assessment approach to the industrial and consumer use of chlorine compounds will ask not what level of exposure to such compounds causes only an "acceptable" level of harm, it will instead seek to demonstrate the existence of effective alternatives for almost all uses of chlorine. Such an approach is precautionary because minimizing harm rather than maximizing social benefits is its watchword. Alternatives assessment also constitutes a step toward *deliberative* precaution because with "broadly based public participation," "a full range of alternatives is more likely to be considered" (O'Brien 1999, 210). Discovering alternatives requires ensuring that policymakers are not exposed to only one side of an issue or hear mainly from those who have an immediate interest in allowing risky activity to go forward. Alternatives assessment highlights choices, thereby enlarging the field for democratic processes of change.

In its commitment to opening risk analysis to outside scrutiny and challenge, alternatives assessment shades over into a third way of making pluralist democracy more deliberative and precautionary. The activities of NGOs can provoke controversy in ways that make government and business elites open risk decisions to wider investigation. Typically, they frame controversies as matters of collective responsibility (Laraña 2001, 36–37). Recourse to publicity campaigns, protest, lawsuits, civil disobedience, and street theater as well as conventional lobbying have made organizations like Greenpeace and Friends of the Earth redoubtable actors in international environmental politics. In 1984, a Natural Resources Defense Council staff member initiated a lawsuit to force the EPA to implement CFC reductions that it had agreed to in earlier international agreements. This pressure was one factor in pushing the United States toward the 1987 Montreal Protocol phasing out most uses of CFCs (Litfin 1994, 70–71). When Greenpeace operatives greeted the first transatlantic shipments of GM soybeans with protests in 1996, they caught public attention more powerfully than had any parliamentary debates up to that point. A newly alert public took matters from there. Protests and a stream of newspaper stories forced governments across Europe to reconsider EU decisions on GMO safety. In countries where electoral rules have allowed Green parties to grow strongest, members of parliament carry the sensibility of the environmental movement directly into legislative politics. In Germany, decades of antinuclear protest culminated in 2002, with the Greens successfully sponsoring a law to phase out nuclear power over twenty years.

Such examples suggest that the existence of a vigorous environmental civil society promotes precautionary policy (Davidson, Barns, and Scibeci, 1997, 341–342). But their vigor depends in part on a political-legal context that recognizes their potential contributions. One reason that Europe is now more precautionary than the United States is that European countries are less reticent about giving public interest and community groups representation on science and technology advisory boards. The United States, in contrast, tends to favor more limited participation in science and technology policymaking. Business leaders, high-ranking military officers, and expert researchers are especially prominent (Sclove 1995b). We have seen how Germany's board overseeing trials of GMOs included members of labor unions and environmental organizations. Even France, whose republican traditions generally favor a close collaboration between national political representatives and experts (L'hexagone privilégie 2000; Boy 1999, 621), has come to include representatives of consumer associations, environmental protection groups, professional agricultural societies, and unions on its committee (the CGB) that oversees the safety of genetic engineering experiments (Dossier de l'environnement 1996). In such ways, representative institutions of pluralist democracies can be structured to include more of civil society.

Furthermore, precaution requires access to information. Effective disclosure requirements—ones that are not riddled with loopholes protecting "trade secrets"—can create more opportunities for preventive interventions, even in a thoroughly pluralist context (Lewis 1999, 246). Becoming alert to potentially anomalous phenomena requires an awareness that some change has actually occurred in one's surroundings. Questioning experts' assumptions about how risks will be handled in real-world situations (for example, whether GM seeds will be stored and spread in the ways that manufacturers suppose) requires having access to those assumptions: listening to them in public hearings or seeing them published. It was scandalous, objected Jean-Jacques Salomon (1999, 20–22), that the location of experimental sites for GM plants could be kept secret in France.[4] If neighbors are not even aware that transgenic plants are in their vicinity, it is much more difficult for them to consider the possibility that some marginal change in their surroundings (say, the diminished vitality of pollinating insects or the spread of a troublesome weed) might be attributable to those plants. Transparency about risk opens space for debate about unexpected consequences. That is why, for instance, labeling, traceability, and public reporting requirements for products carrying potential dangers are precautionary. Not only do they make it possible to locate and recall products that turn out to be dangerous. They also enable citizens and NGOs to track effects independently of government regulators.

If deliberation is about trying to find the common good, not just the largest coalition of interests, then making it possible for groups to challenge government and business decisions, based on their own calculations and toxicological studies, is crucial to the public interest. For example, waste-disposal contractors who incinerate dioxin-contaminated materials must report the characteristics of their incinerators and the materials they propose to burn. Using this information, a Greenpeace scientist was able to demonstrate that the contractor was allowing more dioxin in its emissions than was permitted; the EPA was forced to admit that the Greenpeace calculations were correct (O'Brien 2000, 31–33).

Still, no one should overestimate the precautionary significance of incorporating deliberative elements into pluralist democracy. Prospective bodies like the Office of Technology Assessment and as well as the Parliamentary Office for the Evaluation of Scientific and Technological Choices are all well and good. But their functions are purely advisory. They feed into a political process whose dynamics are essentially unchanged. When it comes time to pass new technology and environmental regulations, decisions will still be made by legislators whose political fate is determined by voters in a small region, under the influence of the usual lobbies and campaign contributors, in the context of national policies prioritizing economic growth and competition. These bodies seldom cause a wholesale reorientation of policy. They are also politically vulnerable. It is worth remembering that in a period of cost cutting and antiregulatory feeling, the U.S. Congress abolished the Office of Technology Assessment in 1995. As for the role of NGOs, Robert Brulle's study of their importance in relation to environmental deliberative democracy ends rather pessimistically. Too often, he concludes, such organizations accept without question the types of scientific discourse that discourage citizen participation in risk decisions (Brulle 2000). They accept "external funding [that draws them] into an existing network of economic and political power" (274). And they develop oligarchic internal structures for their own governance.

Problems of economic bias are endemic to pluralist democracy. But they are only a part of the problem from a precautionary point of view. Assume that a level playing field is assured, such that initial disparities in political and economic power between groups are not allowed to determine the policy outcomes of intergroup bargaining. Even so, many of the precaution-sapping characteristics of familiar pluralist institutions are left unquestioned. Elitism aside, competitive, interest-driven politics still has trouble attending to long-term consequences. It still arbitrates among technologies and practices presented to it by scientists and economic actors, rather than attempting to make collective judgments about the desired direction of change. It leaves intact all the motives for competing groups to use uncertainty as a pretext for delaying measures of environmental protection.

For those attracted to a deliberative ideal, then, there many good reasons to invent models of risk regulation that go beyond those usually offered in pluralist democracies.

Participatory Technology Assessment

Numerous models for increased public participation in confronting environmental risk are available (see Fiorino 1990). Several are highlighted in the work of Richard Sclove.[5] He imagines ways of getting citizens involved in processes of technological research, development, and design. For example, lay advisory panels could be incorporated into the structures of organizations that award grants for scientific research (Sclove 1995a, 211). The aim is to give citizens a say in the direction of technological change *before* what Jonas called the compulsive dynamics of innovation set in. Sclove cites instances of "community-based research." Ordinary citizens in Woburn, Massachusetts, collaborated with scientists from Harvard University to do their own epidemiological studies of the effects of toxic wastes in their community (Sclove 1995a, 200). In a related example, Sclove mentions Dutch experiments with "science shops." Dutch universities set up internal research networks to study questions about the effects of science and technology referred to them by community groups, public interest organizations, and trade unions (Sclove 1995a, 225). Without lapsing into wishful thinking about ordinary citizens' degree of scientific or juridical sophistication, each of these models suggests how the general public can play a more active, prevention-oriented role in evaluating risk-generating practices.

Perhaps the most illuminating model of participatory technology assessment is the consensus conference, noted earlier, which has been used by about a dozen countries in the last twenty years (Joss 1999, 291). It is worth going into greater detail on this model, not because it represents the definitive form of deliberative precaution, but because its carefully designed procedures illuminate with special clarity the breadth of conditions that make citizen participation reasonable and potentially efficacious.

Consensus conferences originated in Denmark—inspired in part by U.S. experiences with panels of doctors assembled to evaluate medical practices (Jorgensen 1995). In 1985, the Danish parliament created a board of technology to develop new procedures aiming to get citizens involved in assessing technologies like nuclear power and biotechnology. The resulting model, the consensus conference, is meticulously organized. Fourteen citizens, chosen either randomly or after newspaper solicitation, comprise a panel. These citizens are given several days of training in the background issues pertaining to the technology in question. They help choose a group of experts, who they will question over several days of debate. The aim of these exchanges is to allow ordinary citizens to help clarify the issues in technoscientific debates, reveal uncertainties and ambiguities, and bring scientists into direct contact with citizen concerns (Un débat public 1998). Finally, the panel puts together a report on the topic and sets out the policy proposals that it deems justified. These proposals are not politically dispositive, but members of parliament are expected to take them into consideration before legislating in reference to the technological option. Denmark has held consensus conferences on subjects as diverse as plant biotechnology, food irradiation, and the future of motor transport (Anderson and Jaeger 1999).

A number of features of consensus conferences are crucial to their counting as a form of deliberative precaution.

First, the participants of the citizens' conference have a certain representativeness. The panelists are no self-selected group of activists or people whose representativeness is simply unknown. A polling company selects the panelists according to criteria designed to assure that participants come from a cross-section of the population. Some allowance for representation in this sense is critical to the panel's political status. One obvious obstacle to deliberative precaution is that it is hard to imagine how to get a large number of people involved in a discussion of the complicated issues involved in technology assessment. That is why it is more typical for contemporary polities to rely on the institutions of representative government and expert consultation. If, however, there is a distinct case for deliberative precaution, and if such deliberations rely on the voices of a small number of citizens, then the Danish solution of seeking a statistically representative sample of citizens is not a bad one.

Second, the consensus model strives to create the conditions for well-informed debate. It does so in two ways. First, procedures regulating the length of presentations and opportunities for cross-questioning help equalize participatory opportunities. There are no hierarchical relations (for instance, employer-employee or expert-nonexpert) or power asymmetries among the panelists, so the pressure for strategic calculation is minimized. Furthermore, the panelists do not merely voice opinions or rehearse ideological positions. The participants are given training in the technical issues before them. There is an educative process involved in which citizens acquire some basic competence in the policy area through interaction with experts. In this way, one of the barriers to deliberative precaution—the need for technical expertise in order to make judgments—is lowered. The barrier is not eliminated, to be sure, but it is lowered enough that ordinary citizens can compete with political professionals for access to a key ingredient of legitimate decision making: the best available knowledge on the subject. In France, a frequent reaction to its 1998 conference on GM crops was satisfaction—if not astonishment—that ordinary citizens could engage so intelligently in a debate on so technical an issue (Callon, Lascoumes, and Barthe 2001, 158ff.; Le Déaut 2001, 18).

Third, throughout the process of organizing the citizens' conference, from training to debate, great emphasis is laid on the neutrality and objectivity of the people involved and the information considered (Boy, Donnet-Kamel, and Roqueplo 2000, 783, 784, 790ff.). The panelists receive information that is assembled in such a way as to alert them to controversy and uncertainty. In the French case, for example, the participants listened to serious critics of GMOs as well as to their defenders. They had a chance to probe and challenge statements. No one charged that the participants were subject to compulsion or systematic deception. Throughout, the conditions of the process encouraged them to reason as concerned citizens, not just as self-interested consumers, employees, or partisans. Deliberative assessment ultimately fosters judgments separating believable information from hearsay and error. This achievement corresponds to the second objective of consequentialist precaution: helping regulatory bodies maintain their independence by exposing their reasoning and sources of information to broader scrutiny.

Fourth, at the conclusion of a conference, the panel renders a finding, including policy recommendations. Although representative democracies provide other opportunities for debate (such as election campaigns, public hearings, letters to the editor, and protests), these less structured forums conclude without anyone crafting a document that reduces multiple opinions to a set of particular proposals. This difference lessens their deliberative significance. No nonpartisan, *collective judgment* takes place. Outcomes are often ambiguous, in just the way that politicians prefer—precisely so that they can claim to have listened to the public without anyone being able to measure their subsequent performance against a set list of measures. The Danish model, in contrast, involves participants in a quasilegislative exercise. The panelists deliberate in view of issuing policy recommendations. This forces them, and anyone who reads their conclusions, to try to arrive at a balanced judgment of all the stakes involved.

Fifth, consensus conferences are presented in ways designed to stimulate discussion in the polity as a whole. In Denmark, consensus conference conclusions are widely publicized. Videos and leaflets are distributed, and local debates are organized (Sclove and Scammell 1999, 262). The French consensus conference was held in the building of the lower house of parliament. This was no gathering of citizens in the street or a town hall. It received national media attention. Subsequent experience with forums for participatory technology assessment confirms that in the absence of a legitimizing stage for the deliberations, public interest in them declines (Whiteside 2003a).

Finally, the citizens' recommendations become part of the public record and are delivered to the parliament. Critics can then seize on citizen proposals that the government ignores and take advantage of their quasilegitimacy to press the government to reconsider. In Denmark, surveys show that members of parliament are interested in consensus conferences—some even attend. There is evidence that subsequent legislation has been affected by the citizens' recommendations (Joss 1998; Sclove and Scammell 1999, 263).

Proposals coming out of consensus conferences have been more precautionary than those generated by the normal regulatory process, without being far-fetched or utopian. Fears that an irrational public might end up endorsing simplistic solutions like outright bans on broad categories of new technologies have not materialized. Germany convened citizen panels in the early 1990s to discuss how to reduce carbon dioxide emissions. The citizens' consensual solution consisted of measures designed to increase energy efficiency such as decreasing fuel consumption by motor vehicles, new standards for insulating and heating buildings, and expansion of renewable energy sources. Citizens helped identify policies that were not only economically and technically feasible but would also enjoy broad popular support (Hörning 1999, 355). The recommendations coming out of France's 1998 citizens' conference on GMOs were quite pragmatic. The citizens called for a clear labeling and separate handling of GMO-containing products—but not for a general moratorium on GMOs. They agreed that in evaluating GMO safety, "it is appropriate to decide on a case-by-case basis" (cited in Le Déaut 1998, 106). They also suggested several modifications of the biotechnology oversight board (CGB), requiring, for instance, that its members reveal their financial and contractual links to outside interests. Meanwhile, France was urged to step up its research efforts, both to develop GMOs and to give it some independence in understanding how to manage them and evaluate their safety. Similarly measured ideas emerged from France's 2002 "public debate" on the field testing of GMOs. Citizens recommended not forbidding open-air experiments but allowing them to proceed only if covered by insurance (Babusiaux et al. 2002, 30–31).

The importance of the consensus conference model is that it presents a well-developed example of deliberative precaution, without suggesting that science can be democratized from one end to the other. Nor does it suppose that the purpose of participatory methods is primarily to oblige decision makers to deal with diffuse cultural understandings of environmental phenomena. Consensus conferences have a more limited function—one that corresponds to the objectives of consequentialist precaution. Consensus conferences can be convened to debate specific, potentially dangerous technologies or environmental trends. Especially significant from a precautionary point of view is that they have the advantage of timeliness. They can be convened at an early stage in the development of a technology—even earlier than the moment when an agency such as the Office of Technology Assessment can issue a report (Sclove and Scammell 1999, 262). Furthermore, they work at augmenting the public understanding of complex phenomena rather than accepting prejudices about laypeople's inability to follow scientific debate. They can be structured to give citizens opportunities to probe the sources of uncertainty in expert testimony. Consensus conferences stimulate public discussion and encourage society as a whole to remain alert to weak signals of environmental degradation.

Still, it would be rash to maintain that consensus conferences are *the* ultimate realization of democratized precaution. Such events are necessarily exceptional. Convened too frequently, they would lose their ability to stimulate broad public discussion. Moreover, for practical reasons, they can fall short of an ideal of the unimpeded discussion of a risk issue. One observer of a consensus conference on biotechnology in Great Britain noted how the introductory speakers framed the event as an opportunity to overcome a deficit of public understanding—not as an occasion when public representatives might expose gaps in expert knowledge (Purdue 1996). Social movements were treated prejudicially as pressure groups rather than more neutrally as NGOs. A study of a consensus conference in New Zealand likewise found that rules designed to guarantee well-informed debate instead ended up turning panelists into passive recipients of expert knowledge (Goven 2002). While various reforms might mitigate some of these problems, their tenacity probably indicates something important about the complementarity of deliberative and pluralist models of democracy.[6]

The type of adversarial confrontation that occurs in the institutions of pluralist democracy is desirable in its own right. It is not merely a second-best, pragmatic substitute for a consensus-oriented deliberative ideal. There are good reasons to have well-organized groups that elaborate their own ethically charged points of view independently of rules designed to minimize conflict. The undiluted strength of their passions can be crucial to uncovering uncomfortable truths that relentlessly "realistic" societies prefer to deny. It is desirable for legislators to draw on multiple forms of expertise, not merely to listen to interest groups and opinionated constituents. No advocate of deliberative precaution should forget the critical role of expert groups like the Intergovernmental Panel on Climate Change—not the general public—in sounding the alarm over global warming.

It is equally true that the clash of adversaries and the consultation of experts are by themselves inadequate substitutes for the ideal of deliberative democracy. For if the economic resources available to various competing groups are grossly unequal, pluralism will tend to validate existing power structures, not challenge the sources of unwanted risk. Where competing groups see politics simply as a field of competition for resources, strategic calculation will take the place of true deliberation about the common good. If representative institutions depend on scientific experts who underestimate the role of social values and general convictions in their testimony about the behavior of natural phenomena, their advice may illegitimately rule out alternative policies that would have been safer.

In other words, even where the institutions of pluralist democracy go unchanged, their legitimacy is inseparable from their ability to live up to consequentialist standards whose features are associated with deliberative democracy. Pluralism loses its luster if it is seen to foster partiality and the systematic distortion of knowledge rather than a respect for truth. The case for competitive, representative politics must in the final analysis rest on its ability genuinely to secure the long-term welfare of the polity, not just to pick winners who manage to delay effective policy from one electoral cycle to the next. Nor will pluralist democracy hold much attraction in the long run if political competition within nation-states leads them to despoil the global environment because the most "rational" strategy for "solving" environmental problems is to displace them onto others. It is only by infusing pluralist democracy with deliberative ideals that we can hope to mobilize the forces of vigilance, skepticism, and public concern to genuine precautionary effect.

Conclusion: Precaution and Environmental Social Learning

In the first half of the twentieth century, a small set of widely shared assumptions kept environmental issues largely out of the political limelight. The belief that environmental degradation, when it occurred, was essentially local and that technological advances would permit us to cope with damages before they became too serious implied that preventive action was superfluous (deFur 1999, 341). It was thought that the current state of scientific knowledge generally sufficed to indicate when regulation was necessary. Nothing like the precautionary principle seemed remotely necessary as long as it was assumed that the environment had a virtually inexhaustible capacity for self-renewal by the processes of assimilation and dispersal.

Soaring rates of economic growth and rapid technological innovation in the 1950s and 1960s brought with them an awareness that human activity could have broad, lasting, and unanticipated detrimental effects on the global environment. The open-air testing of nuclear weapons in the 1950s was revealed to spread dangerous levels of radioactive pollution throughout the Northern Hemisphere. Early warnings that greenhouse gas emissions might provoke climate change date from those years as well. In 1962, Rachel Carson published *Silent Spring,* tracing the connection between the wide use of the pesticide DDT and declining avian populations. Even at low concentrations, this chemical had surprising hormonal effects in birds, decreasing the thickness of their eggshells. Evidence emerged over the next twenty years that persistent toxic chemicals such as dioxins and PCBs spread around the globe and could harm many living creatures, including humans, at extremely low exposure levels.

Meanwhile, the more obvious, cumulative effects of environmental degradation were also making themselves felt. By the late 1960s, the pollution was so severe in Lake Erie that few fish could survive there. In Europe in the 1970s, unanticipated eutrophication and declining fish stocks in the North Sea as well as the withering of forests in Germany provoked an increasing awareness that existing regulations were based on incomplete scientific understandings of ecosystem dynamics. In Europe and the United States, collective experiences in managing pesticides, power-plant emissions, and marine pollution suggested that conventional methods of risk assessment and risk management came up short. Environmental policies that aimed primarily at pollution control—that is, at managing the waste products once they had been generated—increasingly showed themselves inadequate to the task of avoiding serious problems before long-term environmental damage set in (Gottlieb and Smith 1995, 12).

To make good this regulatory deficiency, precautionary decisions began to be taken. Their premises first appeared anonymously in health and environmental regulations in the United States. The principle was finally given a name in Germany. There, Vorsorge was transformed into a general rule for achieving heightened environmental protection. In the 1980s and 1990s, the precautionary principle spread throughout Europe. In the last decade of the twentieth century, nations around the world agreed to use the principle as the basis for settling cases of international environmental degradation where the scientific evidence is incomplete or disputed (Trouwborst 2000). By the year 2000, the precautionary principle had made its way into some sixteen international treaties and documents.[1]

The emergence of the precautionary principle is a classic example of social learning in environmental affairs. Social learning refers to the process by which whole communities, not just individuals, draw lessons from their experiences of success and failure in dealing with challenges, gradually developing their level of moral insight and practical skill. Societies, like individuals, are capable of evolving more sophisticated means of cognition and more rationally defensible rules of social interaction (Habermas 1979, 121–122). The precautionary principle springs from the realization that existing levels of scientific understanding are not always sufficient to allow societies to devise effective, timely strategies for environmental protection. Requiring high levels of scientific proof before acting is in certain cases an *irrational* strategy. Reason—drawing its lessons from experience with long-term, large-scale, cumulative environmental problems—requires prevention rather than after-the-fact reaction. Precaution is a corrective factor built into our societies' means of environmental cognition.

To call precaution rational, moreover, is to assert that it expresses a convincing logic, one that appeals to rational agents generally. No nation alone will be able to control climate change. None will be able to protect its agriculture from a biotechnology experiment gone wrong. In the case of environmental dangers that are serious and irreversible, where an insistence on unchallengeable scientific evidence would delay preventive action past the point where it could be effective, every nation has an interest in finding just directing principles around which a large consensus for precautionary measures could form. The history of the precautionary principle illustrates how rules of social interaction fall increasingly under expectations that they be argued from a universal point of view. We settle conflicts by agreeing to abide by rules that hold all parties equally accountable for their actions. Just as the international recognition of basic human rights represents an advance in humanity's ability to abide by norms of reciprocal accountability, so the precautionary principle reflects an advance in our collective will to make our technological power consistent with ecological well-being.

Social learning on this scale is not a smooth march toward the right and the good. It is a messy, lurching process. The history of human rights since the eighteenth century confirms this. No one should forget that the United Nation's Universal Declaration of Human Rights followed on the Holocaust. Progress does occur; universal recognition does grow. But it does so through crisis, confrontation, backtracking, and the reformulation of principles.

It is in this light that the Bush administration's frontal opposition to the precautionary principle should be seen. That opposition should not be allowed to obscure the advance of precautionary reasoning in the United States. Surveys in the 1990s found Americans worried by global warming and inclined to think that their government should take preventive measures—even before evidence of the danger becomes definitive (Kempton, Boster, and Hartley 1996, 129). Regarding GMOs, Americans are barely aware how pervasive they have become on supermarket shelves. But in a Pew Initiative (2003) survey, 89 percent of the respondents declared that GM foods should not be authorized for sale until the FDA checks their safety. Accordingly, the Clinton administration, with its famously acute ear for public opinion, took nuanced policy positions on precautionary issues. Even as it challenged Europe's ban on importing hormone-treated beef, even as it promoted GMOs, that administration never systematically opposed the precautionary principle. It participated in the development of the Kyoto Protocol on global warming and it finally accepted including the precautionary principle in the Montreal biosecurity protocol in 2000 (Pollack and Shaffer 2000). Toward the end of his tenure, U.S. Secretary of Agriculture Dan Glickman significantly softened his position on applying the precautionary principle to GMOs (Bush's Conservative Team 2000). Even under the administration of George W. Bush, U.S. policy on GMOs has changed—partly as a result of the European unwillingness to import transgenic crops. In 2004, the USDA announced that henceforth, it will examine the possible effects of transgenic crops on the environment, human health, and livestock, not just on plants and insects (USDA to Overhaul GM Regulations 2004). The United States tacitly concedes that its testing of GM crops has been too limited. A new, tiered system of regulations in which some GMOs (those with pharmaceutical or industrial traits) are held to more stringent standards than others is precautionary in everything but the name.

Precaution's name recognition is growing in the United States, too. At the Wingspread Conference, held in Racine, Wisconsin, in January 1998, thirty-two participants—academics, activists, politicians, and others (including some with direct experience with Germany's Vorsorgeprinzip)—put together a declaration calling for implementing the precautionary principle (Raffensperger and Tickner 1999, 349–355). The Wingspread statement embroidered on earlier versions of the principle by emphasizing alternatives assessment and including more democratic structures in environmental decision making (Tickner 2003a, 266). This statement is now regularly referenced in U.S. discussions of precaution. Its conclusions are relayed nationwide by the Science and Environmental Health Network.[2]

Perhaps the most powerful evidence indicating precaution's positive prospects in the United States is the increasing frequency with which the principle is being put forth to guide environmental policy—especially at subfederal governmental levels. As Carolyn Raffensperger and Joel Tickner (1999, 7) report:

> On the state level, at least 25 states have established some type of pollution prevention legislation. California passed Proposition 65, which requires companies and other establishments to label any products that contain substances that could cause cancer or developmental harm. . . . [The Commonwealth of Massachusetts's] Toxics Use Reduction Act requires firms using certain toxic chemicals to identify alternatives to reduce or eliminate their use.

Local governments have followed suit. In June 2003, the city of San Francisco adopted the precautionary principle across the board in its decision making. From transportation to health care to energy policies, this ordinance mandates the assessment of available alternatives, using the best science available, in order to select the one that "presents the least potential threat to human health and the City's natural systems."[3] This duty applies all the way down to city employees making purchasing decisions about janitorial equipment and pesticides. Other local governments that have incorporated the precautionary principle in at least some of their management policies, or are studying doing so, include: Seattle, Washington; Multnomah County, Oregon; Marin County, California; and the Los Angeles County Unified School District (Franzen and Fowler 2004). The Environmental Health Alliance, a coalition of 160 groups, has launched a campaign to change regulations governing the use and disposal of toxic chemicals. As a result, "local jurisdictions in Massachusetts and Maine . . . have passed ordinances banning pesticide use in schools unless deemed absolutely essential" (Baker 2003). All of these developments bring to mind what Sheila Jasanoff (2003, 236) calls the U.S. "precautionary ideal," in which precaution is expressed through notions like the duty of care (to avoid negligence), rationality (to avoid arbitrary decision making), and accountability.

As one would expect in a conflictual learning process, European formulations of the precautionary principle owe something to the U.S. experience as well. It should be remembered that Europeans were partly inspired by the USDA when they created a new European Food Authority. Danish consensus conferences were originally patterned on a U.S. model for consulting physicians about the best medical practices. Moreover, diplomatic dustups with the United States played a role in getting the European Commission to clarify the implications of the precautionary principle. Europeans now routinely include increased scientific study among the precautionary measures to be taken in cases of poorly understood environmental risks. In addition, they recognize the need to evaluate the relative costs of whatever measures are taken. The European Commission's 2000 statement takes pains to ensure that the precautionary principle is not applied in ways that are arbitrary or discriminatory. These commitments respond to U.S. qualms and have drawn (cautious) compliments from U.S. observers (Graham 2002; Wiener and Rogers 2002, 343; Pollack and

Shaffer 2001). In a conflictual learning process, criticisms of the precautionary principle are not simply external to the evolution of the principle itself. They probe and test its application. As a consequence, the principle is made more reasonable and acceptable to all parties whose interests are at stake.

This story of halting social learning says two important things about the precautionary principle. First, in spite of talk of *the* precautionary principle, there is no perfect statement of the principle already out there, just waiting to be found. We are not awaiting some green Moses to lace up his hiking boots, ascend Mount Sinai, and rappel back down with divinely inscribed tablets of environmental law. The precautionary principle is a pragmatically evolving, human principle, born of modern societies' reflections on the nature of new risks. Any particular formulation of it is an attempt to express both as generally and concisely as possible all the considerations pertinent to an extremely complex risk-management situation. It does have certain invariant features. It references the potential for harm to persons and the environment, scientific uncertainty about those harms, and taking anticipatory action. But other considerations like the proportionality and revisability of precautionary measures represent real concerns about the range of measures that can reasonably be allowed to count as precautionary.[4] It is no wonder that there are many different versions of the precautionary principle.

Second, it is important to realize—as U.S. critics too rarely do—that the precautionary principle will never be just a juridical formula, twenty or thirty words long. It is a commitment to develop a wide array of prospective procedures, institutions, and social practices, all of which work together to make societies more responsible in relation to long-term, large-scale, uncertain risks. These range from setting up more comprehensive forms of environmental monitoring to shifting the burden of proof in establishing the safety of a product. They include alternatives assessment as well as new forms of public involvement in risk-regulation decisions.

This ensemble of implications is what makes it appropriate to say that the precautionary *principle* shades off into precautionary *politics*. Precaution is not just for judges, legislators, or policy analysts. It demands new linkages between scientists and laypeople, between political representatives, NGOs, and businesses. The precautionary principle touches the distribution and legitimation of regulatory power throughout society. It affects products that are available in the market and how they are presented. It affects opportunities for citizen consultation. And it affects the allocation of resources for scientific research and how that research is organized. Precaution invokes politics in the noble sense of the term—politics understood as a broadly inclusive, deliberatively engaged activity on behalf of the well-being of the whole community.

This notion of politics is the opposite of that intended by a U.S. official who grumbled, "The precautionary principle . . . substitutes politics for science" (Hegwood 2002). In this perspective, politics is a pejorative term. It signifies decisions dictated by power, not reason. It suggests sordid deal making, catering to partial interests, bureaucratic interference in the sphere of personal choice, and shameless electioneering. From this pejorative notion of politics follow all the charges that the precautionary principle promotes self-defeating safety regulations and disguises protectionist trade policies. Critics claim that only with objective science, quantitative social analysis, and "insulated" decision making can regulatory policy be lifted above politics.

That claim is illusory. In practice, the critics' proposals are no less political than precautionary regulations. There is politics at work when science-based policies are shaped behind closed doors by industrial lobbyists, as in the case of transgenic crop regulations. There is politics when the U.S. Congress mandates research on the consequences of climate change, yet the executive branch fails to follow through with timely studies on the impacts on agriculture, energy, water resources, and biodiversity (Climate Research Faulted 2005). When regulators expressly forbid testing beef for mad cow disease, out of fear that one company's BSE-free labels would hurt the reputation of the rest of the beef industry, that is politics. There is politics at work when U.S. administrations press for science-based risk assessment at an international level, knowing that they represent an economy whose comparative advantage comes from rapid technological innovation and high levels of energy consumption. And no one should ignore that cost-benefit analysis has been part of an antiregulatory political agenda precisely because its cumbersome procedures *slow down* the regulatory process (Ward 1999). Science-based risk assessment does not eliminate politics; it does, however, hide it. That way, decisions can be left to experts, elites, and powerful interest groups.

We do well to understand that *all* risk management is political. Becoming aware of its political character strips away one of the key rhetorical gambits by which partisans of cost-benefit analysis belittle alternative ways of thinking about regulatory action. If all risk management is political, then the debate over the precautionary principle is not between science/knowledge/objectivity, on the one side, and opinion/power/partiality, on the other. It is between competing interpretations of the past and competing political visions of the future.

To get at this political vision, people owe it to themselves and future generations to ask a broad question: What should we learn from the successes and failures of environmental policy in the twentieth century? Is the lesson that governments have regulated too often? Have governments targeted insignificant risks while ignoring major ones? Have they lavished too much money on cleanup and kept consumption levels too low? Or have they foolishly restrained technological innovation and taken away entrepreneurial liberty? Are those really the things that have gone wrong in our world? If so, then a particular vision of what humanity needs now follows suit. We need less regulation and less public influence in establishing government priorities, and more commerce, more consumption, and the more rapid introduction of world-transforming technologies.

This political vision is identical with what German social theorist Jürgen Habermas (1987) calls one-sided rationalization. It assumes that the ultimate role of the modern state is to foster prosperity. Economic growth requires stimulating investment and consumption. Regulation seeks to stabilize the market economy and, in general, favor capital accumulation. In economic reasoning and political strategizing, private interests are given pride of place. At the same time, values that would make society more multidimensional—values pertaining to a more just distribution of goods, protecting nature, enhancing people's capacity for aesthetic appreciation, and developing active citizens—are given less and less significance. Scientific advising is integrated into this one-sided system. Demands for the expert evaluation of social choices effectively delegitimate citizen deliberation. This helps insulate the state from public demands, thus abetting its mission of serving the private interests that are the motor of the economy (Zeitlin 1980, 27–28).

For environmentalists, that vision is a formula for disaster. The closing years of the twentieth century saw increasing evidence of looming catastrophe from global warming, the worldwide environmental diffusion of synthetic organic compounds, and the unprecedented destruction of biodiversity. Nonetheless, international efforts to avert catastrophe have been timid and largely ineffectual (Speth 2004). Understanding what does not work in the current modes of social organization leads to demands for adjustment and adaptation. In the words of Dominique Dron (2000, 113), "The precautionary principle should be analyzed as the collectivity's call for control over its own ends." That control is precautionary politics.

Politics, as Aristotle taught, concerns how a community organizes itself to arbitrate among all the activities that take place within it. Politics is distorted when it is subordinated to any of the other practices—economic, scientific, religious, or expressive—in which its citizens engage. For politics is what establishes the mutually acceptable terms under which all of these practices take place, such that they can coexist in ways consistent with the highest purposes of the whole community. In its deliberative form, precaution means that the community seeks to make science and technology compatible with its highest purposes. Citizens are given an opportunity to reflect on whether they really wish to take the risks that some experiments will impose on them all. With precaution, society resumes a measure of control over the purposes of economic growth. Production must be made compatible with sustainable development by refraining from causing irreversible environmental harm (Zuindeau 1997, 196–197; Dobson 1996, 414).

Most important, the precautionary principle reflects the realization that the whole community now embraces not only fellow citizens in one's own nation-state but also people across the globe and their successor generations. Precautionary politics means that we must take responsibility for maintaining the robustness of the intricately interconnected ecological systems that sustain life on this entire planet—even when we are far from understanding all the conditions that make them thrive. Never before has so much wisdom been required of humanity's slowly advancing capacity for political association.

Notes

Introduction

1. United Nations Environment Programme (UNEP) 1992. Rio declaration on environment and development, Principle 15. Declaration made at the United Nations Conference on Environment and Development, Rio de Janeiro, Brazil, June 14.

2. Sandin (1999) canvases nineteen different versions of the precautionary principle. See also various formulations in Godard (1997a, 37–84) and Raffensperger and Tickner (1999, 256–261).

3. Readers interested less in the underpinnings of the precautionary principle than in the variety of circumstances in which it can be used should consult Raffensperger and Tickner (1999), Tickner (2003b), O'Riordan and Cameron (1994), and European Environment Agency (2001).

Chapter 1

1. Mellon is the director of the Union of Concerned Scientists' agriculture and biotechnology program; Rissler worked at the Environmental Protection Agency (EPA) on biotechnology policies and has a PhD in plant pathology from Cornell University.

2. Here is a not untypical answer from one survey: "I am against [biotechnologies]. We should leave things as they are. You must not upset nature. It gets its revenge." See Cheveigné, Boy, and Galloux (2000, 167–171).

3. The exceptions stem from bacteria or virus-mediated gene flow, mutations, and selective breeding by humans. None of these remotely approximates the speed or species-crossing practice of genetic engineering.

4. See Deborah Whitman, "Genetically Modified Foods: Harmful or Helpful," <http://www.csa.com/hottopics/gmfood/overview/php>. "A GM plant does not require a permit if it meets these 6 criteria: 1) the plant is not a noxious weed; 2) the genetic material introduced into the GM plant is stably integrated into the plant's own genome; 3) the function of the introduced gene is known and does not cause plant disease; 4) the GM plant is not toxic to non-target organisms; 5) the

introduced gene will not cause the creation of new plant viruses; and 6) the GM plant cannot contain genetic material from animal or human pathogens (see <http://www.aphis.usda.gov:80/bbep/bp/7cfr340>)."

5. The Clinton administration was virtually as anxious to foster biotechnology as its predecessors. Procedures for field testing GMOs and approving bioengineered foods were simplified, while an EPA proposal for stricter regulation of pesticide-producing transgenic crops was defeated in Congress.

6. France's request had to go through an additional round of expert investigations after objections from the British government concerning the antibiotic marker. See Roy (2001, 17).

7. This language was inserted into Article 130R of the Treaty of Rome (Gossement 2003, 85).

8. Originally, the CGB was comprised of ten scientists, two representatives of industry, one lawyer, one representative of consumer interests, and one labor representative. In 1996, its composition was enlarged and redistributed. It now includes eleven scientists/biologists/doctors and eight nonscientists (representatives of consumer associations, environmental protection associations, professional agricultural societies, unions, owners groups, and one lawyer).

9. The panel's conclusions are published as an annex titled "Conférence de Citoyens sur l'utilisation des OGM en agriculture et dans l'alimentation" in the report of the Office parlementaire d'évaluation des choix scientifiques et technologiques on GMOs. See Le Déaut (1998, 105–117).

Chapter 2

1. For a powerful critique of cost-benefit methods applied to climate change, see Kysar (2004).

2. That new environmental problems undermine the governmental and insurance industry methods of risk calculation is an important part of Ulrich Beck's (1995, 20–26) famous "risk society" thesis.

3. For empirical evidence relating to this preference, see Kirsch, Nijkamp, and Zimmermann (1988).

4. A belief in the earth's resilience is a feature of the particular type of environmental discourse that John Dryzek (1997, 58) calls "Promethean."

Chapter 3

1. For a discussion of the contents of the Cartagena Protocol, see Falkner (2001).

2. The European Food Authority, however, unlike the USDA, cannot issue food safety regulations; "risk management" remains under the purview of various EU political bodies.

3. *Reserve Mining v. EPA,* reversed by 514 F.2d 492 (8th Cir. 1975) (en banc), cited in Bodansky (1994, 208).

4. The law's more general precautionary provisions concerning food additives remain in force.

5. In the United States, lawsuits against the asbestos industry began in the early 1960s. They pushed the EPA to regulate asbestos starting in 1976. In France, asbestos policy was handled in a much more closed, corporatist fashion up until the mid-1990s. At that time, a change in the French penal code facilitated bringing lawsuits. Lawsuits, victims' associations, and journalists finally forced the issue into the open, and asbestos was banned at the beginning of 1997. See Vogel and Bensedrine (2002, 14–17).

6. This paragraph summarizes information found in Dormont and Hermitte (1999) and European Environment Agency (2001, 157–167).

7. "Die Bundesregierung leitet aus dem Prinzip der Unweltvorsorge das Gebot der Minimierung von Risiken ab" (*Leitlinien der Bundesregierung zur Unweltvorsorge durch Vermeidung and stufenweise Verminderung von Schadstoffen,* BT Drs. 10?5028 [19.09.86] B.II. 1b).

8. On the European side, see Larrère and Larrère (1997, 235ff), Bourg and Schlegel (2001, 167–168); Callon, Lascoumes, and Barthe (2001, 274); Cheveigné, Boy, and Galloux (2000, 189); Lepage and Guery (2001, 118–123); Ewald (1997, 119); Lecourt (1990, 168). Meanwhile, in English, Jonas's ideas are entirely absent from seminal essays like Cameron and Abouchar (1991) and O'Riordan and Jordan (1995). Nor are traces of his work to be found in Goklany (2001) or Sunstein (2005). Jonas merits just one passing reference in a recent collection of essays (Tickner 2003b, 297).

9. European law arguably contains some earlier precedents for precaution, but the formulations are less precise. See Bechmann and Mansuy (2002, 7).

10. Ministerial Declaration, Second International Conference on the Protection of the North Sea, London, November 24–25, 1987.

11. "Community policy in the environmental domain . . . is founded on the principles of precaution and of preventive action" (Article 174, paragraph 2, Treaty of the European Union).

12. See also Attfield (2003, 145); Lepage and Guery (2001, 109).

13. Nonetheless the communication has critics among both skeptics and defenders of the precautionary principle. Skeptics (Majone 2002; Scott and Vos 2002) question whether the commission's criteria are really clear enough to regularize the implementation of the precautionary principle. They complain of the discretion that the European Commission retains to decide for itself the right level of protection for European citizens. They are suspicious of allowing the "public acceptability" of products and practices to count in the determination of risk. They repeat the standard charge that principled precaution ignores the opportunity costs of stalling technological advance. On the other hand, a consistent defender of the precautionary principle, Joel Tickner (2000), faults the commission's communication for making the principle only one tool in risk management rather than its "overall guide." A particular failing of the communication is the absence of any requirement for alternatives assessment prior to initiating potentially harmful activities.

Chapter 4

1. For related criticisms, see Duclos (1993, 194–200); Caillé (2001, 111, 113).

2. With his usual iconoclasm, Latour (2000a, 342) virtually admits this: "I believe . . . that, in spite of appearances, the precautionary principle has little to do with risks, danger, or random factors."

3. One more measure of the remaining distance between the United States and Europe over precaution is that U.S. courts tend to frown on the use of broad categories in regulating chemicals. Instead, "substantial evidence" of a particular chemical's potential to create an environmental or health hazard must be shown before it can be regulated. See Applegate (2000, 431).

4. Stirling is a professor at the Science and Technology Policy Research Center at the University of Sussex.

Chapter 5

1. Defenders of science-based risk assessment generally allow for social scientific ways of counting public opinion: surveys, polls, economic studies of consumers' "willingness to pay" for various goods. These methods treat people's views not as arguments but as quantifiable objects. In this way, however, they give no recognition to the fact that some views have more rational force than others or that people may modify their views as a result of deliberative engagement.

2. Although they mention how "the quality and reliability of knowledge can be improved through a deliberative process," most of their reasoning pertains to matters of legitimacy and trust.

3. For an example of local ecological knowledge affecting an oil pipeline proposal, see Sclove (1995a, 49).

4. The French government reversed this policy in 2001, under pressure from environmental organizations (La justice 2001).

5. Sclove is the executive director of the LoKa Institute, a research and advocacy organization dedicated to making science and technology development responsive to democratically decided social and environmental concerns (see <http://www.loka.org>). Sclove's argument in *Democracy and Technology* (1995a) is considerably broader than my case for a consequentialist democratic precaution. He contends that because technologies structure social relations, citizens must be empowered to evaluate them. This argument appeals most often to the prior, legitimating grounds of democratic decision making. In a later essay with Madeleine Scammell (1999) Sclove relates his ideas more systematically to the precautionary *effects* of public involvement in technological decision making.

6. The political significance of consensus conferences could be increased if parliament were required to debate the citizens' conclusions. Instructions to the participants could be changed in ways that highlighted their role as questioners, not merely as learners. More open-ended, less structured forums for public discussion might be tried. After holding its consensus conference on GM crops, the French

government then held an "Estates-general on food" and a "public debate" on the open-air testing of GMOs. These arenas allowed for much larger numbers of citizens to participate and engage in ethical debate. See Whiteside (2003a).

Conclusion

1. See Carolyn Raffensperger's compilation at <http:// www.biotech-info.net/ treaties_and_agreements.html>.

2. See <http://www.sehn.org/precaution.html>.

3. San Francisco Precautionary Principle Ordinance, section 101. See <http:// temp.sfgov.org/sfenvironment/aboutus/innovative/pp/sfpp.htm>; see also LaFranchi (2005, 716–720).

4. In the version that France added to its constitution in February 2005 (in Berger 2005, 3), it is specified that the precautionary principle calls for "provisional and proportionate measures . . . to prevent damage." These specifications answer critics who feared that precautionary policies might be invoked to stifle all innovation. They establish that precaution does not simply stop action; it requires efforts to *calibrate* policy more carefully to possible dangers. It also urges the adoption of measures that can be *revised* as careful testing and experience confirm or disconfirm hypotheses about harm.

References

Alerte au soja fou. 1996. *Libération,* November 1, p. 1.

Anderson, Ida-Elisabeth, and Birgit Jaeger. 1999. Scenario Workshops and Consensus Conferences: Towards More Democratic Decision-Making. *Science and Public Policy* (October): 331–340.

Applegate, John S. 2000. The Precautionary Preference: An American Perspective on the Precautionary Principle. *Human and Ecological Risk Assessment* 6, no. 3:413–443.

Arendt, Hannah. 1959. *The Human Condition.* New York: Anchor Books.

Attfield, Robin. 2003. *Environmental Ethics.* Cambridge, UK: Polity Press.

Babusiaux, Christian, Jean-Yves LeDéaut, Didier Sicard, and Jacques Testart. 2002. *Rapport à la suite du débat sur les OGM et les essais au champ.* Paris: Ministère de l'Agriculture et de la Pêche and Ministère de l'Aménagement du Territoire et de l'Environnement.

Baghestani-Perrey, Laurence. 1997. Le principe de précaution: Nouveau principe fondemental régissant les rapports entre le droit et la science. *Recueil Dalloz* 41:457–462.

Baker, Linda. 2003. Lois Gibbs' Campaign Urges Caution on Toxic Chemicals. *E/The Environmental Magazine* 14, no. 4. <http://www.emagazine.com/view/?376&src=>.

Barred from Testing for Mad Cow, Niche Meatpacker Loses Clients. 2004. *New York Times,* April 18, p. A14.

Barrett, Katherine, and Carolyn Raffensperger. 1999. Precautionary Science. In *Protecting Public Health and the Environment: Implementing the Precautionary Principle,* ed. Carolyn Raffensperger and Joel Tickner. Washington, DC: Island Press.

Barry, John. 1999. *Rethinking Green Politics.* Thousand Oaks, CA: Sage.

Bauer, Martin, John Durant, and George Gaskell. 1998. *Biotechnology in the Public Sphere: A Comparative Review.* London: Science Museum.

Bechmann, Pierre, and Véronique Mansuy. 2002. *Le principe de précaution: Environnement, santé et sécurité alimentaire.* Éditions du Juris Classeur.

Beck, Ulrich. 1992a. From Industrial Society to Risk Society. In *Cultural Theory and Cultural Change,* ed. Mike Featherstone. Thousand Oaks, CA: Sage.

Beck, Ulrich. 1992b. *Risk Society: Towards a New Modernity.* Thousand Oaks, CA: Sage.

Beck, Ulrich. 1995. *Ecological Enlightenment: Essays on the Politics of the Risk Society.* Atlantic Highlands, NJ: Humanities Press.

Beck, Ulrich. 1996. Risk Society and the Provident State. In *Risk, Environment, and Modernity: Towards a New Ecology,* ed. Scott Lash, Bronislaw Szerszynski, and Brian Wynne. Thousand Oaks, CA: Sage.

Belpomme, Dominique. 2003. *Ces maladies créées par l'homme.* Paris: Albin Michel.

Berger, Blandine. 2005. Du discours au texte: de la méthode d'élaboration de la Charte de l'environnement. *Gazette du palais* (March 19): 2–3.

Bernstein, Steven. 2002. Liberal Environmentalism and Global Environmental Governance. *Global Environmental Politics* 2, no. 3 (August): 1–16.

Bijker, Wiebe. 1997. Démocratisation de la culture technologique. *Revue Nouvelle* 106, no. 9:37–47.

Bodansky, Daniel. 1994. The Precautionary Principle in U.S. Environmental Law. In *Interpreting the Precautionary Principle,* ed. Tim O'Riordan and James Cameron. London: Earthscan.

Boehmer-Christiansen, Sonja. 1994. The Precautionary Principle in Germany: Enabling Government. In *Interpreting the Precautionary Principle,* ed. Tim O'Riordan and James Cameron. London: Earthscan.

Bourg, Dominique. 1996. *Les scénarios de l'écologie.* Paris: Hachette.

Bourg, Dominique. 1998. *Planète sous contrôle.* Paris: Les Éditions Textuel.

Bourg, Dominique, and Daniel Boy. 2005. *Conférences de citoyens, mode d'emploi.* Paris: Éditions Charles Léopold Mayer.

Bourg, Dominique, and Jean-Louis Schlegel. 2001. *Parer aux risques de demain: Le principe de précaution.* Paris: Seuil.

Bourg, Dominique, and Kerry H. Whiteside. 2003. Précaution: Un principe problématique mais nécessaire. *Le Débat* 129 (March–April): 153–174.

Boy, Daniel. 1999. Politiques de la science et de la démocratie scientifique. *Revue Internationale de Politique Comparée* 6, no. 3 (Winter): 613–625.

Boy, Daniel. 2001. Les nouveaux modes de délibération publique. *Risques* 47:110–114.

Boy, Daniel, Dominique Donnet-Kamel, and Philippe Roqueplo. 2000. Un exemple de la démocratie délibérative: la conférence française de citoyens sur l'usage des organismes génétiquement modifiés en agriculture et en alimentation. *Revue française de science politique* 50, no. 4 (August–October): 779–809.

Brave New Farm. 1999. *Time* (January 11): 87.

Bro-Rasmussen, Finn. 2003. Risk, Uncertainties, and Precautions in Chemical Legislation. In *Precaution: Environmental Science and Preventive Public Policy,* ed. Joel Tickner. Washington, DC: Island Press.

Brown, Donald A. 2003. The Precautionary Principle as a Guide to Environmental Impact: Lessons Learned from Global Warming. In *Precaution: Environmental*

Science and Preventive Public Policy, ed. Joel Tickner. Washington, DC: Island Press.

Brulle, Robert J. 2000. *Agency, Democracy, and Nature: The U.S. Environmental Movement from a Critical Theory Perspective.* Cambridge: MIT Press.

Brunel, Sylvie. 2002. OGM et faim dans le monde: pour une charte des aliments essentiels. *Problèmes Économiques* 2.786 (November 27): 28–32.

Bureau, Jean-Christophe, and Stephan Marrette. 2000. Accounting for Consumer Preferences in International Trade Rules. In *Incorporating Science, Economics, and Sociology in Developing Sanitary and Phytosanitary Standards in International Trade,* ed. National Research Council. Washington, DC: National Academies Press.

Bush's Conservative Team Spells Trouble for Europe. 2000. *Independent,* December 24, p. 15

Caillé, Alain. 2001. Une politique de la nature sans politique: A propos des Politiques de la nature de Bruno Latour, *Revue du MAUSS* 17, no. 1:94–116.

Callon, Michel. 1999. Des différentes formes de démocratie technique. *Les Cahiers de la Sécurité Intérieure* 38, no. 4:37–54.

Callon, Michel, Pierre Lascoumes, and Yannick Barthe. 2001. *Agir dans un monde incertain: Essai sur la démocratie technique.* Paris: Seuil.

Cambrosio, Alberto, and Camille Limoges. 1991. Controversies as Governing Processes in Technology Assessment. *Technology Analysis and Strategic Management* 3, no. 4:377–391.

Cameron, James. 1999. The Precautionary Principle. In *Trade, Environment, and the Millennium,* ed. Gary Sampson and W. Bradnee Chambers. New York: United Nations University Press.

Cameron, James, and Julie Abouchar. 1991. The Precautionary Principle: A Fundamental Principle of Law and Policy for the Protection of the Global Environment. *Boston College International and Comparative Law Review* 14, no. 1:1–27.

Canada Stunned as Mad Cow Discovery Leads to Beef Ban. 2003. *Independent* (London) May 24, p. 19.

Can Biotech Crops Be Good Neighbors? 2004c *New York Times,* September 26 (Week in Review), p. 12.

Centre for International Sustainable Development Law. 2002. Legal Brief: Precaution in International Sustainable Development Law. <http://www.cisdl.org>.

Cheveigné, Suzanne de, Daniel Boy, and Jean-Christophe Galloux. 2000. *Les biotechnologies en débat: Pour une démocratie scientifique.* Paris: Balland.

Chine, nouvelle révolution culturelle; OGM. 2002. *Libération,* February 15, p. 24.

Choix technologiques: Comment associer le citoyen? *Les Échos,* November 8.

Christoforou, Theofanis. 2003. The Precautionary Principle in European Community Law and Science. In *Precaution: Environmental Science and Preventive Public Policy,* ed. Joel Tickner. Washington, DC: Island Press.

Climate Research Faulted over Missing Components. 2005. *New York Times,* April 22, p. A20.

Cohn-Bendit, Daniel. 2000. Pour la Troisième Gauche Verte. *Libération,* February 23.

Collier, Christian, Bruno Jullien, and Nicholas Treich. 2000. Scientific Progress and Irreversibility: An Economic Interpretation of the Precautionary Principle. *Journal of Public Economics* 75:229–253.

Collinge, J. 1999. Variant Creutzfeldt-Jakob Disease. *Lancet,* July 24, 317–323.

Colloque de la Villette. 1999. *L'Opinion publique face aux plantes transgéniques: Entre incertitudes et prise de conscience.* Paris: Albin Michel.

Commissariat Général du Plan, Rapport du groupe presidé par Bernard Chevassus-au-Louis. 2001. *OGM et agriculture: options pour l'action publique.* September. La Documentation Française.

Commission européenne. 2000. *Communication de la commission sur le recours au principe de précaution.* Brussels: <europa.eu.int/com/environment/docum/20001_frhtm>.

Commoner, Barry. 2002. Unraveling the DNA Myth. <http://www.mindfully.org/GE/GE4/DNA-Myth-CommonerFeb02.htm>.

Convention on Biological Diversity. 2000. Cartagena Protocol on Biosafety to the Convention on Biological Diversity. <www.biodiv.org/convention/articles.asp>.

Corcelle, Guy. 2001. La perspective communautaire du principe de précaution. *Revue du marché commun et de l'Union Européenne* 7–8:447–454.

Dana, David. 2003. A Behavioral Economic Defense of the Precautionary Principle. 97 *Northwestern University Law Review* 97:1315, 1320–26.

Davidson, Aiden, Ian Barns, and Renato Scibeci. 1997. Problematic Publics: A Critical Review of Surveys of Public Attitudes to Biotechnology. *Science, Technology, and Human Values* 22, no. 3:317–348.

Un débat public sur les plantes transgéniques va être organisé. 1998. *Le Monde,* February 14.

deFur, Peter L. 1999. The Precautionary Principle: Application to Policies regarding Endocrine-Disrupting Chemicals. In *Protecting Public Health and the Environment,* ed. Carol Raffensperger and Joel Tickner. Washington, DC: Island Press.

Delannoi, Gil. 2000. Sagesse, prudence, précaution. *Revue Juridique de l'Environnement,* no. spécial:11–17.

Deléage, Jean-Paul. 1991. *Histoire de l'écologie: une science de l'homme et de la nature.* Paris: La Découverte.

Derboulles, Laurent. 2001. La réception par le parlement français du principe de précaution. *Revue de la recherche juridique et droit prospectif* 26, no. 89:763–796.

Deville, Adrian and Ronnie Harding. 1997. *Applying the Precautionary Principle.* Annandale, Australia: Federation Press.

Dobson, Andrew. 1996. Environment Sustainabilities: An Analysis and a Typology. *Environmental Politics* 5, no. 3:401–428

Dormont, Dominique and Marie-Angèle Hermitte. 1999. Propositions pour le principe de précaution à la lumière de l'affaire de la vache folle. In *Le Principe de Précaution,* ed. Philippe Kourilsky and Geneviève Viney. Paris: Odile Jacob.

Dossier de l'environnement. 1996. Le Courrier de l'environnement de l'INRA. December 12. <http://www.inra.fr/Internet/Produits/dpenv/do12-004.htm>.

Dron, Dominique. 2000. Environnement: Les enjeux du prochain siècle. In *RAMSÈS 2001,* ed. Thierry de Montbrial. Paris: Dunod.

Dryzek, John. 1997. *The Politics of the Earth: Environmental Discourses.* Oxford: Oxford University Press.

Duclos, Denis. 1993. *De la civilité: Comment les sociétés apprivoisent la puissance.* Paris: La Découverte.

Dupuy, Jean-Pierre. 2002. *Pour un catastrophisme éclairé.* Paris: Seuil.

Echols, Marsha. 1998. Food Safety Regulation in the European Union and the United States: Different Cultures, Different Laws. *Columbia Journal of European Law* (Summer): 525–543.

Eckersley, Robyn. 1992. *Environmentalism and Political Theory: Toward an Ecocentric Approach.* Albany: State University of New York Press.

Eckersley, Robyn. 1999. The Discourse Ethic and the Problem of Representing Nature. *Environmental Politics* 8, no. 2:24–49.

Economic Research Service, USDA. 2003. Briefing Room. April 7. <http://www.ers.usda.gov/briefing/AgChemicals>.

Environmental Defense Fund. 2004. Coal-Fired Power Plants are Big Contributors to Sooty Particle Pollution in Eastern States. July 16. <http://www.environmentaldefense.org/article.cfm?ContentID=3842>.

EPA, Industry Will Push to Revise Europe's White Paper Proposal. 2002. *Chemical Week,* March 20: p. 10.

Epstein, Samuel S. 2002. Reversing the Cancer Epidemic. *Tikkun* 17, no. 4:56–61.

EU Fear-Mongers' Lethal Harvest. 2002. *Los Angeles Times,* August 18.

European Environment Agency. 2001. *Late Lessons from Early Warnings: The Precautionary Principle, 1896–2000.* Environmental Issue Report 22, Copenhagen. <http://reports.eea.eu.int/environmental_issue_report_2001_22/en>.

Europe Information Service. 2000. Europolitique: Débats serrés sur le moratoire OGM et la "gouvernance internationale." July 19.

Ewald, François. 1996. Philosophie de la précaution. *L'Année Sociologique* 46, no. 2:383–412.

Ewald, François. 1997. Le retour du malin génie. Esquisse d'une philosophie de la précaution. In *Le Principe de précaution dans la conduite des affaires humaines,* ed. Olivier Godard. Paris: Éditions de la Maison des sciences de l'homme.

Ewald, François, Christian Gollier, and Nicholas de Sadeleer. 2001. *Le Principe de précaution.* Paris: Presses Universitaires de France.

Ewald, François, and Denis Kessler. 2000. Les noces du risque et de la politique. *Le Débat* 3–4, no. 109:55–72.

Ewald, François, and Dominique Lecourt. 2001. Les OGM et les nouveaux vandales. *Le Monde,* September 4, p. 1

Experts: L'impossible indépendance: Collégialité et transparence, gages d'impartialité. 2001. *Les Échos,* April 12, p. 58.

Falkner, Robert. 2001. Genetic Seeds of Discord: The Transatlantic GMO Trade Conflict after the Cartagena Protocol on Biosafety. In *Governing Food: Science, Safety, and Trade,* ed. Peter W. B. Phillips and Robert Wolfe. Montreal: McGill-Queen's University Press.

Faucheux, Sylvie, and Martin O'Connor. 2000. Technosphère vs écosphère: Choix technologiques et menaces environnementales: signaux faibles, controverses et decisions. *futuribles* 251:29–59.

Favret, Jean-Marc. 2001. Le principe de précaution ou la prise en compte par le droit de l'incertitude scientifique et risque virtuel. *Recueil Dalloz* 43:3462–3469.

Federal News Service. 2001. John McLaughlin's "One on One" Guest: EPA Administrator Christine Todd Whitman. August 31.

Ferry, Luc. 1995. *The New Ecological Order.* Chicago: University of Chicago Press.

Fiorino, Daniel J. 1990. Citizen Participation and Environmental Risk: A Survey of Institutional Mechanisms. *Science, Technology, and Human Values* 15, no. 2:226–243.

Fisher, Elizabeth, and Ronnie Harding, 1999. The Precautionary Principle: Towards a Deliberative, Transdisciplinary Problem-Solving Process. In *Perspectives on the Precautionary Principle,* ed. Ronnie Harding and Elizabeth Fisher. Federation Press.

Food and Drug Administration. 1992. *Statement of Policy: Foods Derived from New Plant Varieties.* 57 FR 22984, May 29. Washington, DC: U.S. Dept. of Agriculture.

Food and Drug Administration. 2000. *Precaution in U.S. Food Safety Decision-making: Annex II to the United States' National Food Safety System Paper.* March 3. Washington, DC: U.S. Department of Agriculture. <http://www.foodsafety.gov/~fssyst4.html>.

Franzen, Emily, and Laurie Fowler. 2004. Implementing the Precautionary Principle: A Tool for Georgia's Local Government. <http://www.rivercenter.uga.edu>.

Freestone, David, and Ellen Hey, eds. 1996. *The Precautionary Principle and International Law.* New York: Kluwer Law International.

Gauging GM Risk Proves a Tricky Task. *Financial Times,* October 25, p. 11.

General Accounting Office. 2000. *Environmental Protection Agency: Use of Precautionary Assumptions in Health Risk Assessments and Benefits Estimates.* GAO–01–55. Washington, DC: General Accounting Office.

Genes from Engineered Grass Spread for Miles, Study Finds. 2004. *New York Times,* September 21, p. A1.

Genetic Modification Taints Corn in Mexico. 2001. *New York Times,* October 2, p. F7.

Godard, Olivier. 1997a. L'ambivalence de la précaution et la transformation des rapports entre science et décision. In *Le Principe de précaution dans la conduite des affaires humaines,* ed. Olivier Godard. Paris: Éditions de la Maison des sciences de l'homme.

Godard, Olivier, ed. 1997b. *Le Principe de précaution dans la conduite des affaires humaines.* Paris: Éditions de la Maison des sciences de l'homme.

Godard, Olivier. 1999. De l'usage du principe de précaution en univers controversé. *futuribles* 239–240:37–59.

Godard, Olivier. 2000. Le principe de précaution: Un principe politique de l'action. *Revue Juridique de l'Environnement,* numéro spécial: 127–144.

Godard, Olivier. 2001a. Environnement et commerce international: Le principe de précaution sur la ligne de fracture. *futuribles* 262:37–62.

Godard, Olivier. 2001b. Précaution légitime et proportionnalité. *Risques* 47:95–100.

Goklany, Indur M. 2000. Applying the Precautionary Principle in a Broader Context. In *Rethinking Risk and the Precautionary Principle,* ed. Julian Morris. Oxford: Butterworth-Heinemann.

Goklany, Indur M. 2001. *The Precautionary Principle: A Critical Appraisal of Environmental Risk Assessment.* Washington, DC: Cato Institute.

Gonzalez Vaqué, Luis, Lothar Ehring, and Cyril Jacquet. 1999. Le principe de précaution dans la législation communautaire et nationale rélative à la protection de la santé. *Revue du Marché unique européen* 1:79–128.

Gossement, Arnaud. 2003. *Le principe de precaution: Essai sur l'incidence de l'incertitude scientifique sur la decision et la responsabilité politique.* Paris: L'Harmattan.

Gottlieb, Robert. ed.1995. *Reducing Toxics: A New Approach to Policy and Industrial Decisionmaking.* Washington, DC: Island Press.

Gottlieb, Robert, and Maureen Smith. 1995. The Pollution Control System: Themes and Frameworks. In *Reducing Toxics: A New Approach to Industrial Decisionmaking,* ed. Robert Gottlieb. Washington, DC: Island Press.

Gottlieb, Robert, Maureen Smith, Julie Roque, and Pamela Yates. 1995. New Approaches to Toxics: Production Design, Right-to-Know, and Definition Debates. In *Reducing Toxics: A New Approach to Policy and Industrial Decisionmaking,* ed. Robert Gottlieb. Washington, DC: Island Press.

Gottweis, Herbert. 1998. *Governing Molecules: The Discursive Politics of Genetic Engineering in Europe and the United States.* Cambridge: MIT Press.

Goven, Joanna. 2002. Citizens and Deficits: Problematic Paths toward Participatory Technology Assessment. <http://www.ifz.tu-graz.ac.at/sumacad/02/goven.pdf>.

Government, Chemical Industry Fight EU Proposal on Safety. 2003. Newhouse News Service, June 24, n.p.

Graham, John D. 2002. The Role of Precaution in Risk Assessment and Management: An American's View. January 11–12. <http://www.whitehouse.gov/omb/inforeg/eu_speech.html>.

Graham, John D. 2004. The Perils of the Precautionary Principle: Lessons from the American and European Experience. Heritage lecture, no. 818. January 15. <http://www.heritage.org/Research/Regulation/hl818.cfm>.

Greciano, Philippe. 2001. Sur le principe de précaution en droit communautaire. *Petites affiches* 390, no. 56:4–7.

Green Fades Rapidly to Grey. 2002. *Sunday Tribune* (Dublin), September 1, p. 19.

Guegan, Anne. 2000. L'apport du principe de précaution au droit de la responsabilité civile. *Revue Juridique de l'Environnement* 2:147–178.

Gündling, Lothar. 1990. The Status in International Law of the Principle of Precautionary Action. *International Journal of Estuarine and Coastal Law* 5:23–30.

Habermas, Jürgen. 1979. *Communication and the Evolution of Society.* Boston: Beacon.

Habermas, Jürgen. 1987. *The Theory of Communicative Action, Volume Two: Lifeworld and System: A Critique of Functionalist Reason.* Boston: Beacon.

Hallers-Tjabbes, Cato C. ten. 2003. Science Communication and Precautionary Policy: A Marine Case Study. In *Precaution: Environmental Science and Preventive Public Policy,* ed. Joel Tickner. Washington, DC: Island Press.

Harding, Ronnie, and Elizabeth Fisher. 1999. The Precautionary Principle: Towards a Deliberative, Transdisciplinary Problem-Solving Process. In *Perspectives on the Precautionary Principle,* ed. Ronnie Harding and Elizabeth Fisher. Annandale, Australia: Federation Press.

Hart, Kathleen. 2002. *Eating in the Dark: America's Experiment with Genetically Engineered Food.* New York: Pantheon Books.

Hayward, Tim. 1998. *Political Theory and Ecological Values.* New York: St. Martin's Press.

Hegwood, David. 2002. Confusion on Biotech Affecting Famine, Trade. December 16. <http://www.useu.be/categories/Sustainable%20Development/Dec1602BiotechFamineHegwood.html#remarks>.

Held, David. 2002. Globalization, Corporate Practice, and Cosmopolitan Social Standards. *Contemporary Political Theory* 1, no. 1:59–78.

Hermitte, Marie-Angèle. 1997. Les OGM et la précaution: comme un parfum de nostalgie. In *Génie Génétique: des chercheurs citoyens s'expriment,* ed. Mae-Wantto. Paris: Sang de la terre.

Hermitte, Marie-Angèle, and Christine Noiville. 1993. La dissémination volontaire des organismes génétiquement modifiés dans l'environnement: une première application du principe de prudence. *Revue Juridique de l'environnement* 3:391–418.

Hörning, Georg. 1999. Citizens Panels as a Form of Deliberative Technology Assessment. *Science and Public Policy* 26, no. 5:351–359.

Houdebine, Louis-Marie. 2000. *OGM: Le vrai et le faux.* Paris: Le Pommier-Fayard.

Husset, Marie-Jeanne. 1999. Les citoyens peuvent-ils réellement peser sur la décision: les OGM, un rendez-vous manqué? In *L'Opinion publique face aux plantes transgéniques: Entre incertitudes et prise de conscience,* ed. Colloque de la Villette. Paris: Albin Michel.

International Panel on Climate Change. 2001. *Climate Change 2001: The Scientific Basis.* Cambridge: Cambridge University Press.

International Service for the Acquisition of Agri-biotech Applications. 2004. ISAAA Briefs 32–2004: Preview: Global Status of Commercialized Biotech/GM Crops. <http://www.isaaa.org>.

Jasanoff, Sheila. 1990. *The Fifth Branch: Science Advisers as Policy-Makers.* Cambridge: Harvard University Press.

Jasanoff, Sheila. 1995. Product, Process, or Program: Three Cultures and the Regulation of Biotechnology. In *Resistance to New Technology: Nuclear Power, Information Technology, and Biotechnology,* ed. Martin Bauer. Cambridge: Cambridge University Press.

Jasanoff, Sheila. 2000. Technological Risk and Cultures of Rationality. In *Incorporating Science, Economics, and Sociology in Developing Sanitary and Phytosanitary Standards in International Trade,* ed. National Research Council. Washington, DC: National Academies Press.

Jasanoff, Sheila. 2003. A Living Legacy: The Precautionary Ideal in American Law. In *Precaution: Environmental Science and Preventive Public Policy,* ed. Joel Tickner. Washington, DC: Island Press.

Johnson, Lawrence E. 1991. *A Morally Deep World: An Essay on Moral Significance and Environmental Ethics.* Cambridge: Cambridge University Press.

Joly, Pierre-Benoît. 1999a. Besoin d'expertise et quête d'une légitimité nouvelle: quelles procédures pour réguler l'expertise scientifique? *Revue Française des Affaires Sociales* 53, no. 1:45–52.

Joly, Pierre-Benoît. 1999b. Quand les "candides" évaluent les OGM: la Conférence de citoyens, nouveau monde de démocratie technique our manipulation médiatique? In *L'Opinion publique face aux plantes transgéniques: Entre incertitudes et prise de conscience,* ed. Colloque de la Villette. Paris: Albin Michel.

Joly, Pierre-Benoît. 2000. Les OGM dans l'agriculture et dans l'alimentation: le face à face États-Unis/Europe. *Science et société: Cahiers français* 294:53–59.

Joly, Pierre-Benoît, Gérald Assouline, Dominique Kréziak, Juliette Lemarié, Claire Marris, and Alexis Roy. 2000. *L'innovation controversée: le débat public sur les OGM en France.* INRA Collectif sur les Risques, la Décision et l'Expertise. Grenoble: Institut National de la Recherche Agronomique.

Jonas, Hans. 1979. *Das Prinzip Verantwortung: Versuch einer Ethik für die technologische Zivilisation.* Frankfurt am Main: Insel Verlag.

Jonas, Hans. 1984. *The Imperative of Responsibility: In Search of an Ethics for the Technological Age.* Chicago: University of Chicago Press.

Jorgensen, Torben. 1995. Consensus Conferences in the Health Care Sector. In *Public Participation in Science: The Role of Consensus Conferences in Europe,* ed. Simon Joss and John Durant. London: Science Museum.

Joss, Simon. 1998. Danish Consensus Conferences as a Model of Participatory Technology Assessment: An Impact Study of Consensus Conferences on Danish Parliament and Danish Public Debate. *Science and Public Policy* 25, no. 1:2–22.

Joss, Simon. 1999. Public Participation in Science and Technology Policy and Decision-Making: Ephemeral Phenomenon or Lasting Change? *Science and Public Policy* 26, no. 5:290–293.

Joss, Simon, and Arthur Brownlear. 1999. Considering the Concept of Procedural Justice for Public Policy and Decision-Making in Science and Technology. *Science and Public Policy* 26, no. 5:321–330.

Joss, Simon, and John Durant. 1995. *Public Participation in Science: The Role of Consensus Conferences in Europe.* London: Science Museum.

La justice impose la transparence sur les OGM. 2001. *Le Figaro,* March 2.

Kempton, William, James S. Boster, and Jennifer Hartley. 1996. *Environmental Values in American Culture.* Cambridge: MIT Press.

Khachatourians, George G. 2001. How Well Understood Is the "Science" of Food Safety? In *Governing Food: Science, Safety, and Trade,* ed. Peter W. B. Phillips and Robert Wolfe. Montreal: McGill-Queen's University Press.

Kilama, John. 2003. Barriers to U.S. Food Trade Foreign Food Assistance. *Federal Document Clearing House Congressional Testimony.* March 26.

Kirsch, Guy, Peter Nijkamp, and Klaus Zimmermann, eds. 1988. *The Formulation of Time Preferences in a Multidisciplinary Perspective.* Aldershot, UK: Gower Publishing Company.

Kourilsky, Philippe. 2002. *Du bon usage du principe de précaution.* Paris: Odile Jacob.

Kysar, Douglas. 2004. Climate Change, Cultural Transformation, and Comprehensive Rationality. *Boston College Environmental Affairs Law Review* 34:555–590.

Lafond, François. 2001. The Creation of the European Food Authority: Institutional Implications of Risk Regulation. *Notre Europe: European Issues* 10 (November).

LaFranchi, Scott. 2005. Surveying the Precautionary Principle's Ongoing Global Development: The Evolution of an Emergent Environmental Management Tool. *Boston College Environmental Affairs Law Review* 32:679–720.

Laraña, Enrique. 2001. Reflexivity, Risk, and Collective Action over Waste Management: A Constructive Proposal. *Current Sociology* 4, no. 1:23–48.

Larrère, Catherine, and Raphaël Larrère. 2000. Les OGM entre hostilité de principe et principe de précaution. *Cités: Philosophie, Politique, Histoire* 4:40–53.

Larrère, Catherine, and Raphaël Larrère. 1997. *Du bon usage de la nature: Pour une philosophie de l'environnement.* Paris: Aubier.

Lascoumes, Pierre. 1996. La précaution comme anticipation des risques résiduels et hybridation de la responsabilité. *L'Année Sociologique* 46, no. 2:359–382.

Lascoumes, Pierre. 1997. La précaution: Un nouveau standard de jugement. *Esprit* (November): 129–140.

Lash, Scott, Bronislaw Szerszynski, and Brian Wynne. 1996. *Risk, Environment, and Modernity: Towards a New Ecology.* Thousand Oaks, CA: Sage.

Latour, Bruno. 1991. *Nous n'avons jamais été modernes*. La Découverte.

Latour, Bruno, Cécile Schwartz, and Florian Charvolin. 1991. Crises des environnements: Défis aux sciences humaines. *Futur antériur* 6:28–56.

Latour, Bruno. 1993. Arrachement ou attachement à la nature? *Écologie Politique* 5:15–26.

Latour, Bruno. 1994. Esquisse d'un parlement des choses. *Écologie Politique* 10:97–115.

Latour, Bruno. 1999a. *Pandora's Hope: Essays on the Reality of Science Studies.* Cambridge: Harvard University Press.

Latour, Bruno. 1999b. *Politiques de la nature: Comment faire entrer les sciences en démocratie.* Paris: La Découverte.

Latour, Bruno. 2000a. Du principe de précaution au principe du bon gouvernement. *Etudes* 3934:339–346.

Latour, Bruno. 2000b. Prenons garde au principe de précaution. *Le Monde,* January 4.

Latour, Bruno. 2000c. When Things Strike Back: A Possible Contribution of "Science Studies" to the Social Sciences. *British Journal of Sociology* 51, no. 1:105–123.

Lecourt, Dominique. 1990. *Contre la peur.* Paris: Hachette.

Le Déaut, Jean-Yves. 1998. *De la connaissance des gènes à leur utilization.* Vol. 1. Tome I. National Assembly No. 1054, Senate No. 545. July 8.

Le Déaut, Jean-Yves. 1999. Choix technologiques, débat publique et décision politique. In *L'opinion publique face aux plantes transgéniques: Entre incertitudes et prise de conscience.* Colloque de la Villette. Paris: Albin Michel.

Le Déaut, Jean-Yves. 2001. Le débat nécessaire entre le politique et le citoyen. *Risques* 47:115–120.

Lemieux, Cyril, and Yannick Barthe. 1998. Les risques collectifs sous le regard des sciences du politique. *Politix.* 44, no. 4:7–28.

Leone, Julien. Les OGM à l'épreuve du principe de précaution. *Petites Affiches* 388, no. 164:12–16.

Lepage, Corinne, and François Guery. 2001. *La politique de précaution.* Paris: Presses Universitaires de France.

Levidow, Les, Susan Carr, David Wield, and Rene von Schomberg. 1997. European Biotechnology Regulation: Framing the Risk Assessment of an Herbicide-Tolerant Crop. *Science, Technology, and Human Values* 22, no. 4:472–505.

Levidow, Les, and Claire Marris. 2001. Science and Governance in Europe: Lessons from the Case of Agricultural Biotechnology. *Science and Public Policy* 28, no. 5:345–360.

Levins, Richard. 2003. Whose Scientific Method? Scientific Methods for a Complex World. In *Precaution: Environmental Science and Preventive Public Policy,* ed. Joel Tickner. Washington, DC: Island Press.

Lewis, Sanford. 1999. The Precautionary Principle and Corporate Disclosure. In *Protecting Public Health and the Environment: Implementing the Precautionary*

Principle, ed. Carolyn Raffensperger and Joel Tickner. Washington, DC: Island Press.

Lewontin, Richard. 2001. Genes in the Food! *New York Review of Books,* June 21, 81–84.

L'hexagone privilégie le recours au couple expert-élu. *Les Échos,* November 8.

Litfin, Karen T. 1994. *Ozone Discourses: Science and Politics in Global Environmental Cooperation.* New York: Columbia University Press.

Lomborg, Bjorn. 2001. *The Skeptical Environmentalist: Measuring the Real State of the World.* Cambridge: Cambridge University Press.

Losey, John E., Linda S. Rayor, and Maureen E. Carter. 1999. Transgenic pollen harms monarch larvae. *Nature* 214:399.

Lovelock, James. 1995. *Gaia: A New Look at Life on Earth.* Rev. ed. Oxford: Oxford University Press.

Lucchini, Laurent. 1999. Le principe de précaution en droit international de l'environnement: ombres plus que lumières. *Annuaire Français de Droit International* 45:710–731.

Lynch, Diana, and David Vogel. 2000. Apples and Oranges: Comparing Regulation of Genetically Modified Food in Europe and the United States. Paper presented at the annual meeting of the American Political Science Association, Washington, DC.

Majone, Giandomenico. 2002. What Price Safety? The Precautionary Principle and Its Policy Implications. *Journal of Common Market Studies* 40, no. 1:89–109.

Maréchal, Jean-Paul. 1999. Biodiversité: Faut-il craindre des dérives mercantiles? *Problèmes économiques,* no. 2.628 (August 25): 29–31.

Marris, Claire, and Pierre-Benoît Joly. 1999. La gouvernance technocratique par consultation? Interrogation sur la première conférence de citoyens en France. *Les Cahiers de la Sécurité Intériure* 38, no. 4:97–124.

Marris, Claire, Brian Wynne, Peter Simmons, and Sue Weldon. 2001. *Public Perceptions of Agricultural Biotechnologies in Europe.* Final report of the PABE Research Project, funded by Commission of European Communities, contract no. FAIR CT98–3844 (DG 12–SSMI). December.

Martin-Bidou, Pascale. 1999. Le principe de précaution en droit international de l'environnement. *Revue générale de droit international public* 103, no. 3:631–666.

Mazurek, Janice, Robert Gottlieb, and Julie Roque. 1995. Shifting to Prevention: The Limits of Current Policy. In *Reducing Toxics: A New Approach to Policy and Industrial Decisionmaking,* ed. Robert Gottlieb. Washington, DC: Island Press.

Miller, Henry, and Gregory Conko. 2000. Genetically Modified Fear and the International Regulation of Biotechnology. In *Rethinking Risk and the Precautionary Principle,* ed. Julian Morris. Oxford: Butterworth-Heinemann.

Miller, Henry, and Gregory Conko. 2001. The Perils of Precaution: Why Regulators' "Precautionary Principle" Is Doing More Harm Than Good. *Policy Review* 107:25–39.

Ministère de l'Écologie et du Développement Durable. 2003. Rapport de la Commission Coppens de préparation de la Charte de l'Énvironnement. Paris, France. <http://www.charte.environnement.gouv.fr>.

Ministère de l'Économie, des Finances et de l'Industrie. 2000. Brefs rappels sur les OGM. July. <http://www.finances.gouv.fr/ogm/ogm_bref.htm>.

Mironesco, Christine. 1998. Parliamentary Technology Assessment of Biotechnologies: A Review of Major TA Reports in the European Union and the USA. *Science and Public Policy* (October): 327–342.

Morris, Julian. 2000a. Defining the Precautionary Principle. *Rethinking Risk and the Precautionary Principle,* ed. Julian Morris. Oxford: Butterworth-Heinemann.

Morris, Julian, ed. 2000b. *Rethinking Risk and the Precautionary Principle.* Oxford: Butterworth-Heinemann.

National Academy of Sciences. 1987. *Introduction of Recombinant DNA-Engineered Organisms in the Environment: Key Issues.* Washington, DC: National Academies Press.

National Academy of Sciences, Committee on Genetically Modified Pest-Protected Plants. 2000. *Genetically Modified Pest-Protected Plants: Science and Regulation.* Washington, DC: National Academies Press.

National Research Council. 1989. *Field Testing Genetically Modified Organisms: Framework for Decision.* Washington, DC: National Academies Press.

Noiville, Christine. 2000. Principe de précaution et OMC: le cas du commerce alimentaire. *Journal du droit international* 127, no. 2:263–297.

Noiville, Christine. 2002. Le Principe de précaution: quelles perspectives d'avenir? *Cahiers français* 1–2, no. 306:36–42.

Noiville, Christine. 2003. *Du bon gouvernement des risques. Le droit et la question du risque acceptable.* Paris: Presses Universitaires de France.

Noiville, Christine, and Jean-Pierre Gouyon. 1999. Principe de précaution et OGM: le cas du maïs transgénique. In *Le principe de précaution,* ed. Philippe Kourilsky and Geneviève Viney. Paris: Odile Jacob.

Nordlee, Julie, Steve Taylor, Jeffrey Townsend, Laurie Thomas, and Robert Bush. 1996. Identification of a Brazil Nut Allergen in Transgenic Soybeans. *New England Journal of Medicine* 334, no. 11:688–692.

O'Brien, Mary. 1999. Alternatives Assessment and the Precautionary Principle. In *Protecting Public Health and the Environment,* ed. Carol Raffensperger and Joel Tickner. Washington, DC: Island Press.

O'Brien, Mary. 2000. *Making Better Environmental Decisions: An Alternative to Risk Assessment.* Cambridge: MIT Press.

Organisation for Economic Cooperation and Development. 2001. *OECD Environmental Outlook.* Paris: OECD Publishing.

O'Riordan, Tim, and James Cameron, eds. 1994. *Interpreting the Precautionary Principle.* London: Earthscan.

O'Riordan, Tim, and Andrew Jordan. 1995. The Precautionary Principle in Contemporary Environmental Politics. *Environmental Values* 4:191–212.

O'Riordan, Tim, and Andrew Jordan. 1999. The Precautionary Principle in Contemporary Environmental Politics and Policy. In *Protecting Public Health and the Environment: Implementing the Precautionary Principle,* ed. Carolyn Raffensperger and Joel Tickner. Washington, DC: Island Press.

Paarlberg, Robert. 1999. Lapsed Leadership: U.S. International Environmental Leadership since Rio. In *The Global Environment,* ed. Norman Vig and Regina Axelrod. Washington, DC: Congressional Quarterly Press.

Padioleau, Jean-Gustave. 2000. La société du risque, une chance pour la démocratie. *Le Débat* 109:39–54.

Paillotin, Guy. 1998. L'émergence des biotechnologies en agriculture. *futuribles* 53–56.

Passmore, John. 1974. *Man's Responsibility for Nature.* New York: Charles Scribner's Sons.

Pelt, Jean-Marie. 2000. *Plantes et aliments transgéniques.* Paris: Fayard.

Pew Initiative on Food and Biotechnology. 2003. Public Sentiment about Genetically Modified Food: September 2003 Update. <http://pewagbiotech.org/research/2003update/>.

Phillips, Lord of Worth Matravers, June Bridgeman, and Malcolm Ferguson-Smith. 2000. *The BSE Inquiry Report: Evidence and Supporting Papers of the Inquiry into the Emergence and Identification of Bovine Spongiform Encephalopathy (BSE) and Variant Creutzfeldt-Jakob disease (vCJD) and the Action Taken in Response to It up to 20 March 1996.* London: Her Majesty's Stationery Office.

Phillips, Peter W. B. 2001. Food Safety, Trade Policy, and International Institutions. In *Governing Food: Science, Safety, and Trade,* ed. Peter W. B. Phillips and Robert Wolfe. Montreal: McGill-Queen's University Press.

Pollack, Mark A., and Gregory Shaffer. 2000. Biotechnology: The Next Transatlantic Trade War? *Washington Quarterly* 23, no. 4:41–54.

Pollack, Mark A., and Gregory Shaffer. 2001. The Challenge of Reconciling Regulatory Differences: Food Safety and GMOs in the Transatlantic Relationship. In *Transatlantic Governance in the Global Economy,* ed. Mark A. Pollack and Gregory Shaffer. Lanham, MD: Rowman and Littlefield.

Pons, Alain. 1995. Vico: de la prudence à la providence. In *De la prudence des Anciens comparée à celle des Modernes. Sémantique d'un concept, déplacement des problématiques,* ed. André Tosel. Paris: Les Belles Lettres.

Les pouvoirs publics constatent la colonisation des cultures par les OGM. 2001. *Le Monde,* July 26, p.5.

Precaution Is for Europeans. 2003. *New York Times,* May 18. (Week in Review), p. 14.

La première conférence sur les plantes transgéniques a mis en lumière les craintes et les interrogations des citoyens. 1998. *Les Échos,* June 22, p. 8.

Purdue, Derrick. 1996. Contested Expertise: Plant Biotechnology and Social Movements. *Science as Culture* 4, no. 25:526–545.

Le Puy-de-Dôme, champ d'opposition entre anti et pro-OGM. 2005. *Le Monde*, June 18.

Radé, Christophe. 2000. Le principe de précaution: Une nouvelle éthique de la responsabilité? *Revue Juridique de l'Environnement*, no. spécial: 75–89.

Raffensperger, Carolyn, and Joel Tickner, eds. 1999. *Protecting Public Health and the Environment: Implementing the Precautionary Principle.* Washington, DC: Island Press.

Redesigning Nature: Hard Lessons Learned. 2001. *New York Times*, January 25, p. A1.

Reiss, Michael J., and Roger Straughan. 1996. *Improving Nature? The Science and Ethics of Genetic Engineering.* Cambridge: Cambridge University Press.

Remond-Gouilloud, Martine. 1996. Entre science et droit, le mirage de l'exactitude. *La jaune et la rouge* 513:25–27.

Les risques orphelins: Quand les assureurs réchignent à assurer. 2001. *Les Échos*, December 5, p. 58.

Rissler, Jane, and Margaret Mellon. 1996. *The Ecological Risks of Engineered Crops.* Cambridge: MIT Press.

Roqueplo, Philippe. 1997. *Entre savoir et décision, l'expertise scientifique.* Paris: Institut National de la Recherche Agronomique.

Roy, Alexis. 2001. *Les experts face au risque: le cas des plantes transgéniques.* Paris: Presses Universitaires de France.

Sadeleer, Nicholas de. 1999. *Les principes de pollueur-payeur, de prévention et de précaution.* Brussels: Bruylant.

Sadeleer, Nicholas de. 2001a. Les avatars du principe de précaution en droit public: effet de mode ou révolution silencieuse? *Revue française de droit administratif* 17, no. 3:547–562.

Sadeleer, Nicholas de. 2001b. Le statut juridique du principe de précaution en droit communautaire: du slogan à la règle. *Cahiers du droit européen* 37, nos. 1–2:91–132.

Sagoff, Mark. 1988. *The Economy of the Earth.* Cambridge: Cambridge University Press.

Salomon, Jean-Jacques. 1999. Pour une éthique de la science: De la prudence au principe de précaution. *futuribles* 245:5–28.

Sandin, Per. 1999. Dimensions of the Precautionary Principle. *Human and Ecological Risk Assessment* 5:889–908.

Sclove, Richard. 1995a. *Democracy and Technology.* New York: Guilford Press.

Sclove, Richard. 1995b. Put Democracy into R&D. *Christian Science Monitor*, October 30, p. 19.

Sclove, Richard, and Madeleine Scammell. 1999. Practicing the Principle. In *Protecting Public Health and the Environment: Implementing the Precautionary Principle*, ed. Carolyn Raffensperger and Joel Tickner. Washington, DC: Island Press.

Scott, Joanne, and Ellen Vos. 2002. The Juridification of Uncertainty: Observations on the Ambivalence of the Precautionary Principle within the EU and the WTO. In *Good Governance in Europe's Integrated Market,* ed. Christian Joerges and Renaud Dehousse. Oxford: Oxford University Press.

Seralini, Gilles. 2000. *OGM: Le vrai débat.* Paris: Flammarion.

Speth, James Gustave. 2004. *Red Sky at Morning.* New Haven, CT: Yale University Press.

State Department Transcript. 2002. U.S. Agriculture Chief Stresses Importance of New Technology; Sec. Veneman Addresses Food Policy Research Group. December 9. <http://canberra.usembassy.gov/hyper/2002/1209/epf109.htm>.

Stirling, Andrew. 2000. Sciences et risques: aspects théoriques et pratiques d'une approche de précaution. In *Le principe de précaution: Significations et conséquences,* ed. Edwin Zaccai and Jean-Noël Missa. Brussels: Université de Bruxelles.

Sullivan, Roger J. 1977. *Morality and the Good Life: A Commentary on Aristotle's Nicomachean Ethics.* Memphis, TN: Memphis State University Press.

Sunstein, Cass R. 2002. *Risk and Reason: Safety, Law, and the Environment.* Cambridge: Cambridge University Press.

Sunstein, Cass R. 2005. *Laws of Fear: Beyond the Precautionary Principle.* Cambridge: Cambridge University Press.

Taking No Chances, Disaster-Conscious Firms Treat Global Warming as a Reality. 2001. *Washington Post,* June 26, p. E01.

Teitel, Martin, and Kimberly A. Wilson. 1999. *Genetically Engineered Food: Changing the Nature of Nature.* Rochester, VT: Park Street Press.

Tengs, Tammy O., and John D. Graham. 1996. The Opportunity Costs of Haphazard Social Investments in Life-Saving. In *Risks, Costs, and Lives Saved: Getting Better Results from Regulation,* ed. Robert W. Hahn. Oxford: Oxford University Press.

Testart, Jacques. 2001. Les OGM, un vandalisme libéral. *Libération,* December 7.

Tickner, Joel. 2000. Precautionary Principle: Current Status and Implementation. *Synthesis/Regeneration* 23 (Fall). <http://www.greens.org/s-r/23/23-17.html>.

Tickner, Joel. 2003a. Precautionary Assessment: A Framework for Integrating Science, Uncertainty, and Preventive Public Policy. In *Precaution: Environmental Science and Preventive Public Policy,* ed. Joel Tickner. Washington, DC: Island Press.

Tickner, Joel, ed. 2003b. *Precaution: Environmental Science and Preventive Public Policy.* Washington, DC: Island Press.

Tickner, Joel, Carolyn Raffensperger, and Nancy Myers. 1999. *The Precautionary Principle in Action: A Handbook.* Windsor, ND: Science and Environmental Health Network. <http://www.biotech-info.net/handbook.pdf>.

Tocqueville, Alexis de. [1835] 1969. *Democracy in America.* Ed. J. P. Mayer. Garden City, NY: Doubleday Anchor.

Trouwborst, Arie. 2000. *Evolution and Status of the Precautionary Principle in International Law.* Norwell, MA: Kluwer Law International.

Underwriters Refuse Cover for GM Farmers. 2003. *Guardian,* October 16, p. 6.

Underwriters Refuse Cover for GM Farmers: Leading Agricultural Insurers Liken Risk of Association with New Crops to Thalidomide and Terrorism. 2003. *Observer* (London), October 16, p. 10.

United Nations Environment Programme (UNEP). 1992. Rio Declaration on Environment and Development. <http://www.unep.org/Documents.multilingual/Default.asp?DocumentID=78&ArticleID=1163>.

United Nations Millennium Ecosystem Assessment. 2005. *Living beyond our Means: Natural Assets and Human Well-being* (Statement of the Millennium Assessment Board). <http://www.millenniumassessment.org/en/Products.BoardStatement.aspx>.

USDA to Overhaul GM Regulations. 2004. *Chemical Week,* January 28, p. 10.

Victor, David. 2000. Risk Management and the World Trading System: Regulating International Trade Distortions Caused by National Sanitary and Phytosanitary Policies. In *Incorporating Science, Economics, and Sociology in Developing Sanitary and Phytosanitary Standards in International Trade,* ed. National Research Council. Washington, DC: National Academies Press.

Vig, Norman, and Herbert Paschen, eds. 2000. *Parliaments and Technology: The Development of Technology Assessment in Europe.* Albany: State University of New York Press.

Vogel, David. 2001. Ships Passing in the Night: GMOs and the Politics of Risk Regulation in Europe and the United States. <http://www.insead.fr/events/gmoworkshop/papers/1_Vogel.pdf>.

Vogel, David, and Jabril Bensedrine. 2002. Comparing Risk Regulation in the United States and France: Asbestos, AIDS, and Genetically Modified Agriculture. *French Politics, Culture, and Society* 20, no. 1:13–29.

Vogel, David. 2003. The Hare and the Tortoise Revisited: The New Politics of Consumer and Environmental Regulation in Europe. *British Journal of Political Science* 33, no. 4:557–580.

von Moltke, Konrad. 1988. The Vorsorgeprinzip in West German Environmental Policy. In *The Royal Commission on Environmental Pollution, Twelfth Report: Best Practicable Environmental Option.* London: Her Majesty's Stationery Office.

Ward, Halina. 1999. Science and Precaution in the Trading System. International Institute for Sustainable Development and the Royal Institute of International Affairs. <http://www.iisd.org/pdf/sci_precaution.pdf>.

Weale, Albert. 1992. *The New Politics of Pollution.* Manchester: Manchester University Press.

Whiteside, Kerry H. 2002. *Divided Natures: French Contributions to Political Ecology.* Cambridge: MIT Press.

Whiteside, Kerry H. 2003a. French Regulatory Republicanism and the Risks of Genetically Modified Crops. *French Politics* 1:153–174.

Whiteside, Kerry. 2003b. Humanisme et Terroir: The Culture of Genetically Modified Crops in France. *French Politics, Culture, and Society* 21, no. 3:73–90.

Wiener, Jonathan B., and Michael D. Rogers. 2002. Comparing Precaution in the United States and Europe. *Journal of Risk Research* 5, no. 4:317–349.

Wildavsky, Aaron. 1995. *But Is It True? A Citizen's Guide to Environmental Health and Safety Issues.* Cambridge: Harvard University Press.

Wildavsky, Aaron. 2000. Trial and Error versus Trial without Error. In *Rethinking Risk and the Precautionary Principle,* ed. Julian Morris. Oxford: Butterworth-Heinemann.

Wynne, Brian. 1996. May the Sheep Safely Graze? A Reflexive View of the Expert-Lay Knowledge Divide. In *Risk, Environment, and Modernity: Towards a New Ecology,* ed. Scott Lash, Bronislaw Szerszynski, and Brian Wynne. Thousand Oaks, CA: Sage, 1996.

Zaccai, Edwin, and Jean-Noël Missa. 2000. *Le principe de précaution: Significations et conséquences.* Brussels: Université de Bruxelles.

Zeitlin, Maurice. 1980. *Classes, Class Conflict, and the State: Empirical Studies in Class Analysis.* Cambridge, MA: Winthrop.

Zhao, Jian-Zhou, Jun Cao, Hilda L. Collins, Sarah L. Bates, Richard T. Roush, Elizabeth D. Earle, and Anthony M. Shelton. 2005. Concurrent use of transgenic plants expressing a single and two *Bacillus thuringiensis* genes speeds insect adaptation to pyramided plants. *Proceedings of the National Academy of Sciences,* June 14, 102(24):8426–8430.

Zuindeau, Bertrand. 1997. Le développement durable: Une introduction générale. *Environnement: Représentations et concepts de la nature,* ed. Jean-Marc Besse and Isabelle Roussel. Paris: L'Harmattan.

Zwanenberg, Patrick van, and Erik Millstone. 2001. "Mad Cow Disease" 1980s–2000: How Reassurances Undermined Precaution. In *Late Lessons from Early Warnings: The Precautionary Principle 1896–2000,* ed. European Environment Agency. Environmental Issue Report 22, Copenhagen.

Index

Urban and Industrial Environments
Series editor: Robert Gottlieb, Henry R. Luce Professor of Urban and Environmental Policy, Occidental College

Maureen Smith, *The U.S. Paper Industry and Sustainable Production: An Argument for Restructuring*

Keith Pezzoli, *Human Settlements and Planning for Ecological Sustainability: The Case of Mexico City*

Sarah Hammond Creighton, *Greening the Ivory Tower: Improving the Environmental Track Record of Universities, Colleges, and Other Institutions*

Jan Mazurek, *Making Microchips: Policy, Globalization, and Economic Restructuring in the Semiconductor Industry*

William A. Shutkin, *The Land That Could Be: Environmentalism and Democracy in the Twenty-First Century*

Richard Hofrichter, ed., *Reclaiming the Environmental Debate: The Politics of Health in a Toxic Culture*

Robert Gottlieb, *Environmentalism Unbound: Exploring New Pathways for Change*

Kenneth Geiser, *Materials Matter: Toward a Sustainable Materials Policy*

Thomas D. Beamish, *Silent Spill: The Organization of an Industrial Crisis*

Matthew Gandy, *Concrete and Clay: Reworking Nature in New York City*

David Naguib Pellow, *Garbage Wars: The Struggle for Environmental Justice in Chicago*

Julian Agyeman, Robert D. Bullard, and Bob Evans, eds., *Just Sustainabilities: Development in an Unequal World*

Barbara L. Allen, *Uneasy Alchemy: Citizens and Experts in Louisiana's Chemical Corridor Disputes*

Dara O'Rourke, *Community-Driven Regulation: Balancing Development and the Environment in Vietnam*

Brian K. Obach, *Labor and the Environmental Movement: The Quest for Common Ground*

Peggy F. Barlett and Geoffrey W. Chase, eds., *Sustainability on Campus: Stories and Strategies for Change*

Steve Lerner, *Diamond: A Struggle for Environmental Justice in Louisiana's Chemical Corridor*

Jason Corburn, *Street Science: Community Knowledge and Environmental Health Justice*

Peggy F. Barlett, ed., *Urban Place: Reconnecting with the Natural World*

David Naguib Pellow and Robert J. Brulle, eds., *Power, Justice, and the Environment: A Critical Appraisal of the Environmental Justice Movement*

Eran Ben-Joseph, *The Code of the City: Standards and the Hidden Language of Place Making*

Nancy J. Myers and Carolyn Raffensperger, eds., *Precautionary Tools for Reshaping Environmental Policy*

Kelly Sims Gallagher, *China Shifts Gears: Automakers, Oil, Pollution, and Development*

Kerry H. Whiteside, *Precautionary Politics: Principle and Practice in Confronting Environmental Risk*